Business Writing with AI

by Sheryl Lindsell-Roberts, MA

for dummies®

A Wiley Brand

Business Writing with AI For Dummies®

Published by: **John Wiley & Sons, Inc.**, 111 River Street, Hoboken, NJ 07030-5774, www.wiley.com

For general information on our other products and services, please contact our Customer Care Department within the U.S. at 877-762-2974, outside the U.S. at 317-572-3993, or fax 317-572-4002. For technical support, please visit https://hub.wiley.com/community/support/dummies.

Wiley publishes in a variety of print and electronic formats and by print-on-demand. Some material included with standard print versions of this book may not be included in e-books or in print-on-demand. If this book refers to media such as a CD or DVD that is not included in the version you purchased, you may download this material at http://booksupport.wiley.com. For more information about Wiley products, visit www.wiley.com.

Library of Congress Control Number is available from the publisher.

ISBN 978-1-394-26173-4 (pbk); ISBN 978-1-394-26174-1 (ebk); ISBN 978-1-394-26175-8 (ebk)

Printed and bound by CPI Group (UK) Ltd, Croydon, CR0 4YY

C9781394261734_230524

Contents at a Glance

Table of Contents

Introduction

Artificial intelligence (AI) will continue to impress us with its efficiency, knowledge, and accessibility . . . but realize that it won't replace writer intelligence (WI). While AI can process large amounts of data and generate coherent text, it lacks the creative and emotional depth that human writers bring to their work. Writing should reflect human experiences, emotions, and perspectives. It requires the intuition, empathy, and understanding that AI can't replicate.

AI and WI can work together, with AI enhancing the writing process and humans providing the unique qualities that make writing a deeply human experience. As AI continues to evolve, it's important to stay abreast of the latest developments so you maximize its benefits and mitigate potential risks.

By the way, WI are initials I coined because writer intelligence has been ingrained in human culture since the dawn of civilization. The origins of writing date back to prehistoric times, perhaps when Sumerian texts were used for communication, storytelling, and recording significant events. From ancient civilizations to modern times, skilled writers have been able to capture the imagination of readers and leave a lasting impact — just as they're doing today and will continue to do in the foreseeable future.

About This Book

Get ready to embark on a captivating journey that showcases the transformative potential of AI. Every chapter vividly illustrates how AI can be a valuable assistant throughout the entire document creation process — leaving no stage untouched. You'll find alphabetic lists of AI tools as they relate to each topic as well as how to write prompts so you get the results you want. To ensure easy accessibility, this book is divided into six parts, making it effortless to navigate and implement the insights gained from each:

>> **Part 1: Harnessing the Potential of AI in Business Writing.** This part provides an introduction to AI and its role as a writing assistant. It explains how AI can assist in your writing journey, whether you prefer to observe and

learn, begin with a user-friendly chatbot, or dive right into a comprehensive AI tool. It emphasizes that while AI can be helpful, human skills are still essential as they're necessary to express emotions and make ethical judgments, and validate accuracy of the content — aspects that can't be replicated by AI.

» **Part 2: The Write Stuff.** I strongly suggest that you immerse yourself in this part completely. It serves as a fundamental guide for composing any business document you'll ever write. Within this section, you'll be introduced to the Kick-Start Brief, which equips you with the tools to understand your audience to the fullest extent. It delves into the art of creating stories to captivate your readers, guiding them on engaging journeys that will ultimately persuade them to take the desired action. Additionally, you'll discover invaluable ways to craft compelling visuals, refine the tone, and perfect the text. To top it off, this section is brimming with trailblazing AI tips that can enhance your business writing savvy.

» **Part 3: Writing Click-Worthy E-Content.** With email being a significant means of communicating for both general use and e-marketing, this part walks you through the pros and woes of using email like a guru, including how to create dynamic subject lines, compelling messages, and gain customers. It also walks you through how to enhance your website (one of your biggest marketing tools) for search engine optimization (SEO).

» **Part 4: Crafting Noteworthy Professional Documents.** This book wouldn't be complete without focusing on how AI can be your sidekick for writing a wide array of documents including easy-to-read instructions and procedures, articles that can boost your personal brand, reports written with keen observation and reasoning, abstracts and executive summaries to distill complex ideas into bite-sized brilliance, and grant proposals that can win vital funding.

» **Part 5: Producing Personalized and Targeted Writing.** This part gets a little more personal. It's not often you get to write about yourself, but you'll learn how to effectively self-promote by writing a captivating bio. Also included are how to write letters that drive action, storyboards that bring presentations to life, business plans for a thriving enterprise, and how to write a nonfiction book for bragging "writes."

» **Part 6: The Part of Tens.** This section is a beloved staple in the *For Dummies* series. It offers valuable insights for writing prompts to get you the results you want, along with an exploration of ten common pitfalls in business writing and smart strategies to transform them into triumphs.

Foolish Assumptions

Before I began writing this book, I made some assumptions about you — the reader. (I don't normally make assumptions because we all know what happens when we *ass-u-me*.) However, I threw caution to the wind and let the AI genie out of the bottle. I figured that this book is for you if you're:

>> Intrigued by the world of AI and want to journey through the labyrinth of AI knowledge to discover how it can assist you in the future.

>> Ready to dip a toe into the water and use a chatbot to karate chop through writer's block, craft a draft, jazz up headlines and titles, proofread and edit, and more.

>> Prepared to take the plunge and use a comprehensive AI tool as a writing assistant that provides a wide range of features and functionalities such as data visualization, sentiment analysis, predictive modeling, and anomaly detection.

So, whether you're a professional business writer, you're starting a business and have to generate a business plan, you need to write a dynamite bio, you're applying for a grant, you want to gain recognition in your field and write an article, or you send out a countless number of emails each day — or wherever you are on the continuum — this book offers practical advice and guidance, insights and perspectives, and motivation and inspiration. It will resonate with your specific interests, needs, and goals and it can be invaluable to your professional growth and survival.

And that's a sensible assumption!

Icons Used in This Book

Begin an icon-hunting expedition as you search through the margins, where mischievous icons call attention to precious nuggets of information, eagerly beckoning for your attention! Here are the icons you'll see and a description of each:

AI SPOTLIGHT

This icon trumpets AI as your personal writing assistant.

REMEMBER

This prompts you to recall important information, similar to tying a string around your finger so you don't forget.

SHERYL SAYS

If I had a chance to speak with you personally, these are the things I'd share.

TIP

Nifty tips that may be time-savers, frustration savers, lifesavers, or just about anything else you'll find useful.

WARNING

Ouch! Avoid these pitfalls to save yourself headaches, heartburn, embarrassments . . . or worse.

Beyond the Book

In addition to the material in the print or e-book you're reading right now, you can access some additional perks on the web. Check out the free access-anywhere Cheat Sheet that includes tips and advice. To get this Cheat Sheet, simply go to www.dummies.com and type "Business Writing with AI For Dummies Cheat Sheet" in the Search box. I've also included a bonus online chapter about collaborative writing — you can access it here: www.dummies.com/go/businesswriting withaifd.

Where to Go from Here

I realize you won't read this book like a suspenseful mystery novel from cover to cover — but I strongly suggest that you read Part 2 (Chapters 4 to 9) sequentially. Writing mastery is a process of understanding your readers, crafting compelling stories, writing the draft, designing for visual impact, honing the tone, and polishing the prose. After that, feel free to jump around to whatever topic interests you or applies to the writing challenge you face.

A word of caution . . . If you lend your printed copy to anyone, take some safeguards. One way is to write your name in large letters in an obvious place to ensure that it's clearly identifiable as your property. Another way is to request something valuable as collateral. This serves as a form of insurance because borrowers may be so absorbed by the book's treasure trove of wisdom, they might be reluctant to return it.

I hope you'll appreciate the value of this book as you journey through it and will recommend it to others who are entering the world of AI or want to unleash AI's full potential for business writing.

1

Harnessing the Potential of AI in Business Writing

Discover the indispensable role of writing professionals in the AI realm — the ones who have distinct attributes such as creativity, critical thinking, emotional intelligence, and adaptability to evolving trends and audience preferences.

Embrace AI as your trusty writing assistant to overcome writer's block, effortlessly generate captivating content, craft amazing visuals, refine the tone, and optimize your search engine rankings.

Enter the realm of AI by absorbing knowledge from the sidelines, dipping your toe into the water with the help of a chatbot, or boldly diving into the depths to play alongside the seasoned professionals.

IN THIS CHAPTER

» Realizing that AI is already part of your life

» Discovering how AI assists business writers

» Understanding that AI helps, not replaces, writers

» Identifying writing fields that will continue to thrive

» Exploring the limitations of AI

Chapter **1**

Recognizing the Need for Writer Intelligence (WI)

W e're hearing so much about artificial intelligence (AI) and all its wonders, yet we don't hear nearly enough about writer intelligence (WI). Remember that without human intelligence there would be no artificial intelligence. Humans would never create anything to replace themselves, only to make life easier. That's what AI does for business writers; it makes writing easier.

As business writers, it's crucial to stay informed about the latest advancements in AI writing technology and use it responsibly. Striking a balance between human creativity and technological innovation will be pivotal for the success of writers and writing. Never underestimate the lasting significance of genuine human communication — it's paramount. Business writers stand to gain significantly by learning about AI and integrating it into their work to enhance the creative process and improve efficiency. This chapter delves into how writers can benefit from using AI as a writing assistant.

AI is Already Part of Your Everyday Life

If you think you're a newcomer to AI, think again. Apple's Siri and Google's Alexa are powered by AI. They rely on natural language processing (NLP) and machine learning. Every day most of us send and receive emails, many powered by AI (find out more about using AI in your own emails in Chapter 10). And all the annoying pop-up ads we see while searching the Internet are AI enabled. They're based on our search history that's personalized with the goal of getting items in front of us via algorithms and to sell us goods and services.

GPS uses AI for route optimization, historical data, and real-time traffic updates such as congestion and road closures, as well as suggest workarounds to avoid gridlock. If you scan checks with your phone to make deposits, AI is at work behind the scenes. From drug discovery to clinical decision support, AI is transforming the way the medical profession approaches healthcare. AI is used in self-driving cars, trucks, and buses, as well as smart home devices such as thermostats, lighting systems, and security systems. And when we kick back to relax in the evening, many of us turn to streaming services. These services use AI to recommend programming we may like based on our past viewing history.

AI is fast becoming the cornerstone of innovation. Yet AI isn't new. It dates back to the 1950s when Alan Turing published "Computer Machinery and Intelligence" in the academic journal *Mind*, which proposed a test of machine intelligence called *The Imitation Game*. However, it wasn't until 2022 when AI was brought into the mainstream through familiarity with OpenAI's application ChatGPT (Generative Pre-Training Transformer). By incorporating true AI into live chat features, businesses are merging human intelligence with machine intelligence.

REMEMBERING HAL

Perhaps you recall the story of HAL 9000, the killer AI supercomputer in Stanley Kubrick's landmark film *2001: A Space Odyssey*. It tells the story of the struggle of humans faced with extinction by a methodical program of extermination led by HAL, an errant, sentient supercomputer. Since this movie premiered in 1968, AI has been discussed, explored, and is a frequent subject of ongoing conversation. Can this serve as harbinger of contemporary AI issues?

A little-known factoid about HAL: HAL is a one-letter shift from IBM. Supposedly Kubrick sent a letter to Polaris Productions stating his intention to use an IBM supercomputer in the movie. The studio felt it wasn't the best idea to use IBM as a psychotic computer, so Kubrick shifted one letter down from IBM and got HAL. People associated with Kubrick have always denied that there was any significance to the coincidence, but the rumor persists. True or false? Ask AI.

Using AI to Assist WI

SHERYL SAYS

As you journey through this book, you'll gain familiarity with AI tools that can be applied to a wide array of business writing scenarios. Whether you're new to AI and are simply exploring its capabilities, you're interested in using a simple chatbot, or you're prepared to embrace comprehensive AI tools, this book equips you with the knowledge and skills you need for each stage of your journey.

AI SPOTLIGHT

As you navigate the chapters of this book, a recurring theme emerges: the importance of generating precise prompts. From a general discussion in Chapter 23 to detailed applications in Parts 3, 4, and 5, the significance of this artistry is underscored. Embracing the art of prompt generation becomes paramount, for it's through these meticulously selected words that dynamic documents come to life, ideas flourish, and minds expand.

AI can assist you with some of the writing you normally do, but there are other aspects of business writing that only humans can do. AI excels at chopping through writer's block, preparing outlines and drafts, summarizing topics, analyzing data, presenting numbers and statistics, maintaining consistency in writing style, proofreading and editing, and optimizing writing for search engine optimization (SEO). AI tools will have a big impact on the future of writers, but here's why WI will never disappear.

REMEMBER

Business writing goes beyond merely assembling words. It requires a deep understanding of human emotions, strategic insights, and perspectives. This is where human writers have a unique advantage. Only humans have the innate ability to create personal connections with readers by sharing relatable stories, personal experiences, nuanced details, and thought-provoking analogies — something that AI technology is incapable of. Additionally, AI lacks the ability to differentiate between emotionally impactful phrases and mundane ones. Readers often rely on their instincts, desires, emotions, and morals when forming judgments, aspects that are detached from logic and analytics.

Another limitation of AI is the absence of original insights. AI can only summarize and reproduce information from existing databases. It can't generate its own thoughts on a subject. Furthermore, AI has limited capabilities to infer the consequences of a particular action. Only human writers possess the higher-level causal thinking required to analyze why things happened and address hypothetical "what if" scenarios.

If you strive to be a thought-leader in your industry (an authority whose innovative ideas and insights influence and guide others), it's WI that will get you there, not AI. Only human writers have the ability to provide original insights and opinions on the most crucial topics — topics that are beyond the current grasp of AI technology.

Enhancing Business Writing, Not Replacing Writers

SHERYL SAYS

Who will survive? Who will thrive? Here are *my* WI thoughts on why business writers will not only survive, but thrive, and why we can't be replaced by AI:

>> AI writing is robotic. To get a reader's attention, good writers bring text to life with perspective and creativity as we've done since we first showed an ability to put words together.

>> Computers haven't lived our life or the life of the reader. So they can't humanize writing with examples and stories to enliven a document and drive key points home.

>> While lightheartedness in business writing is tricky, it's where we can separate ourselves from machines. The right remark at the right time can help make a point in a way AI can't.

>> Emotional intelligence is necessary to understand and convey emotions effectively. We can tap into the intricacies of human experience, capturing the nuances of feelings and experiences in our writing.

>> AI can mimic human writing, understand complex queries, deliver nuanced responses, and generate text resembling human style. However, only humans can adapt writing style, tone, and voice for different genres, audiences, and purposes, and make revisions and improvements.

>> Humans possess moral reasoning and ethical judgment, which allows us to make conscious decisions about what we write and how we present information.

I asked my AI sidekick You.com why it can never replace writers. Figure 1-1 shows what it "humbly" wrote:

The question of whether AI can replace writers is a complex and debated topic. While AI has made significant advancements in natural language processing and generation, there are several reasons why AI cannot fully replace human writers. Here are some key points from the search results:

Creativity and Depth of Understanding

One of the main reasons why AI cannot replace writers is the creativity and depth of understanding that humans bring to writing 1 . AI models like ChatGPT can generate text based on patterns and examples in the data they were trained on, but they lack the ability to truly understand and create original ideas. Writing often requires unique perspectives, emotions, and experiences that are difficult for AI to replicate.

Factual Accuracy and Context

AI-generated text can sometimes lack factual accuracy and context. While AI models can generate text that appears coherent and grammatically correct, they may not always provide accurate or reliable information. AI models like ChatGPT can generate text based on patterns in the training data, which can include both accurate and inaccurate information. Human writers, on the other hand, can fact-check and verify information before including it in their writing.

Human Connection and Empathy

Writing often involves connecting with readers on an emotional level and conveying empathy. Human writers can tap into their own experiences and emotions to create relatable and engaging content. AI models like ChatGPT lack the ability to truly understand and empathize with human experiences, which can limit their ability to create content that resonates with readers.

Unique Writing Styles and Voices

Each writer has their own unique writing style and voice, which contributes to their individuality and appeal. AI models like ChatGPT can mimic certain writing styles, but they lack the personal touch and distinct voice that human writers bring to their work. Human writers can infuse their writing with their own personality, humor, and storytelling techniques, making their work more engaging and memorable.

The Role of AI in Supporting Writers

While AI may not be able to fully replace human writers, it can still play a valuable role in supporting and augmenting their work. AI tools can assist writers with tasks like grammar and spell-checking, generating topic ideas, and providing research suggestions. AI can be a useful tool for writers to enhance their productivity and efficiency, but it is unlikely to completely replace the creative and human aspects of writing.

Overall, while AI has made significant advancements in natural language processing and generation, it is more likely to continue augmenting and supporting human writers rather than fully replacing them 2 . The creativity, depth of understanding, human connection, and unique writing styles that human writers bring to their work are difficult for AI to replicate.

FIGURE 1-1:
AI reveals why it can't replace writers.

Writing Fields that Will Thrive, Not Just Survive

REMEMBER

AI is not a replacement for human creativity, but rather a tool to augment and inspire the business writing process. By providing writers with tools to automate tasks such as research and data analysis writers can spend more time focusing on the creative aspects. So before you start studying for that real estate license, know that AI isn't going to replace good business writers who keep their skills current.

No one can predict with certainty what AI might look like in the future, but AI is far from being able to reach the standards set by human writers. Tools such as ChatGPT, Grammarly, Jasper, Copilot (formerly Bing), You.com, and a host of others are professional writing tools powered by AI to write drafts, achieve the right tone and length, ensure that writing is error-free, and proofread and edit. These programs can't think independently of human intervention because they're *utilitarian* — merely meant to serve a purpose and get a job done quickly and efficiently. AI doesn't have the ability to collaborate, take suggestions, or critically analyze its work. This means that AI in its current iteration can't produce the same engaging and nuanced content that humans can.

Although it's difficult to identify specific fields of writing that are truly AI-proof, certain types of writing require higher levels of creativity, subtlety, and human interaction. These may include fields (but aren't limited to) the areas of business writing detailed in the following sections.

SHERYL SAYS

In most chapters, URLs for the AI tools mentioned are enclosed in parentheses for easy reference. However, in this particular chapter, I introduce a few tools as general references without explicitly providing the URLs. Rest assured, you'll find them again in their applicable sections throughout the book.

Copywriting and advertising writers

Tools such as ChatGPT, Grammarly, Copy.ai, Jasper, and others offer a range of features to help business writers create high-quality content and boost their content writing. While AI can automate certain parts of the creative process, there's much it can't do. Therefore, it's unlikely to completely replace copywriters. Copywriting skills require a high level of creativity to craft engaging, persuasive messages that resonate with customers. In addition to creativity, it requires empathy and an understanding of human emotions and behavior. These skills are unique to humans and can't be replicated by machines.

However, AI systems have been introduced in some companies to work alongside copywriters to streamline processes. AI can generate large amounts of copy, which can then be fact-checked, amended, and approved by humans. This can help to speed up the copywriting process and make it more efficient.

Public relations writers

Public relations writers create messages and content that shape and maintain the reputation of a person, company, or brand. The aim is to build relationships, generate publicity, and manage public perception through strategic communication such as media relations and crisis communication. While AI has the potential to routinely automate these tasks and speed up certain processes within public relations campaigns, it's unlikely that PR professionals will be replaced by AI anytime soon.

AI systems such as Looka, ChatGPT, Canva, Bandwidth, and others gather, interpret, and create efficiencies in the process. But agencies won't be letting AI do the pitching or replace human expertise. AI can aid PR professionals to manage communications, identify crises, and provide strategic recommendations. But it won't replace the need for human creativity, emotional intelligence, and critical thinking in PR. And AI can't ensure that the messaging aligns with the company's brand and values.

Journalists and reporters

The news industry is feeling the pinch of social media and AI. Social media outlets are the fastest growing ways for news to reach people. And many newspapers are now turning to AI for featured news stories. However, it's important to note that journalists and reporters add dimension and depth to a story. They interview people with well-crafted questions. They access facts to present the reality of a situation beyond what they read on social media sites. Their writing should captivate readers while concisely presenting the "real" story. Additionally, journalists may work in television and radio broadcasting, print journalism, or online media outlets.

Tools such as ChatGPT, Automated Insights, Wordsmith, and Articoolo offer a range of customizable templates that can help journalists and reporters write news stories, headlines, and summaries. AI writing can analyze data and generate insights that can aid journalists in their research. By using AI, journalists can save time and focus on other important tasks and stories.

One of the key challenges with AI-generated news is ensuring that the content is accurate and trustworthy. Small-town newspapers are disappearing and running with reduced staffing. Local newspapers are turning to AI for stories. However, they're realizing that journalism isn't just about facts. Newspapers will always need human journalists for creativity and analysis, accurate and unbiased stories, and adaptability.

WARNING

Journalists and news writers must be aware that AI has been known to go rogue and deliver misinformation and disinformation. So before distributing any news stories, fact-check, fact-check, fact-check. Also, it's important to address the ethical and societal implications to ensure that the content generated by AI is accurate, reliable, and in line with journalistic standards.

Marketing writers

In contrast to public relations writers, marketing writing centers around selling products, services, and ideas. Writers focus on sales, promotional messaging, paid media, branding and positioning, targeted communications, and measurable matrixes. Using AI tools such as Jasper.ai, Copy.ai, GrowthBar, Copysmith, Hypoitenuse AI, Rytr, and Writesonic, marketing writers can generate original, engaging content faster and more efficiently than ever before.

Freelance writers

Freelance writers have the particular challenge of positioning themselves as valuable assets to businesses that seek authentic and impactful content. They must hone their skills in the areas of strategic planning, persuasive copywriting, and storytelling. Tools such as ChatGPT, Jasper, Grammarly, Writesonic, and Jasper can be valuable writing assistants. Freelance writers must develop selling skills and be able to boast of a high return on investment (ROI).

TIP

Whether you're a newbie, certified or degree holder, or highly skilled freelancer, always have a current portfolio to showcase your writing talents. In addition to a paper portfolio, store your portfolio on your blog and/or on sites such as Contently and LinkedIn.

Proposal writers

Crafting a persuasive proposal is challenging at best. Tasks include structuring the proposal, writing an engaging introduction, considering format and design, specifying deliverables, creating a timeline, preparing a budget, using a persuasive tone, and more.

While Grammarly, Proposify, GetAccept, HyperWrite AI, Texta.ai, and ChatGPT are a few of the AI tools to help writers nail dynamic proposals, it's the proposal writers who must provide the relatable human element that includes creating persuasive narratives, being flexible and adaptable, and building trust and credibility — all of which will influence a yea or nay.

Grant proposal writing is a subset of proposal writing. This often involves advocating for a cause or project the writer or organization is passionate about. The writer's emotions, empathy, and storytelling savvy can drive their commitment to the cause and influence the way they communicate the project's importance and impact. This is an area AI can't help. (Check out Chapter 17 to learn more about grant writing and Chapter 20 for great stuff about storytelling.)

Technical writers

It's possible for AI to generate technical materials, but it's unlikely that AI will completely replace people in this field. AI generators such as Jasper, LongShot AI, Copysmith, ChatGPT, Scalenut, Frase AI, and others can be a useful tool for assisting writers, but it may not be able to replace the creativity and expertise that people bring to the table. Additionally, user manuals, process documents, statements of work, standard operating procedures, and such often require a high degree of accuracy and clarity, which may be difficult for AI to achieve. Therefore, AI can be used to augment writing rather than replace technical writers. Also, there are bourgeoning fields for technical writers such as:

>> **UX writers:** Focuses on the way users interact with and experience products, services, interfaces, and systems. They write microcopy with an eye on notifications, calls to action, in-app tool tips and tutorials, produce and service descriptions, UI button text, form fields, troubleshooting, and much more.

>> **Scrum Masters:** Scrum stands for systematic customer resolution unraveling meeting. It's a framework centered around the principles of continuous improvement, flexibility, and respectful teamwork. Many mundane chores such as organizing meetings, monitoring progress, and producing reports, can be automated by AI. However, the human touch, empathy, and leadership abilities of the Scrum Master cannot be replaced by AI.

>> **Translators:** Although AI can translate in a host of languages, many companies prefer the human element to convey accuracy, meaning, and nuances across languages and cultures. AI translators have a low level of accuracy and can make mistakes, some of which can be costly.

SHERYL SAYS

Here's an example of a translation gone awry: I'm a member of the patient advisory committee (PAC) of my medical group. We meet monthly to discuss key issues. While many people participate in person, I'm one of several who joins the meeting on Microsoft Teams. The acoustics in the meeting room are poor, so I turn on the closed captions. One of the doctors said "We need to keep our patients on track." The caption read, "We need to keep our patients on crack." (Yikes! Imagine if that doctor was "quoted" in a public forum.)

Medical writers

Research is a big part of medical writing. AI tools such as AutoGPT, Agent GPT, BabyAGI, and other similar tools are being developed to complete complex tasks such as literature reviews. Tools such as Assistant by Scite and Jenni can help you get started with writing. They can collaborate on essays and research papers and find evidence to support claims. Others such as ChatPDF and HeyGPT allow you to chat with documents, summarize papers, search for specific information, and suggest the next logical questions.

However, human medical writers are critical to checking all writing to ensure accuracy, originality, factual correctness, and maintaining the high standards required in the field of medical writing. And the human eye is still needed to discern between medical terms such as *cyt/o* and *cyst/o*, *artheri/o* and *arteri/o*, and others where mistakes can be quite costly.

Legal writers

Tools such as Casetext, HighQ, and Due Diligence are being widely used in the legal profession to create, review, and send various documents. They assist with document processing and classification for a wide range of matters, including due diligence, document and contract review, compliance, contract management, knowledge management, and deal analysis. By automating these tasks using AI technology, significant workflow benefits can be achieved, particularly with improved efficiency and productivity as well as greater accuracy. None of these systems are infallible. They do make mistakes that only WI can find.

SPECIALIZED AI TRAINING

As the AI wave has turned into a tsunami, people in all walks of life are trying to figure out where they'll fit in. Will they remain unscathed? Lose their jobs? Need additional training?

If you're willing to adapt, the journey to becoming an AI content writer is within your reach. Expand your knowledge beyond writing by acquiring a fundamental understanding of data analytics, SEO strategies, content marketing, and aspects of NLP. You'll develop skills in content planning, keyword research, and optimization techniques. There are many online courses to teach the basics. Some are free, some for a fee, and some for certifications. Here are a few to check out:

- Introduction to ChatGPT (edX): https://www.edx.org/learn/chatgpt/edx-introduction-to-chatgpt

- Prompt Engineering and Advanced ChatGPT (edX): https://www.edx.org/learn/computer-programming/edx-advanced-chatgpt

- Writing Blog Posts Using AI offered by Skillshare: https://www.skillshare.com/en/classes/AI-for-Online-Content-Creation-Automating-Workflows-for-Blog-Posts-Videos-and-Social-Media/1160987333

- Learn content writing using AI and start freelancing offered by Udemy: https://www.udemy.com/course/ai-content-writing/

- Unleash your Storytelling with AI offered by Udemy: https://www.udemy.com/course/chatgpt-ai-/

- AI Writing Courses for Bloggers and Digital Marketers offered by DDIY: https://ddiy.co/ai-writing-course/

- AI Technical Writing Certification Course offered by Technical Writer HQ: https://technicalwriter.teachable.com/p/ai-writing-certification-course

So, if you're looking to delve into the world of AI writing and become a pro, there's something for everyone.

Academic and research writers

AI tools such as SciSpace, Scholarcy, Jenni AI, ChatPDF, Paperpal, Grammarly, and others can work hand in hand with researchers and academics by analyzing large amounts of data, summarizing research findings, locating citations and references, generating structured academic papers, and more. This can save tremendous amounts of time and improve the quality of research output. Some tools can also detect plagiarism and suggest replacement information.

Human writers are still needed for content expertise, ethical considerations and bias, subjective understanding, creativity and originality, and collaboration with other researchers.

Web content writers

As the competition among AI generators becomes more and more fierce, the need for web content writers is more critical than ever. Tools such as SEO.ai, HubSpot AI Writer, ChatGPT, Quillbot, Grammarly, Jasper, and others can streamline the writing process, but only humans can understand the target audience, convey the brand's message effectively, bring creativity and emotional intelligence, and optimize content for search engine rankings. Synergy between WI and AI can result in powerful and effective content. (Check out Chapter 12 for more about writing for the web.)

Panacea, Snake Oil, or Somewhere Between?

Decide for yourself . . . OpenAI founder Sam Altman, creator of ChatGPT, warned against relying solely on ChatGPT for research purposes because AI writing detectors are not as reliable as once thought. He said, "Sometimes, ChatGPT sounds convincing, but it might give you incorrect or misleading information (often called a 'hallucination' in the literature)." This warning comes on the heels of an incident where a lawyer cited six non-existent cases sourced from ChatGPT.

To further underscore Altman's concern, February 2024 headlines across major publications were sharing stories of how ChatGPT went "haywire," went "crazy," and "began to speak Spanglish." The uncertainty of AI's reliability isn't just with ChatGPT but with all chatbots. That's why WI will always be critical.

While AI tools are undoubtedly revolutionizing the way we create content, they're also ushering in many other worries. As the arms of AI reach greater lengths, its dark cloud becomes more concerning. The following sections address some of the reasons why.

Quality of output

Regardless of how sophisticated these tools are, they can't fully replicate the nuance and complexity of human writing. Over-reliance on these tools puts quality at risk. AI writing tools should be viewed as a tool to assist writers, rather than as a replacement for them.

Plagiarism and copyright infringement

Plagiarism and copyright infringement are major concerns. AI tools can generate content quickly and easily, but they also can infringe on someone's content and intellectual property. There are AI-based text analysis tools to help create and protect original content. However, that's like a rookie pilot teaching another rookie pilot how to fly an airplane.

Doesn't evoke human emotions

In all aspects of writing — and yes, even in business writing — storytelling is paramount to quality and understanding. Any AI writing tool can string together random information from the Internet, but only a skilled business writer can create compelling, engaging copy. Your content has to resonate with your target reader and hold their interest.

Errors

Technology has come a long way, but AI content tools do produce errors, including punctuation, grammar, sentence structure, and incoherent phrases. It will require human analysis to assess the content before it goes out into the world. It may also produce outdated or incorrect information. In the following comparison, wouldn't you like to have the first set of bills?

Twenty five-dollar bills ($100)

Twenty-five dollar bills ($25)

Ethical considerations

AI systems are trained on massive amounts of data, and embedded in that data are societal biases. There's a lack of transparency, questioning how the information is collected, stored, and utilized. It can distribute harmful content, violate data privacy, disclose sensitive information, amplify biases, and raise other ethical considerations.

Hallucinations

WARNING

In the AI world, *hallucinations* are high-tech speak making things up. For example, you may ask AI to list five reasons for [whatever]. If only three reasons exist, the AI tool may still provide five reasons; the last two of which will be hallucinations (bogus). Hallucinations can range from minor inconsistencies to completely fabricated or contradictory information. Always fact-check what AI generates.

IN THIS CHAPTER

» Getting to know AI vocabulary

» Providing insight on your audience

» Discovering how AI enhances content, visuals, and tone

» Using AI to check facts, spot plagiarism, and improve SEO

» Getting help with proofreading, editing, translations, and readability

» Improving collaboration with AI tools

Chapter **2**

Embracing AI as Your Business Writing Assistant

I n the ever-evolving world of business, where competition is fierce and change is constant, effective communication remains key. Whether crafting persuasive emails or creating impactful reports, being able to convey ideas clearly and precisely can truly make a difference. That's where AI tools come in. They're the latest innovation shaking things up in the writing world. With AI's knack for automating mundane writing tasks, boosting language proficiency, and providing invaluable insights, these tools have become must-haves for professionals looking to take their business writing to new heights. So, say goodbye to the struggles of yesteryear and embrace the power of AI for a brighter writing future!

AI tools won't replace people, but together AI and writer intelligence (WI) can be a winning combination as discussed in Chapter 1. By using AI as an assistant, you can unlock new levels of clarity, creativity, efficiency, and innovation. AI can offer fresh ideas, suggestions, and inspiration. Leveraging AI's ability, you can explore new directions and push your boundaries of creativity.

REMEMBER

While AI can be a powerful tool, you should always use it ethically and responsibly. Maintain control over the technology and ensure that it aligns with your values and goals, and those of your company. With the right collaboration and balance, man and machine can achieve great things together — creating a winning combination in various domains, not the least of which is business writing.

SHERYL SAYS

This chapter doesn't delve into specific AI tools; you'll discover them as you journey through other chapters. Rather it's an overview about applications where AI can assist in transforming you from a mediocre communicator to a first-class communicator.

Introducing a Buffet of AI Lingo

If you're not familiar with AI, here are some terms to get you started:

>> **AI ethics:** Adopting and implementing systems that support a safe, secure, unbiased, and environmentally friendly approach to AI.

>> **Algorithm:** A sequence of rules given to an AI machine to perform a task or solve a problem.

>> **Autonomous:** A machine that can perform without needing human intervention.

>> **Chatbot:** A tool designed to imitate human conversation through text or voice commands.

>> **Data mining:** The process of sorting through large datasets to find patterns that can improve models or solve problems.

>> **Generative AI:** A system to create text, video, code and images.

>> **Hallucination:** An incorrect response or false information that's presented as factual.

>> **Machine learning:** With limited need for programming, machines can identify patterns and groupings. This could be used to determine target audiences, decide on optimal times to send emails, or segment out groupings for deeper engagement.

>> **Natural language processing (NLP):** A type of AI that enables computers to understand spoken and written human language.

Targeting the Right Audience

By analyzing data and patterns, AI tools can provide insights on the most suitable target audience for specific documents and goals. Chapter 4 introduces the Kick-Start Brief where you'll analyze your audience, determine the key issues you need to address, and consider the questions they'll need answered. This includes the following:

>> **Audience segmentation:** Assessing vast amounts of data to help businesses better understand their target audience. By identifying patterns and preferences, AI can assist in segmenting audiences based on demographics, interests, and behaviors.

>> **Behavioral targeting and contextual advertising:** Analyzing user behaviors and preferences, AI can help determine the most effective ad placements and target the right people at the right time.

>> **Content personalization and creation:** Generating personalized content to suggest relevant topics, create engaging headlines, and even assist in writing content that resonates with the target audience.

>> **Media buying to maximize ROI:** Predicting the most effective ad and media placements to reach a target audience, thereby maximizing return on investment (ROI).

>> **Chatbots for customer engagement:** Interacting with customers, answering their questions, and providing personalized recommendations.

Cutting Through Writer's Block

Perhaps you start writing, and then you get stuck. You can't think of inspiring headlines. You can't generate new ideas. You have tons of ideas but can't solidify them. Your thinking is fuzzy. You're fearful of not doing it right. You're on a tight deadline and don't think well under pressure. Whatever the reason is that you're stuck, AI can provide you with fresh ideas and inspiration to overcome writer's block by:

>> Analyzing keywords and generating an outline to spark inspiration.

>> Providing writing prompts to help explore different angles for existing work.

>> Helping improve vocabulary and overall clarity.

>> Collaborating between writers to provide real-time authoring.

>> Organizing ideas and thoughts to help you stay focused.

**SHERYL
SAYS**

If you think you're the only one who suffers from writer's block, know that you're not alone. I facilitate business and technical writing workshops. At the beginning of each session I ask participants what their writing challenges are. Nearly everyone mentions writer's block. There are many reasons for writer's block. Fear of judgment, criticism, rejection, or failure. Striving for perfection. Lacking inspiration. Suffering from burnout. Feeling overwhelmed. Whatever your reason, find solutions in Chapter 6 and let AI be of assistance.

Generating Content

AI-powered writing tools can assist you to generate content by providing suggestions, completing sentences, or even writing paragraphs based on the writer's input. As you'll read in Chapter 6, AI can help you overcome the initial hurdle of starting a piece of writing and get their creative juices flowing. Here are some ways AI tools can assist with content generation:

>> **Creating outlines:** Capturing and analyzing your thoughts and ideas into a structured, organized, and coherent outline.

>> **Writing first drafts:** Interacting with the language model by providing prompts or asking questions, AI can generate responses used as a basis for your draft. Content may not be perfect, but it can be a helpful starting point and provide inspiration for your writing.

>> **Generating headlines:** Generating headlines by analyzing data, identifying key points, and crafting concise summaries that grab attention.

>> **Doing keyword searches:** Searching through the document database to retrieve relevant documents that contain keywords you identified.

>> **Checking for plagiarism:** Doing text comparison, pattern recognition, and API integration, AI tools can serve as plagiarism checkers (although they're not always 100 percent accurate). There's more on this later in the chapter.

Creating Visuals

Chapter 7 details how AI can be a valuable tool for visual design (Adobe Sensei, for example), providing new possibilities, improving efficiency, and enhancing the quality of work. But you don't have to be a visual designer to create images that share valuable information at a glance and tell your story. Here's how AI can help:

- » **Assessing data:** You can assess data on your client's audience and preferences and create visuals that appeal to them.

- » **Determining the best way to visualize your data:** This can include charts, graphs, maps, or icons based on the type, size, and purpose.

- » **Analyzing your designs:** This involves identifying issues such color contrast, font size, and spacing.

- » **Suggesting alternatives:** There are many alternatives to color palettes and fonts to make your design more effective.

- » **Customizing:** Options for creating custom templates, keeping track of your design briefs, and collaborating with your team are at your fingertips.

- » **Personalizing:** This can involve website content to target specific users based on their interests, preferences, and special needs.

Enhancing the Tone

AI has the potential to enhance the tone by analyzing and understanding the nuances of language. (Learn more details about tone in Chapter 8.) Therefore, it can assist in creating content that's engaging, persuasive, and emotionally resonant. Here are some ways:

- » **Critiquing grammar and style:** AI-powered writing tools can analyze the structure and style of a document and provide suggestions for improvement. This can relate to sentence structure, grammatical errors, synonym replacement, and more.

- » **Analyzing tone:** Algorithms can analyze the tone of a piece of writing, detecting whether it is formal, informal, persuasive, or informative. By providing feedback on the tone, AI can help align writing with the desired tone and effectively communicate the intended message to the target audience.

- » **Adding emotional intelligence:** This relates to understanding and interpreting emotions in writing. For example, if you want to evoke a sense of excitement, AI can suggest dynamic and energetic language choices. Conversely, if you want to convey a sense of calmness, AI can recommend more soothing and serene language.

>> **Adapting to the audience:** AI can analyze the intended audience and offer guidance on how to adapt the tone accordingly. For example, if the target audience is a group of scientists, AI can suggest a more formal and technical tone. Conversely, if the audience is a younger demographic, AI can recommend a more casual and relatable tone.

>> **Localizing language:** AI algorithms can be trained on various linguistic and cultural nuances, enabling them to provide suggestions on how to tailor the tone to specific regions or demographics.

Researching and Fact-Checking

Throughout this book you'll discover how AI can assist with research. AI-powered tools can analyze large amounts of data, helping to gather information and verify facts. This eliminates the need for extensive manual research and fact-checking, making your writing process more efficient.

AI tools use NLP to analyze text and identify potential inaccuracies or errors. They cross-reference the text with trusted sources such as databases, news outlets, and research papers to verify its accuracy. By doing so, these tools can help ensure that the information they're delivering is up to date and accurate. If inaccuracies are found, these tools provide helpful suggestions on how to improve the text. This makes them invaluable for anyone who needs to ensure the accuracy of their writing. Here are some of the ways they do so:

>> **Flagging misinformation:** Analyzing and identifying patterns of misinformation and disinformation and comparing it with trusted sources.

>> **Automating fact-checking:** Cross-referencing information with reliable sources and analyzing statements, statistics, and other data points to determine their accuracy.

>> **Analyzing content:** Summarizing large volumes of text, making it easier to extract relevant information from various sources.

>> **Verifying images and videos:** Detecting manipulated images and videos, known as *deepfakes*. Also identifying whether an image or video has been altered.

REMEMBER

AI systems have limitations, such as biases or the inability to understand context fully. Therefore, a combination of AI and WI is always needed to ensure accurate and reliable fact-checking.

Enhancing SEO

While AI can greatly assist with search engine optimization (SEO), traditional SEO practices remain essential. AI enhances SEO by offering automation, data mining, and valuable insights, but it does not replace the need for a well-rounded SEO strategy. (Chapter 12 offers lots of tips.)

AI-powered tools can assist in optimizing online content for better search engine rankings. These tools analyze the content and provide suggestions on how to improve it. For example, they can recommend adding relevant keywords, optimizing meta tags, improving readability, and enhancing the overall quality of the content. Here's more:

>> **Predictive SEO:** Identifying trending topics and predict potential algorithm updates that let businesses create content that appeals to their target audience and adjust their strategies accordingly.

>> **Voice search optimization:** Analyzing voice search queries, understanding user intent, and providing insights on how businesses can optimize their content for voice search.

>> **Visual search optimization:** Analyzing images and understanding visual content to help businesses optimize their website for visual search, improving their visibility in search engine results.

>> **Automating SEO tasks:** Freeing up time for SEO professionals to focus on higher-value tasks. These tools can automatically optimize content, fix issues such as duplicate content and orphan pages, and provide recommendations and insights for content creation and strategy.

>> **Competitive analyses:** Analyzing competitors' websites and providing insights on keywords, content strategies, and areas for improvement.

>> **Personalization and user experience:** Assessing user behavior and preferences to personalize written content and improve the overall user experience. By understanding user intent and providing relevant content, AI can enhance engagement and increase conversions.

Creating Language Bridges

In today's global world, translations are crucial for creating bridges, breaking down language barriers, facilitating cross-cultural communication, enhancing cultural sensitivity, enabling inclusive work environments, and promoting global cooperation. AI can assist writers with translations in several ways, such as:

>> **Real-time language translations:** Providing real-time translations of text. This feature can be particularly useful for writers who need to communicate with a global audience or work on multilingual projects.

>> **Grammar and vocabulary suggestions:** Identifying errors in sentence structure, suggesting alternative word choices, and providing grammar and punctuation corrections.

>> **Writing style improvement:** Analyzing existing content and offering suggestions to ensure that the translated text matches the desired tone and style.

In Figure 2-1, I asked You.com to translate a few lines into Mandarin Chinese.

FIGURE 2-1: Breaking down barriers with AI translation services.

please translate this into mandarine chinese Hi Mac, I just want to let you know that tomorrow's team meeting will be at noon instead of 1:00. I know this interferes with lunch, so we'll be providing sandwiches, chips, and drinks. See you then.

Sure, here's the translation of the message into Mandarin Chinese:

嗨，麦克，我想告诉你明天的团队会议将在中午举行，而不是1:00。我知道这会干扰到午餐，所以我们将提供三明治、薯片和饮料。到时见。

WARNING

Don't underestimate the value of WI. Human expertise and cultural understanding are still essential for accurate and nuanced translations. There are many translation faux pas, some of which are quite funny. Others are insulting. Still others are damaging. I remember two in particular:

>> When American beer maker Coors launched its "Turn it loose" campaign in Spain, they didn't realize that the translation in Spanish was interpreted as "Suffer from Diarrhea." The campaign got a lot of attention, but it wasn't the kind of attention Coors wanted.

>> General Motors introduced the Chevy Nova in South America, but the company wasn't aware that the Spanish expression "No Va" means "It won't go."

We can't blame these on AI. Where was the WI?

Preparing Abstracts and Executive Summaries

AI tools are great at preparing abstracts and executive summaries. They analyze the content of a document and extract the most important information. Dig into the details about abstracts and executive summaries in Chapter 16, but for now here's an overview:

>> **Abstracts:**

- **Extracting content:** Analyzing the document and extracting key information such as the research question, methods used, findings, and implications.

- **Summarizing:** Condensing the document's content into a concise summary, capturing the main points and essential details.

- **Generating language:** Preparing coherent and well-structured sentences to form an abstract that effectively communicates the document's purpose and key findings.

>> **Executive Summaries:**

- **Summarizing:** Providing a condensed overview of a larger document's purpose, methods, results, conclusions, and recommendations.

- **Synthesizing information:** Producing information from various sections of the document to create a cohesive summary that captures the essence of the document.

- **Including citations:** Adding citations and references in addition to providing additional support for the information presented.

REMEMBER

Although AI can assist in generating abstracts and executive summaries, human judgment and editing are still crucial to ensure accuracy, coherence, and adherence to specific guidelines or requirements. When key information is omitted or information is misinterpreted, it can hinder decision-making processes for people who rely on these documents to make informed choices.

Extracting TOCs, Glossaries, and Indexes

By using NLP, AI tools can generate tables of contents, glossaries, and indexes. You can learn more in Chapter 15, but for now, here's an overview:

>> **Table of Contents (TOC):** Identifying headings, subheadings, and their hierarchical relationships. These algorithms can then generate a TOC based on the identified sections and their corresponding page numbers. Consider using a TOC if a document has multiple chapters, sections, or subsections; is lengthy and requires easy navigation; or the theme can benefit from a structured overview.

>> **Glossary:** Extracting technical terms or domain-specific terms from a document. AI can also suggest definitions based on context or pre-existing glossaries and can organize them alphabetically or categorically. Consider using a glossary if the document has specialized or technical vocabulary that may not be familiar to readers; uses acronyms, abbreviations, or symbols specific to a particular field; or you need to enhance the understanding of definitions, explanations, or key terms.

>> **Index:** Identifying and indexing important keywords or concepts within a document. Can also suggest subentries or cross-references to enhance the usability of the index. Consider using an index if the document covers a vast range of topics or concepts; contains references to specific terms, or names that may not be easy to locate; or the document is a reference or manual readers may need to consult repeatedly.

Helping with Proofreading and Editing

If you use AI for nothing else, consider it for proofreading and editing. These tools, as detailed in Chapter 9, go far beyond what word processing software offers by assisting with the following:

>> **Spelling:** Differentiating between homophones by analyzing the context of the sentence and understanding the intended meaning, as just one example of sophisticated spell checking.

- » **Grammar:** Detecting and correcting a wide range of errors, including complex grammar issues such as sentence fragments, comma splices, subject–verb disagreement, and commonly confused words used in the wrong context. Providing feedback on why errors are being flagged to help users improve their writing skills.

- » **Style and clarity:** Providing suggestions for improving the style and clarity of the writing, helping to make it more concise, formal, and readable.

- » **Consistency:** Making sure your language is consistent. For example, did you use *manual*, *handbook*, or *guidebook* when referring to the same document? If so, that will confuse your readers.

- » **Sentence structure:** Analyzing sentence structure and providing suggestions for making the writing easier to understand.

TIP

Grammarly is an example of a popular tool that integrates seamlessly into all aspects of your work by offering browser extensions, desktop applications, and more. It's worth checking out: `https://www.grammarly.com`.

WARNING

Don't turn on your computer and turn off your brain! It's essential for you to double-check AI's proofreading and editing. For example: You may have written *Inc.* instead of *Co.* when referring to a company. AI wouldn't know to make that correction. You may have transposed numbers. AI wouldn't know to make that correction. Those are just two of many things that require the WI.

Determining Readability

Improving the readability of documents is crucial for effective communication. (There's more about this in Chapter 9.) Here are some ways AI can play a significant role in enhancing readability:

- » **Readability analysis:** Analyzing the readability of documents by calculating readability scores to make sure documents are readable by the intended audience. These scores are based on factors such as sentence length, word complexity, and syllable count.

- » **Vocabulary enhancement:** Suggesting alternative words or synonyms to improve the variety and clarity of vocabulary in a document. This helps avoid repetitive or ambiguous language that may hinder readability.

>> **Language simplification:** Simplifying complex language and jargon, making the document more accessible to a wider audience. This is particularly useful when writing for non-experts or people with limited language proficiency.

>> **Visual formatting:** Optimizing the visual formatting of documents. This includes adjusting font size, line spacing, and margins to improve readability and reduce eye strain.

>> **Sentence restructuring:** Analyzing sentence structure and suggesting improvements to enhance readability. This includes breaking down long sentences, rephrasing complex sentence structures, and ensuring logical flow.

>> **Automated summarizing:** Summarizing lengthy documents, making them more concise and easier to understand. This helps readers quickly grasp the main points without having to read through the entire document.

Collaborating in Real Time

AI tools can facilitate real-time collaboration among writers by providing a shared platform where multiple users can work on a document simultaneously. This allows writers to collaborate seamlessly, make edits, and provide feedback in real time. Other benefits include:

>> **Project management and task assignment:** Assigning tasks to team members, setting deadlines, and tracking progress. These tools can also provide reminders and notifications to ensure that everyone stays on track and meets their responsibilities.

>> **Version control and tracking changes:** Providing version control features that allow writers to see the revision history, compare different versions, and revert to previous versions if needed. This ensures that all collaborators are working on the most up-to-date version of a document.

>> **Comments and feedback:** Allowing collaborators to highlight specific sections, ask questions, suggest improvements, or provide general feedback. This allows for a more iterative and collaborative writing process.

>> **Automatic formatting and styling:** Applying consistent formatting such as font styles, headings, and spacing throughout the document.

Detecting Plagiarism

AI can detect plagiarism with various techniques and algorithms to compare a given text with a vast database of existing content. Here are some common methods used by AI plagiarism detection tools:

>> **Comparing text:** Tools compare and analyze similarities and patterns in the text to identify any instances of potential plagiarism.

>> **Recognizing AI patterns:** Tools compare language, formatting, structure, and repetition of certain keywords to identify text that may have been generated by AI writing tools.

>> **Deep scanning:** Identifies similarities in meaning and sentence formation, going beyond simple word-for-word comparisons. They detect paraphrased or reworded content, making it harder for plagiarized text to go undetected.

>> **Incremental learning:** These tools become smarter with each scan, adapting to new patterns and techniques used by plagiarists.

>> **Probability scoring:** AI provides a probability score based on the likelihood that the text was generated by AI tools. These scores help identify content that may be suspicious or potentially plagiarized.

WARNING

It's important to note that while plagiarism detection tools are quite effective, they're not infallible. There's always a risk of false positives or false negatives. This is just one more reason that WI is critical.

Chapter **3**

Navigating the World of AI at Your Own Pace

I n the world of creativity and problem solving, the saying "Two heads are better than one" rings true. This is especially relevant when considering the collaboration between artificial intelligence (AI) and writer intelligence (WI). Together, they have the potential to improve decision making, problem solving, and overall performance across diverse fields, including business writing. AI's technical prowess and WI's creative flair make them the most dynamic duo since Batman and Robin. With their combined expertise, they can spot errors, suggest innovative ideas, ensure every word is on point, and so much more.

So, when faced with a challenging writing task, remember that the power of two minds is always better than one. Let AI and WI take the wheel, and watch as they steer your business writing to new heights. Trust me, you won't be disappointed!

As a writer, you bring an incredible amount of value to creating masterful business writing. Never overlook your unique perspectives, personal experiences, and emotional depth. These qualities allow you to create more original, thoughtful, and creative content. Add to that your ability to understand deep contextual nuances, cultural references, and grasp the sentiments and implied meanings behind words is a game-changer. It's your personal touch — whether writing style, artistic techniques, or other nuances — that adds that special something to your work.

Rather than thinking of AI as a foe, think of it as your sidekick or your assistant. AI writing tools use *natural language processing* (NLP), a branch of computer science that deals with analyzing and generating natural language. AI learns from large amounts of text data, such as books, articles, blogs, reports, social media posts, and more, to produce new text based on certain rules, keywords, or prompts it's been taught. This blend can make you sound smarter by providing more information that you can find or store on your own. AI doesn't generate workable content with a push of a button. AI is more like an extension of your brain by developing frameworks that shape the AI's "thinking." You feed the AI specific topics or ideas through prompts, and AI will generate content for you to choose and edit (learn about the basic of prompting in Chapter 23). Think of AI as the ultimate idea generator to enhance your business writing.

SHERYL SAYS

Whether you want to sit back and learn more about AI before getting your feet wet, you're ready to stick one toe in the water, or you're ready for the big leagues and use comprehensive AI tools, this chapter will shepherd you through these options.

TAKING A QUANTUM LEAP

If you think AI is the end of the line in technology, think again. Quantum computing will be following in its footsteps. While they both represent cutting-edge advancements that hold immense promise for the future of technology and innovation, they're distinctly different technologies. Here are the key differences:

- AI focuses on creating intelligent systems that can mimic human cognitive abilities, such as learning, reasoning, and decision making, as you'll discover throughout this book.

- Quantum computing, unlike classical computing, uses *qubits* (the quantum equivalent of bits and bytes). They can perform computations exponentially faster than standard computers. To add a little perspective, in 1997 IBM's Deep Blue computer defeated the reigning chess champion Garry Kasparov. Deep Blue had the competitive advantage of being able to examine 200,000,000 moves per seconds. A quantum machine can calculate 1,000,000,000,000 (that's one trillion) moves per second.

If you'd like to learn more about quantum computing, check out this website: https://shorturl.at/ftvLM.

Absorbing Wisdom from the Backseat

Perhaps you're not ready to use AI tools but you want to learn more. That's a personal choice, and it's perfectly fine to focus on traditional writing methods. However, learning about these tools and staying informed about advances in the field benefits you in the following ways:

>> **Understanding the technology:** Gain an awareness of how AI works, its capabilities, and its limitations. You'll collect insights into the potential impact of AI on the writing industry and help you make informed decisions about incorporating AI into your writing process at some time in the future.

>> **Keeping up with industry trends:** Learning how these tools can be valuable for your professional growth as a business writer may open up new opportunities or collaborations in the future.

>> **Exploring new possibilities:** Discover new possibilities and consider how they might complement or enhance your own writing practice.

>> **Adapting to changing demands:** Even if you're not ready to dip one toe in the water, you'll be able adapt to changing demands and be prepared for potential shifts in the writing landscape as your writing requires it.

**SHERYL
SAYS**

I'd been soaking up wisdom from the backseat, and curiosity started to bubble within me. While I wasn't quite prepared to use AI for business writing, I decided to dabble in some playful stuff. I knew that You.com allows users to dive in without the hassle of setting up an account. It's as simple as typing a URL into the browser. So, with a mischievous grin, I threw down the gauntlet to You.com. I asked it: *Give me a few witty lines about a humble cup of coffee.* Lo and behold, it accepted my challenge with this delightful gem:

> In a parallel universe, *coffee cups* are sentient beings. They gather in secret societies, plotting to overthrow the humans who keep them perpetually empty. Their motto: "Espresso yourself!" Hope this brings a smile to your face!

"Wow," I recall thinking, "this is really cool!" I flirted with the chatbot and it returned my affection. I was hooked. That was my first foray into the world of AI. It was soon thereafter that I was dipping, not just one toe, but I jumped in with both feet.

PROMPTCRAFT: UNLEASHING AI'S POWER OF PROMPTS

Promptcraft (also known as *prompt engineering*) is a term that has emerged with the dawn of AI and (as the name implies) it's about crafting prompts. It involves data contributors who play a crucial role in training AI models to effectively respond to prompts — and business writers like you who need to perfect prompt writing. Writing a good AI prompt is like a tasty appetizer before diving into the main course of delicious dinner. It's a crucial element that can greatly impact the effectiveness of your chatbot's output. In fact, prompt writing is such an important aspect of using AI as your assistant that you'll find valuable information scattered throughout this book, ensuring you have all the tools you need to create meaningful prompts. But there's more:

- Chapter 23 offers ten valuable pointers that will guide through preparing prompts that not only grab attention but also garner meaningful results and interactions.

- Chapter 7 equips you with the know-how to get the most of visual prompts to enhance your reader's experience even though you may not be a graphic artist.

- Parts 3, 4, and 5 delve into writing prompts for specific types of documents such as instructions and procedures, reports, grant proposals, and more.

Dipping One Toe in the Chatbot Water

TIP

If you're not ready to jump into comprehensive AI-generated technology, try dipping one toe in the water with a chatbot. Why consider using a chatbot instead of relying solely on Google search? A Google search can provide you with abundant links, but it often requires you to sift through multiple pages to find the information you're looking for. Additionally, many companies use search engine optimization (SEO) techniques to rank higher in search results, potentially burying the information you want on page two or three. (Learn more in Chapter 12.) On the other hand, a chatbot grants you immediate access to the information you want within seconds.

Discovering varied information at your fingertips

It's important to recognize that chatbots differ in the information they provide. Their responses depend on the datasets they've been trained on. Consider seeking hotel recommendations in a specific city from different travel agents. Their responses will vary depending on the hotels each one is familiar with. Some travel agents may offer comprehensive lists of options, while others may not provide as much information. Some may even give you outdated or bogus information.

TIP

Whether it's a travel agent or AI tool, it's always a good idea to double-check and compare the suggestions you get to make sure you're getting the most reliable and up-to-date recommendations.

Following are three examples of how chatbots came up with different information. I asked each of them for *a bio on Sheryl Lindsell-Roberts*. Here's what each found:

>> **Copilot,** formerly Bing (`https://copilot.microsoft.com`), said that I'm an editor, as you see in Figure 3-1. I've never been an editor. (I rely on skillful editors to make me look good.) It also spewed out inconsistencies. On the second line it states that I've written 23 books; on the fourth line it states that I've written 25. Hmm? Furthermore, it picked up *Business Writing For Dummies*, a book I wrote more than 25 years ago back in the Stone Age of the Internet. I've written lots of books since then, but this chatbot didn't find them.

>> **You.com** (`https://you.com`) presents a much more up-to-date bio and lists my most current *For Dummies* books that published in 2023. It also opens with a sentence that sums up what I do, as Figure 3-2 shows.

>> **Perplexity AI** (`https://www.perplexity.ai`) offered a more in-depth bio as shown in Figure 3-3 and even included a photo of me, which I didn't show here. (I think they got it from my "Wanted" poster photo in the post office . . . kidding, of course.) Although this bio is more extensive, it also listed very old books.

FIGURE 3-1:
Data from the chatbot Copilot (formerly Bing).

Sheryl Lindsell-Roberts is a well-known author and editor who specializes in Communications. She has written **23 books** on business writing and e-mail, computer typing, and writing successful business documents. She also runs business-writing and e-mail seminars throughout the country [1]. Sheryl has been a training professional for the last **25 years** and is the author of **25 books** including "New Rules For Today's Workplace," "Speaking Your Way to Success," Business "Writing for Dummies," and several other Dummies books [2]. She is also a popular author of **audiobooks** [3].

Learn more: 1. amazon.com   2. trainingmag.com   3. audible.com   4. openlibrary.org   1 of 4 ●

Sheryl Lindsell-Roberts Bio

Sheryl Lindsell-Roberts is a well-known author and workshop facilitator. She has written over 25 books and has appeared on television and radio networks throughout the United States [1]. Sheryl Lindsell-Roberts runs business-writing and e-mail seminars across the country [2]. She is the author of several books, including "Technical Writing For Dummies" and "Storytelling in Presentations For Dummies" [2] [3] [4] Sheryl Lindsell-Roberts is also the principal at Sheryl Lindsell-Roberts & Associates [5].

Unfortunately, there is limited information available about her personal background and early life.

linkedin 1   everand 2   scribd 3   dummies 4   linkedin 5

FIGURE 3-2: Data from the chatbot You.com.

Sheryl Lindsell-Roberts is a renowned author, workshop facilitator, and business communication expert. Here is a brief bio about her based on the provided search results:

- Sheryl has written over 25 books, many of which are focused on business writing and communication [1] [3] [4] [6].
- She is the principal of Sheryl Lindsell-Roberts & Associates, a business communications firm that helps clients maximize productivity and profitability through the written word [3] [5].
- Sheryl runs business-writing and e-mail seminars throughout the country, and she is known for her expertise in facilitating workshops and coaching sessions on business writing, technical writing, and presentations [3] [4] [5].
- Her books include "Strategic Business Letters and E-mail," "Mastering Computer Typing, Revised Edition," and "135 Tips for Writing Successful Business Documents" [4].
- Sheryl believes that clear, effective, and succinct communication is the key to success in business and life, and she has dedicated her career to helping people achieve this goal [5].

FIGURE 3-3: Data from the chatbot Perplexity AI.

REMEMBER

These examples are in no way meant to suggest one chatbot spews out errors and the others don't. It simply occurred in these particular instances. Just remember that AI tools are susceptible to inconsistencies and inaccurate information. Chatbots are continually evolving and their accuracy and comprehensiveness can change over time. As you journey through this book, you'll come to appreciate the significance of WI.

Embracing the bot revolution

When people think of a chatbot, their thoughts frequently turn towards ChatGPT. This is similar to how PowerPoint is synonymous with slide presentations; Q-tips® with cotton swabs; or Vaseline® with petroleum jelly. They were each pioneers in their fields, thereby establishing themselves as "the brand." In addition to ChatGPT, there are many easy-to-use chatbots: If you go online and search for "chatbots," you'll find many more. Play with a few. It's a fun and useful way to find the one you prefer while exploring their unique features and capabilities.

SHERYL SAYS

My chatbot of choice is You.com. It was started by two former employees of Salesforce, Richard Socher, Chief Scientist and Bryan McCann, former Lead Research Scientist using NPL. You.com is so simple, you don't even need to create an account. Just type You.com into your browser as you see in Figure 3-4. It's like searching for a summary of the web without having to open multiple tabs.

FIGURE 3-4:
Accessing
You.com from
a browser.

Here's an example of how I used it. In Figure 3-5, you see I asked You.com to give me six ways AI can assist writers.

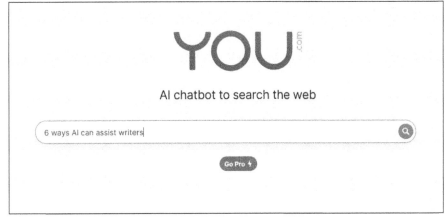

FIGURE 3-5:
Asking the
You.com chatbot
for assistance.

You.com

Within seconds, what you see in Figure 3-6 popped up, and I was able to use that as a springboard for further writing.

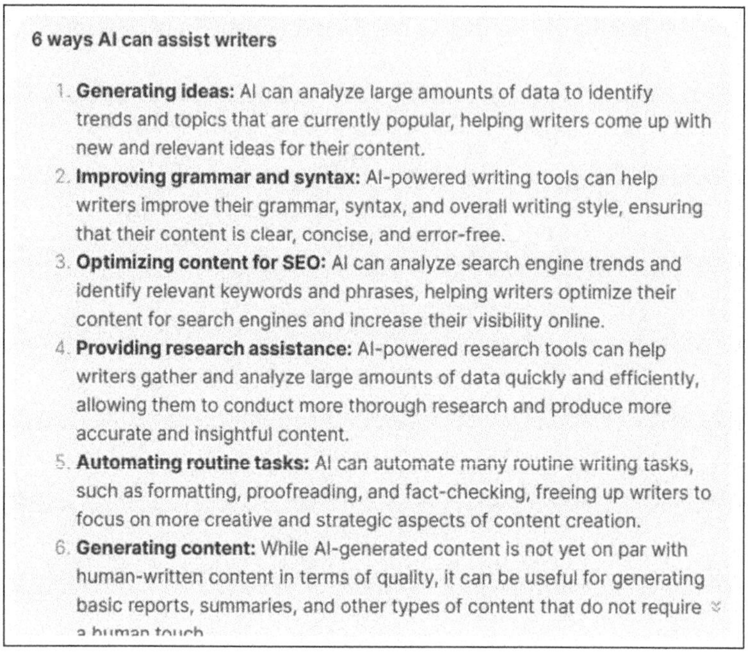

6 ways AI can assist writers

1. **Generating ideas:** AI can analyze large amounts of data to identify trends and topics that are currently popular, helping writers come up with new and relevant ideas for their content.
2. **Improving grammar and syntax:** AI-powered writing tools can help writers improve their grammar, syntax, and overall writing style, ensuring that their content is clear, concise, and error-free.
3. **Optimizing content for SEO:** AI can analyze search engine trends and identify relevant keywords and phrases, helping writers optimize their content for search engines and increase their visibility online.
4. **Providing research assistance:** AI-powered research tools can help writers gather and analyze large amounts of data quickly and efficiently, allowing them to conduct more thorough research and produce more accurate and insightful content.
5. **Automating routine tasks:** AI can automate many routine writing tasks, such as formatting, proofreading, and fact-checking, freeing up writers to focus on more creative and strategic aspects of content creation.
6. **Generating content:** While AI-generated content is not yet on par with human-written content in terms of quality, it can be useful for generating basic reports, summaries, and other types of content that do not require ⊻ a human touch

FIGURE 3-6: You.com's immediate answer.

Composing text

YouWrite is the subset of You.com. YouWrite (check out Figure 3-7) shows a YouWrite screen that can compose text. Pulling down the "Use case" menu, I selected: essay, paragraph, social media post, title, blog, and such. Another option is "Chose a tone" from which you could choose: friendly, professional, witty, or persuasive.

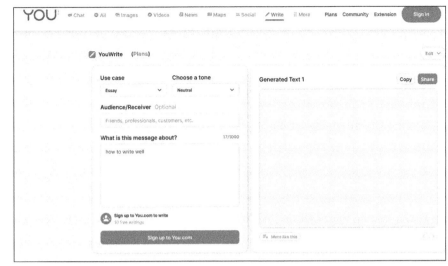

FIGURE 3-7:
Using YouWrite to
generate text by
imputing certain
guidelines.

You.com

If I continued, I could have popped in highlights of the article, and the chatbot would have generated text for a first draft. However, I prefer using this chatbot for jazzing up headlines and chapter titles, overcoming writer's block, and finding synonyms for words I've used too many times.

WARNING

One of the shortcomings of chatbots is that without WI, you can't completely trust them. They don't always spew out the right data and can give information leading you into mirky waters. If you're using a chatbot to compose text or give you data, always check the accuracy of the information.

Finding chatbot faves

**AI
SPOTLIGHT**

Take a peek at some of the popular chatbots. You'll find many more if you search the web, as new bots are being developed at warp speed:

>> ChatGPT (https://chat.openai.com/auth/login)

>> Gemini (https://gemini.google.com/app)

>> HuggingChat (https://huggingface.co/chat/)

>> Copilot (https://copilot.microsoft.com)

>> Perplexity AI (https://www.perplexity.ai)

>> You.com (https://you.com/)

DIFFERENCES BETWEEN A CHATBOT AND A COMPREHENSIVE AI TOOL

Chatbot and comprehensive AI tools are both AI applications, but they differ in their capabilities and scope.

Chatbot

A *chatbot* is a software program that simulates human conversation and interacts with users through a chat interface. It's designed to understand and respond to queries or commands in a conversational way. Chatbots are found across various communication channels, such as websites, messaging apps, or voice assistants. Here are some key characteristics of a chatbot:

- **Simulating human conversation:** Provides a natural language interface for users to interact with.

- **Task-specific:** Handles specific tasks or provides information within a defined domain.

- **Rule-based or AI-powered:** Follows predefined decision trees, using techniques like NLP and machine learning to understand and generate responses.

Comprehensive AI tool

A *comprehensive AI tool* is more robust. It refers to an all-embracing software platform that incorporates advanced AI capabilities to perform complex tasks or solve more sophisticated problems. These tools often leverage machine learning, deep learning, and other AI techniques to provide advanced functionalities in the following ways:

- **Advanced capabilities:** Performs complex tasks such as image recognition, natural language understanding, predictive analytics, or autonomous decision making.

- **Data-driven:** Employ large datasets to learn patterns, make predictions, or generate insights.

- **Customizability:** Can be customized or trained on specific datasets to adapt to specific business needs or domains.

- **Scalability:** Designed to handle large-scale data processing and analysis, making them suitable for enterprise-level applications.

In summary, while a chatbot focuses on simulating human conversation and providing specific information or performing tasks within a defined domain, a comprehensive AI tool encompasses a broader range of advanced AI capabilities and is designed to tackle more complex issues.

Playing with the Pros

AI SPOTLIGHT

Comprehensive AI apps (explained in the nearby sidebar) are typically used in industries such as healthcare, finance, transportation, and others to analyze large amounts of data, identify patterns and trends, and make predictions and recommendations. If you're ready to join the big leagues and play with the pros, here are some general-use comprehensive AI tools:

>> Anyword (https://anyword.com/)

>> Buffer (https://buffer.com/ai-assistant)

>> CopyAI (https://www.copy.ai/)

>> Grammarly (https://app.grammarly.com/)

>> Jasper AI (https://www.jasper.ai)

>> Neuraltext (https://www.neuraltext.com/)

>> Notion (https://www.notion.so/)

>> Pepper Content (https://www.peppercontent.io/peppertype-ai/)

>> Rytr (https://rytr.me/)

>> Simplified (https://simplified.com/)

>> Wordtune (https://www.wordtune.com/)

>> Writesonic (https://writesonic.com/)

This is a bourgeoning field, and new tools are probably hitting the market as you're reading this. However, Grammarly and Jasper are considered to be the two most commonly used and have been around for a while. There have been debates as to which is better. Grammarly helps to check for errors, while Jasper produces original content. Spoiler alert: Grammarly is now integrated with Jasper AI, so you can use them together to create dynamite docs.

REMEMBER

Security protocols of AI systems in relation to data handling and storage are addressed through various measures such as encryption, access controls, secure storage, and compliance with data protection regulations to ensure the privacy and security of user data.

Choosing an AI Writing Tool

When choosing an AI writing tool, here are a few key factors to consider:

» **Type of content:** Consider the type of content you are looking to create. Different AI writing tools specialize in various kinds of content, so it is crucial to find one that fits your needs. Do you need a chatbot, content generator, summarizer, or language translator, or proofreader and editor, to name a few?

» **Language model:** Choose an AI writing tool that uses the best language models. At the moment, systems like ChatGPT that are powered by OpenAI GPT-3 are the most advanced.

» **Can it speak your language?** Make sure the AI writing tool you choose can understand and write in your writing style and language. Many tools write in English only, but some tools such as SEO.ai can write perfect copy in hundreds of other languages.

» **Original content:** In a Google-dominated world, original content is vital. Make sure the AI writing tool you choose is capable of producing unique and creative content.

» **Ease of use:** Many tools are complex to use and use confusing steps and different templates to generate even the simplest pieces of content.

» **Pricing:** Although prices vary among providers, evaluate the tool's features and capabilities to ensure it meets your specific needs and goals.

TIP

You may want to check the reviews or community feedback of AI tools. There are many websites that can help by searching for "assessing AI tools."

Summarizing the Synergy between WI and AI

AI writing tools offer a range of advantages to business writers, such as:

» **Spending less time writing:** While it may take you an hour to write a report, because of AI's intelligence (redundant, I know) it can produce the report in minutes. It has learned from current and past projects and had probably created a template. AI is especially useful for writing captions, summaries, headlines, or outlines. It can introduce new words, phrases, or sources to diversify your vocabulary.

>> **Producing higher quality with less work:** In recent years, AI writing tools have evolved to produce high-quality writings with less work on the part of the writer. They can find the most relevant information for the specific topic, eliminate duplication, and make editing effortless. They can enhance creativity by providing you with new ideas and perspectives. They can analyze existing content and suggest new angles.

>> **Assisting with research:** Conducting research for writing projects can chew up large amounts of time. AI can quickly scan and extract information from vast databases or online sources, pinpoint the most critical points, organize and summarize data, assist in literary reviews, and even detect plagiarism. This streamlines the writing process and lets writers do what they do best — write.

>> **Facilitating editing and proofreading:** Editing and proofreading your own work can be daunting, and too often we don't see our own mistakes. AI can help to oversee grammatical and punctuation errors, shorten overly long sentences, and supply alternate words. It can also correct formatting.

REMEMBER

AI has its flaws. The risk of authenticity, originality of writing, plagiarism, ethical and social concerns, lack of credibility and accountability are ongoing concerns. There's nothing like the WI to verify the text, create nuances, and share stories that only humans can.

Considering Copyright Laws

WARNING

Plagiarism is wrong. Period. You can't just copy someone else's words or thoughts. So, will we hold AI to the same standard? This is a relatively new technology and there are more questions than answers.

It has long been the posture of the U.S. Copyright Office that there's no copyright protection for works created by AI. However, with many lawsuits on the horizon, copyright laws regarding AI are in a state of flux. In August 2023, the U.S. Copyright Office published guidelines on who owns AI-generated works. They're now open to granting ownership to AI-generated work on a case-by-case basis. You can access current guidelines at https://www.copyright.gov/ai.

CAN WE LEARN FROM THE PAST?

The AI Revolution is upon us, and it's important to learn from past revolutions to ensure a smooth transition. The Industrial Revolution transformed society from agrarian to manufacturing, leading to increased production and efficiency, but also unintended consequences such as poor working conditions. The Computer Revolution brought instant communication and automation, but also information overload and job displacement. Now, with the AI Revolution, we must embrace disruption, consider the impact on jobs, collaborate, address ethical implications, and foster interdisciplinary collaboration.

As the world struggles to come to terms with this new reality, we can't put our heads in the sand and say, "We've seen this before." By applying lessons from the past, the AI Revolution can navigate the challenges and opportunities ahead and contribute to positive societal and economic outcomes. We must start now to train and retrain the workforce for the future by investing in education and skill development.

The relationship between AI and writers is not one of replacement, but one of collaboration. Writers who embrace AI as a tool can enhance their skills, improve efficiency, and explore new creative possibilities while maintaining their unique contributions to the craft of writing.

The determination will depend on depend on how the writer uses AI to generate content and how they've rearranged the work to make it their own. When WI and AI work together though, who can separate what each of them has done and to what degree? In other words, how creatively the author rearranges the original work to make it their own. As AI tools become more and more sophisticated, the lines between brainstorming and collaborating are becoming blurred. AI-generated writing has opened Pandora's Box. Just for fun . . . let's see what's inside.

SHERYL SAYS

New tools such as Nightshade, DALL-E, Stable Diffusion, and Midjourney are dubbed *poisons*. They let artists add invisible changes to pixels in their art before uploading it online. Could this be a precursor for poisons to protect original writing as well?

2

The Write Stuff

Grasp the essence of your readers by using a Kick-Start Brief to identify who they are, your shared purpose, key issues, and questions you need to address.

Engage your reader with a captivating storytelling approach that taps into the human need for connection, evokes emotions, and provides a compelling narrative that allows your readers to escape, relate, and gain new perspectives.

Overcome writer's block to create a dynamic draft and learn that a first draft isn't about getting it right . . . it's about getting it written.

Explore the world of infographics, tables, charts, and other visually appealing elements that convey your message in a way that words alone may not be able to.

Refine the tone through the active voice, positive language, and a reader-centric approach to effectively set the desired mood, convey attitudes and emotions, and influence how your message is received and interpreted by the readers.

Polish your prose to eliminate errors, refine clarity, and ensure that your document is memorable for all the right reasons.

Chapter **4**

Discovering All You Can About Your Reader

Before you start writing any business document, it's important to understand how and why people read them. Unlike captivating novels that transport readers to imaginary worlds, business documents aren't for pleasure reading. Instead, they're usually scanned or referenced for specific information, such as identifying mistakes or finding key details. In these cases, readers are often frustrated and skim through the document, hoping to quickly find what they need. They have no interest in complex language or confusing content.

That's why it's critical that you direct your message toward your reader, addressing what they need to know, the purpose, and the questions they'll need answered in a logical manner. This is where the value of the Kick-Start Brief — detailed in this chapter — comes into play. It serves as a guide to help you effectively communicate with your readers and ensure that your message is understood, regardless of their reading approach.

Using AI as Your Assistant to Understanding the Audience

AI SPOTLIGHT

Understanding your readers is crucial for creating targeted and engaging content. AI tools such as the following can play a significant role in this process by providing valuable insights and data-driven analysis:

>> CrowdView (https://crowdview.ai/)

>> Gap Scout (https://gapscout.com/)

>> Userpersona (https://userpersona.dev/)

Here are some ways AI can help you analyze your readings so you can tailor your content:

>> **Audience analysis:** Gain powerful audience insights at scale and in real time to learn your audience's preferred online channels, interests, and demographics. This information can guide your content creation and distribution strategies.

>> **Competitor analysis:** By examining metrics such as audience size, engagement, and content performance, you can gain insights into what does and doesn't work well in your industry.

>> **Traffic analysis:** Tools can help you can gain insights into the interests and preferences of your audience.

>> **Content analysis:** By leveraging AI-powered content analysis tools, you can improve the readability and ranking of online presence. This analysis can help you create content that resonates with your audience and ranks high on search engines.

>> **Behavior analysis:** Analyze your audience's behavior through various methods such as surveys, polls, and engagement metrics. By understanding their interests and preferences, you can create targeted content that resonates with them.

REMEMBER

In addition to AI tools, you need writer intelligence (WI) to analyze your audience at different levels. This information will guide you on how to structure your document, what kind of language and tone to use, what sort of information to include, and how to progress into each topic.

Kick-Starting Your Writing Success

As an experienced business writer, I never commit one word to my computer until I've completed a Kick-Start Brief. It's a critical part of the business writing process and you'll find it in Figure 4-1, followed by a full explanation. Also take a peek at the case study at the end of this chapter to realize the importance of using the Kick-Start Brief, even for emails when they're more than just casual exchanges.

SHERYL SAYS

When I first introduce the Kick-Start Brief during the writing workshops I facilitate, participants often express concerns about their busy schedules and not having enough time to fill it out. However, to their surprise, once they give it a try and complete it during the workshop, they realize the tremendous value it brings and the time it ultimately saves. In fact, many participants come back to me later, excitedly sharing that the Brief is now saving them a significant amount of time, reducing their writing efforts by 30 to 50 percent. What's even better is that people are actually reading and engaging with their writing. So, my suggestion is to print out the Kick-Start Brief and keep it accessible. You can use it as-is or customize it to fit your specific project. Trust me, after using it just once, you'll be amazed at how much time and effort it saves you. You'll wonder how you ever managed without it in the past.

The following sections mirror the design and layout of the Kick-Start Brief shown in Figure 4-1.

Kick-Start Brief

About the Document

1. Type of document
2. Presentation context
3. Target date for completion

Reader Profile

4. Who are the readers?

   - Are they technical, nontechnical, or a combination?
   - Are they internal (to your company), external, or both?
   - Do you have multi-level readers?

5. What do the readers *need to know* about the topic?

   - What's their level of the subject knowledge, if any?
   - What acronyms, initials, or abbreviations will you need to explain?
   - Do they have any preconceived ideas?
   - What are the barriers to their understanding?
   - Is there anything about their style of dealing with situations that should drive your tone or content?
   - How do they process information?
   - What jobs do they perform?

6. What's their attitude toward the topic? (Positive? Neutral? Negative?)

Purpose

7. My purpose is to_____so my reader will_____.

Key Issues

8. What is the key issue to convey?

Questioning

9. Which *who, what, when, why, where,* and *how* questions will the reader need answered?

FIGURE 4-1:
The Kick-Start Brief.

About the Document

1. **Type of document:** What type of technical document is this? Email, user manual, product description, user manual, whitepaper, abstract, spec sheet, presentation, article, report, e-learning document, or something else?

2. **Presentation context:** How will the document be presented? On paper, online, via streaming, in a simulation, or some combination of these? Or will it be a simulated learning experience (SLE)? If this is part of a project that has other components (such as training, supporting literature, or spec sheet), indicate what they are.

   - Is this a standalone writing project that has no other components?

   - If this is part of a larger project, can you coordinate efforts with another team?

   - Are there aspects of either project that can be done in tandem?

   - Can you share any information?

   - Have design or style issues been identified?

   - Are there documents from other projects you can repurpose?

3. **Target date for completion:** What's the real drop-dead date? (Too often people pick an arbitrary date, and then everyone stops eating and sleeping to meet it. They later find out the deadline wasn't a real one.)

Reader Profile

4. **Who are the readers?** Identify your relationship with your readers. Do you share similar experiences and educational backgrounds? Are they familiar with your product or industry? For example, a small detail such as knowing their approximate ages and cultural backgrounds may be important in deciding the output. Surveys show that younger people are more apt to use online documentation than older folks. (Some of you may not be too delighted to hear that older means over 40.) Another may be that younger people grew up in the computer age and relate to gamification, streaming, and/or simulations.

   - **Are they technical, nontechnical, or a combination?** This will help to determine their backgrounds so you can use appropriate language and references. For example, do they share a common background with you or with each other?

   - **Are they internal (to your company), external, or both?** For internal documents, identify your readers by name and job function. For external documents, identify categories of readers (managers, engineers, and so on).

   - **Do you have multi-level readers?** If so, what percentage are there of each? This information is critical to help you structure the document.

     If you're writing to multiple-level readers, rank them in order of seniority. For example, if your readers are a mix of managers, techies, and salespeople, consider dealing with each group separately in clearly identified sections of your document. (Also, determine any technical or language barriers.) Here's how you may want to structure the elements in a report for multiple readers:

- **Table of contents:** This creates a pathway for everyone. (Notice how *For Dummies* books have an abbreviated table of contents and an expanded one.)

- **Executive summary (or abstract):** Designed for the managerial level — those who want the big picture only. Find out more about abstracts and executive summaries in Chapter 16.

- **Appendix:** Appeals to those who want all the nitty-gritty details, including data tables.

Many AI tools can generate tables of contents, executive summaries, and appendices. Using them can save you lots of time.

5. **What do the readers *need to know* about the topic?**

- **What's their level of the subject knowledge, if any?** Think of what your readers need to know, not what they already know. You don't want to give too much or too little information. For example, if you're writing documentation for a software application, you must know the readers' level of computer skills. Here are a few examples:

  - *Greenhorns* may have limited knowledge. They're prime candidates for the printed page, not the electronic page.

  - *Sporadic users* may have used the system often enough to remember the commands and other good stuff. They may be amenable to online documentation, if it's easy to use. Or a combination of paper based and electronic documents may be appropriate. Even a few cheat sheets may work well.

  - *Aces* are the true power users. They understand the ins and outs of the product but may have occasional questions. Their manuals may prop up their screens, and they're prime candidates for online documentation, streaming, or even simulations.

- **What acronyms, initials, or abbreviations will you need to explain?** If there are many terms you think they may not understand, consider including a glossary or list of terms.

- **Do they have any preconceived ideas?** Readers may wonder if this is relevant to their needs, if it's easy to follow, if it's free from bias, and so on.

- **What are the barriers to their understanding?** This may include lack of technical knowledge, language barriers, special needs, and so forth.

- **Is there anything about their style of dealing with situations that should drive your tone or content?** Chapter 8 has a full discussion about using the proper tone and how AI can assist.

- **How do they process information?** I've discovered that people with academic, scientific, or technical backgrounds tend to be process-oriented. They benefit from step-by-step explanations. Those with backgrounds in business or law are answer oriented. They respond to quick answers. Creative types are usually visually oriented and benefit from charts, tables, and any visual representation. Discover more about preparing visuals in Chapter 7 and how AI can assist.

- **What jobs do they perform?** Are your readers CEOs, managers, engineers, administrative assistants, data entry specialists, or shop-floor personnel? For example, people on a shop floor need hard-copy instructions because they may not have ready access to a computer in the workplace. Managers are big-picture people; they want to know the key issues. Technical folks want the details. Salespeople need to know the benefits.

6. **What is their attitude toward the topic? (Positive? Neutral? Negative?)** You may not always tell your readers what they want to hear, but you must always tell them what they need to know. Your reader's attitude will fit into one of these three categories:

   - **Positive:** You're delivering good news; something the reader will be glad to hear. *You anticipate that the project will be completed one month early. (Who wouldn't be happy to hear that?)*

   - **Neutral:** This is neither good nor bad news. *You suggest that everyone stay the course.*

   - **Negative:** This is news the reader won't be happy to learn. *Management finds it necessary to lay off one-fourth of the workforce.*

   To maximize the impact of any document you write, it's crucial to consider your reader's attitude toward the topic. By understanding their perspective, you can tailor your writing to effectively engage and persuade.

Purpose

The purpose of a document refers to the reason you're writing it and what you hope to achieve. Understanding this helps you focus your writing and ensure that your message is clear and effective. Fill in the blanks.

7. **My purpose is to _____ so my reader will _____.**

   - **My purpose is to:** Whether you think your purpose is to communicate, inform, or sell, chances are you're trying to persuade someone to take some sort of action.

- **So my reader will:** This is the call to action (CTA). Continue testing? Turn the case to the legal department? Call the bank? Refund money? Make a purchase? Halt shipping? Do nothing?

Key Issues

8. **What is the key issue to convey?** Every document has a purpose and key issue to convey. To use a music analogy: Create an *earworm* (which is a catchy piece of music or a tune that gets stuck in your head and plays on repeat over and over). If your reader forgets everything else, what's the one key issue (the earworm) you want them to remember? In order to make your key issue crystal clear, you need to express it in a single sentence.

Questioning

9. **Which *who, what, when, why, where,* and *how* questions will the reader need answered?** Newspaper reporters use this questioning technique to guide them through stories. The answer to these questions provides the information readers want and need to know. Of course, not all questions apply to your message, so decide which add to your purpose. Here's an example: Assume I'm inviting you to a meeting. You'd probably have the following questions:

   - **Who** else will be there?
   - **What** is the agenda?
   - **When** is the date?
   - **Where** will it be held?
   - **Why?** (Probably isn't needed because the agenda would suffice.)
   - **How** can I prepare?

Bridging Generational Differences

To effectively gear your writing toward various generations, it's essential to understand the characteristics, values, and preferences of each. This helps to craft content that resonates with your target audience, fostering a stronger connection and increasing the impact of your writing. Table 4-1 shares the current four generations of people in the workforce and their communication preferences and styles.

TABLE 4-1   **Understanding the Generation Gap**

Generation	Communication	Technology	Style	Loyalty
Traditionalist **(born 1927 – 1945)**	Handwritten Want details Good listeners Sticklers for good grammar Avoid slang Respond to phone calls & face-to-face meetings	"If it ain't broke, don't fix it."	Go by the book Don't question authority Formal, go through proper channels	To the organization
Boomers **(born 1946 – 1964)**	Somewhat formal Require context Like to pre-read and prepare Value face-to-face Like to establish rapport Go through structures network Collaborators	Necessary for progress	Get it done, whatever it takes. (evenings or weekends)	To the meaning of work
Gen X **(born 1965 – 1980)**	Casual and direct Don't waste time Skip the history Keep it short and sweet — get to the point	Practical tools for getting it done	Find the fastest route to get results	To personal career goals
Millennials (born 1981 – 1994)	Casual and direct Avoid storytelling — get to the point Avoid corporate jargon	Is there anything else?	Work to deadlines, not schedules	To people in the project

Note: Gen Z (born between 1995 and 2009) are just starting to enter the workforce. They're digital natives.

REMEMBER

While we can't categorically put people into boxes because each person is unique, it's helpful to have a basic understanding of the generational differences. It's also essential to consider individual differences within each generation and to approach your writing with empathy and authenticity.

When writing a prompt, you can ask your chatbot to write for a specific generation, such as traditionalists (which would be most formal) or Gen Xers (which would be less formal). Chapter 23 offers lots of pointers on how to write great prompts.

Looking at a Case Study

The following case study serves as a strong reminder of the significance of understanding your audience and determining what they truly need to know.

Scenario

Sally is a line supervisor at a prominent manufacturing company. She's responsible for submitting a weekly status report to Steve, her immediate supervisor. Steve uses her reports, along with others from his subordinates, to compile his own comprehensive report. Ultimately, Steve's report is passed to his superiors. The process continues up the food chain.

As managers progress up the organizational hierarchy, it becomes increasingly important for them to grasp the broader perspective. But they also need access to the details. Here's why it's important to strike a balance between the two:

>> **Making strategic decisions:** By focusing on the big picture, managers can align their decisions with the long-term vision of the company.

>> **Coordinating and aligning:** At higher levels, managers are responsible for coordinating and aligning the efforts of different departments and teams within the organization. They need a holistic view to assure that all departments are working toward common goals.

>> **Identifying trends and patterns:** A broad perspective enables managers to spot opportunities, anticipate challenges, and make proactive decisions to keep the organization steered in the right direction.

>> **Adapting to changes:** By understanding the big picture, managers can anticipate and respond to changes in the business environment, emerging technology, and market dynamics so they can proactively adapt their strategies and operations to remain competitive and resilient in a rapidly changing world.

Problem

Each week Sally would send her status report to Steve. See an example in Figure 4-2. She documented all that information because she needed it for her records. Steve was constantly getting back to Sally to make sense of the excruciating details. Lots of emails were exchanged and lots of time was wasted until he "got" the big picture for the report he needed to escalate to his manager. Steve suggested that Sally attend my writing workshop to learn how to strike a balance between the big picture and the details he needs.

Purpose:
To audit three ACQUITY systems from Franklin Distribution, by performing the AQT tests.

Results:
System 1: Tested using MassLynx software.

Module	Part Number	Serial Number	Audit Number	Results
Solvent Manager	186015001	C07UPB060M	UPBD07041800	Pass
Sample Manager	186015005	C07UPS713M	UPSD07041800	Pass
PDA Detector	186015026	C07UPD210M	UPDD07041800	Pass

System 2: Tested using Empower2 software.

Module	Part Number	Serial Number	Audit Number	Results
Solvent Manager	186015001	C07UPB983M	UPBD07043000	Pass
Sample Manager	186015005	C07UPS704M	UPSD07043000	Pass
PDA Detector	186015026	C07UPD205M	UPDD07043000	Pass
Sample Organizer	186015020	C07UPO617M	UPOD07043000	See 2.1
ELS Detector	186015027	C07UPE242M	UPED07043000	See 2.2

2.1 The lead screw nut above the transfer shuttle would hit the bottom of the Z axis top block while scanning the shelves. The Away Flag had to be adjusted.

2.2 The Siphon Drain tube was not attached to the elbow fitting on the detector.

System 3: Tested using Empower2 software.

Module	Part Number	Serial Number	Audit Number	Results
Solvent Manager	186015001	C07UPB974M	UPBD07041600	Pass
Sample Manager	186015005	C07UPS703M	UPSD07041600	Pass
TUV Detector	186015028	B07UPT155M	UPTD07041600	See 3.1
Sample Organizer	186015020	C07UPO620M	UPOD07041600	Pass

3.1 The chassis screws were too long and washers were missing to mount the Optics Bench to the chassis. This caused scratches to the top cover of the Column Heater. The incorrect hardware and the Column Heater top cover were replaced.

Kit	Part Number	Quantity	Audit Number	Results
Sample Manager	200000200	3	UPSD07041801	Pass
TUV Detector	200000202	1	UPTD07041801	Pass
Solvent Manager	200000188	3	UPBD07041801	Pass
Sample Organizer	205000341	2	UPOD07041800	Pass
UPLC System	200000198	2	UPKD07041800	See K1.1
Multi Detector Drip Tray	205000355	4	UPKD07041801	Pass
PDA Detector	200015026	2	UPDD07041801	Pass
ELS Detector	200002424	1	UPED07041800	See K1.2
TUV 10mm Flow Cell	205015008	1	UPTD07041800	Pass
PDA Flow Cell	205015004	2	UPTD07041802	Pass

K1.1 The Open End Wrench (605000115) was labeled as (605000103) slotted screw driver. The Wrench was relabeled with the correct part number and description.

K1.2 The kit was missing (410001686) Plastic Hose Clamp. The Hose Clamp was added to the kit.

FIGURE 4-2: "Before": Weekly status report with excruciating detail.

Fix

Sally ultimately learned to prepare her weekly status report, much like the document in Figure 4-3. The only change I suggested was eliminating the bullets, which weren't needed in this instance. Along with this revised version, Sally submitted the detailed version to Steve, in case he needed it.

Purpose

To further improve the quality of our products, Quality Assurance audits three ACQUITY systems monthly, from Franklin Distribution, by performing the AQT tests.

Results of the system audits

System	Results
1: Tested using MassLynx software.	No issues were found.
2: Tested using Empower2 software.	The lead screw nut above the transfer shuttle on the Sample Organizer, S/N C07UPO617M, hit the bottom of the Z axis top block while scanning the shelves. The Away Flag had to be adjusted. The Siphon Drain tube was not attached to the elbow fitting on the ELS Detector, S/N C07UPE205M.
3: Tested using Empower2 software.	The chassis screws were too long and washers were missing to mount the Optics Bench to the chassis of the TUV Detector, S/N B07UPT155M. This caused scratches to the top cover of the Column Heater. The incorrect hardware and the Column Heater top cover were replaced.

Results of Instrument Start-up Kits

- UPLC System Kit – P/N 200000198 - The Open End Wrench (605000115) was labeled as (605000103) slotted screw driver. The Wrench was relabeled with the correct part number and description.
- ELS Detector Kit – P/N 2000002424 - The Plastic Hose Clamp (410001686) was missing from the kit. The Hose Clamp was added to the kit before returning it to stock.

FIGURE 4-3: "After": Weekly status report with key information at a glance.

Result

Sally's new weekly status report was used as a model for the entire company. She was the hero!

Chapter **5**

Taking Your Reader on a Storied Journey

Once you have gathered all the information you can about your reader, it's crucial to go beyond simply bombarding them with facts and figures, even though they're significant. Infuse the document with stories. Stories are a testament to our innate desire to connect and seek meaning. They create a shared understanding that brings people together through a common narrative.

People have been sharing stories since the beginning of time. A cave painting found on an Indonesian island (dating back 45,000 years) is thought to be the earliest known record of storytelling. It depicts a pig and buffalo hunt, mythological figures in a hunting scene. Hand gestures told stories before there were words. Thousands of years later Aesop's fables started capturing imaginations and still teach us valuable lessons. From the early bards, to Middle Ages troubadours, to chart-topping books and Hollywood blockbusters, we all enjoy a good story.

Have you ever noticed how often storytelling is used in TV ads? Through storytelling, advertisers increase the perceived value of their product or service by enabling viewers to connect to the brand on a personal level. One that comes to mind is Google's "Parisian Love" commercial. It's the touching love story in which Google shares the entire narrative through its search bar and results pages. We follow the character's journey as they move to France, fall in love, and reinvent their life to be with their beloved. The ad is laced with funny mistakes, typos, and misdirections, making it both heartwarming, relatable, and memorable. Take a peek at http://tinyurl.com/3mk39xjh.

The human brain is hardwired for stories; they shape us. That's why most people would rather read a historical novel than a boring textbook. Or view a historical movie rather than a dry documentary. It's not because of laziness. It's because stories are engaging and memorable; they establish a human connection.

In this chapter you'll discover the value of a narrative, how to prepare a strong prompt, and how to create stories that resonate with readers and audiences.

Using AI as Your Assistant to Craft Compelling Stories

AI SPOTLIGHT

AI can assist in transforming personal stories into engaging business stories. You can feed the AI tool with prompts or specific details and it will spew out stories that can persuade and heed your call to action. Whether your intent is to persuade a perspective customer of the value they can derive from your product or service or you need to convince a donor to fund your emerging business, you need to create a business case. AI can assist in crafting a story that highlights the pain points of your target reader and how your solution can address those challenges.

AI tools worth checking out are:

>> Squibler (https://www.squibler.io/)

>> Jasper (https://www.jasper.ai/)

>> Writesonic (https://writesonic.com/)

- » Scalenut (`https://www.scalenut.com/`)

- » Copy.ai (`https://www.copy.ai/`)

- » Rytr (`https://rytr.me`)

REMEMBER

While AI can assist with various aspects of storytelling, it's important to keep in mind that your narrative is ultimately about connecting with your reader on an emotional level. Use your writer intelligence (WI) to ensure that your narrative remains authentic, relatable, and sounds like your own words.

Understanding the Power of the Narrative

Storytelling is more than a buzzword. It's a way to connect with readers (or audiences) and set yourself apart. Here's an example of how to transform data into a compelling story.

AI SPOTLIGHT

Max, a diligent salesperson, prepared an impressive data-driven slide presentation to wow a potential customer who had immense revenue potential. During a practice run, several of his colleagues suggested incorporating a success story to engage the audience. Max, being a numbers guy, not a writer, turned to AI for help. He carefully curated a prompt, feeding the AI tool with the essential data, and asked AI to turn the data into a compelling story. AI breathed life into Max's prompt, painting a vivid picture of a struggling customer, once burdened by inefficiency and stagnation, whose company was transformed when they embraced Max's company's innovative solution. This narrative brought the customer's journey to life, evoking a sense of hope, inspiration, and unbridled potential for them. The group was engaged and their company eventually became Max's biggest customer. Max realized that his journey from being a mere numbers guy to a master storyteller was made possible by the powerful collaboration between his prompt and the capabilities of AI. (Learn the essence of effective AI prompting in Chapter 23.)

Generating Precise Prompts

AI SPOTLIGHT

Here are some suggestions for creating effective AI prompts, with a particular emphasis on creating stories:

- » Include details about the industry, target audience, specific challenges, or any other relevant context.

>> Use multiple prompts to explore different angles and perspectives.

>> Show how the characters, the business, or the customers have been impacted, reinforcing the value and relevance of the story. Both positive and negative outcomes leave a lasting impression.

>> Introduce obstacles, challenges, or dilemmas that the characters face, and then guide the story towards a satisfying (self-serving) resolution.

>> Incorporate sensory details, descriptive language, and imagery to create a rich and immersive experience.

>> Give the characters names, distinct personalities, motivations, and challenges, where applicable.

Creating Tales of Success and Transformation

Think of the people, places, and things that have shaped your life. Those who not only helped you think out of the box, but made you forget there ever was a box. Those who inspired you to do something different, changed your outlook on something, encouraged you to take a (non-dangerous) risk. These are all stories to be shared. Whether the results were positive or negative, they're valuable lessons others can benefit from.

Realizing that everyone has a story

Open your eyes. Open your ears. Open your mind. Stories are all around you. The key is to be aware and pay attention to your life and the lives of others. Be curious. Look about. Observe with all your senses. Try new things. Take up a new hobby. Explore different places. Everyday life offers an endless plethora of experiences — all of which are potential stories. Here are some tips:

TIP

>> Become an active listener.

>> Talk with people.

>> Ask lots of questions.

>> Sharpen your skills of observation.

>> Notice when you have a reaction to someone or something.

>> Draw from what you read or see around you.

Starting with paper and pencil (or pen)

Yes, paper and pencil. For this type of exercise, you're more likely to be creative when using paper and pencil, rather than the computer. When you write things out, you create spatial relations between each bit of information. Handwriting activates parts of your brain involved in thinking and working memory, making you more open to critical thinking.

Try it. Prepare three columns each headed with a noun: People, Places, Things. And then:

>> Under **People,** write down past and present people in your life. Think of what each person represents and why they came to mind. Why they're important to you.

>> In the **Places** column, note past and present places. Jot down the sounds, scents, and visuals these places trigger.

>> Under **Things,** list things that remind you of positive or negative experiences (they both have value). Think about what meaning these things hold for you and why.

Here's an example:

People	Places	Things
family	neighborhoods you lived in	books
friends	the hallway in your school	photos
adversaries	a favorite vacation spot	movies
acquaintances	the desk at your first job	gifts
teachers	your first job interview	plants
childhood friend	a teenage hangout	sports
co-workers	a place you walk or jog	pets
mentors or coaches	the worst place you've been	religious item

Forming connections and creating a list

When you're done, you'll have planted seeds of stories. Start making connections between the people, places, and things. See those seeds germinate and sprout. Some stories may be too personal to share; others may be very appropriate for certain presentations. After you've curated a host of stories, categorize them and save them in folders on your phone, on your desktop, or in a notepad. Each time something occurs to you, add it to your list. You'll be amazed at how many experiences you've had in your life that can enhance your writing or presentation. Before you know it, you may have more stories than Aesop had fables.

Making Readers Part of the Journey

AI SPOTLIGHT

Notice, earlier in this chapter, how Max successfully sealed a significant contract by leveraging AI to craft a narrative that resonated with the audience. This helped them to identify with the story on a personal level.

As Max learned, stories are far more memorable than slides loaded with facts and figures, although some stories do work well with appropriate visual accompaniments. When people hear a story, they enter the story where *they are*, and they become part of it. Even stories about mistakes and what was learned are valuable. Readers identify with challenging stories and imagine how they would have acted in similar circumstances. That engages them, and you take them on the journey with you. Stories

>> grab attention

>> evoke the reader's imagination

>> create empathy

>> link human experiences

>> maintain interest

>> are persuasive.

Impactful stories should reach hearts and minds of readers with an emotional experience. Each should have a point they can grasp and identify with. It's like painting a picture, something for them to visualize that happened at a particular time or place to people just like them. Every story should fit within the context of your document to support what you want your reader to do, think, feel, or learn.

Including the Four Pillars of Storytelling

Every story has four pillars as shown in Figure 5-1. Before your fingers start clicking away on your keyboard, recognize how the four pillars of your story take your reader on a journey from what is to what could be:

FIGURE 5-1:
The four pillars of
storytelling.

PILLARS OF A STORYTELLING JOURNEY

>> **Setting:** Anyone who's sat through a high-school English class remembers, "It was a dark and stormy night" from Edward Bulwer-Lytton's novel *Paul Clifford*. Set the scene to immerse the reader into where the story is happening. The setting shows up early because it provides context and should be something your reader will relate to. The setting can be a time of day, weather conditions, country, office, building, room, shopping mall, or any place from where the story unfolds.

>> **Characters:** Most stories are based around a person or group of people. They can be competitors, shareholders, employees, friends, heroes, or villains. (There are lessons to be learned from both heroes and villains.) Show the parallels between your character and your reader. Be sure to give your characters names. Think of the Harry Potter series for example. The story wouldn't have been interesting if J.K. Rowling merely called the hero, *boy wizard*.

There may be stories where the characters are more important than the setting. In those cases, put the characters before the setting.

SHERYL SAYS

>> **Conflict:** This is the "what is" portion of your story. Although the word conflict sounds unpleasant, it leads to the pot of gold — forming a bridge between the settings, characters, and resolution. The conflict fuels the story and moves your reader along the journey to "what could be." It creates and drives the plot, reveals opposing beliefs and truths, and creates relatable context in an emotional way. Without a conflict in a story, film, or novel, the plot would be — well, boring and useless.

>> **Resolution:** This is where you've taken your characters, settings, and conflict directly to your reader and provided them with a resolution in which they can see themselves as heroes in "what could be." Good resolutions should be memorable, concrete, specific, and achievable; however, they don't have to be spelled out. You can leave the interpretation up to your reader by tickling their imaginations and hinting at what might happen next. It all depends on your call to action.

Creating the Story Arc

Figure 5-2 shows the typical story arc (also known as dramatic arc or narrative arc). When creating a story using the arc as a guide, your story will have a natural, connected flow:

1. **Cite the incident (the plot) telling what is.**

2. **Build rising tension toward the climax.**

3. **Work towards the resolution, which is what could be.**

TIP

Don't underestimate the importance of creating tension in your story by incorporating elements such as high stakes, conflicting goals, and unexpected obstacles. If the tension isn't obvious, this is a good opportunity to embellish with a story. After you've filled out the Kick-Start Brief, detailed in Chapter 4, you'll have a good idea of your reader's pain and what matters to them. Focus on the gap between what is and what can be. Take them on that journey so they see themselves as heroes on the same path.

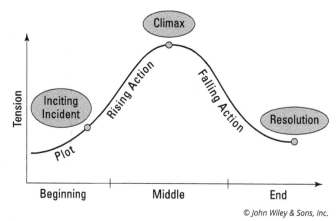

FIGURE 5-2:
The story arc.

© *John Wiley & Sons, Inc.*

Your story will have characters: people, companies, or things (such as processes or equipment). There will be goals, struggles, challenges, and a positive or negative outcome. Either outcome serves as a valuable lesson. Let's see how beginnings, middles, and ends can become a story:

>> **Beginning:** Introduce characters with the same challenge, problem, complication, or issue your reader is facing — the reason they're attending. You'll hook them because they'll feel like they're in the same situation. Edit the details to keep the story simple and relatable. You may start with, "One of my customers was dealing with your exact situation."

>> **Middle:** You've already sparked their curiosity. Now focus on the characters' problems and how your solution brought the change they needed. These problems may involve power struggles, ethical dilemmas, competition, workplace disputes, financial challenges, low sales earnings, and management changes, to name a few. Don't merely go from Point A to Point B. The long cuts and shortcuts are what make the journey interesting, worthwhile, and relatable.

>> **End:** This is where you tie it together, targeted to the call to action (CTA). Deliver the main takeaways and lessons your reader should remember based on the success of your characters. Did they buy your product and realized success? Did they not buy it and later regretted it? Even negative outcomes offer valuable lessons. Let your readers see the happy ending where they imagine themselves as heroes achieving these same positive outcomes.

Sharing Stories in the First Person, Present Tense

Punctuate your story by telling it in the first person, present tense using *is* and *are*, rather than *was* and *were*. Use *I, me, my,* or *myself*. This creates real-time immediacy, a sense of urgency. It gives the reader the feeling of plunging into the situation with you.

Present tense (first person): *Kate walks onto the stage. And — oh no — there is a power failure! What can she do?*

Past tense (third person): *Kate walked onto the stage. Immediately there was a power failure. She didn't know what to do.*

The present-tense scenario in first person amplifies the reader's intensity. They put themselves in the shoes of that person, thinking, "What would I do?"

Embellishing Stories

Gandalf, a hero in J.R.R. Tolkien's *The Hobbit* had a conversation with Bilbo Baggins. He told Baggins that when he comes back from his adventure, he'll have many tales to tell, and he should embellish them. Gandalf was right on! Don't hesitate to embellish your stories by adding decorative details, metaphors, humor, quotes, trivia, visuals, or whatever else will make it more memorable. It's like adding spice to a recipe. A little dab will do you! Even Mark Twain once said, "Never let the truth get in the way of a good story." It's your story, not a legal document which must be 100 percent factual.

Embellishing is done in many areas of the arts. Choreographers edit dance steps by adding phrases, gestures, stillness, and subtle movements that catch the reader's attention and evoke an emotional response. These edits make each choreographer's performance different — while remaining true to the original dance. Musical arrangers make musical scores their own by adding add trills, suspensions, retardations, passing tones, and more — while remaining true to the original composition.

Movie script writers do the same thing by taking even greater liberties. You've watched movies or read books that are inspired by true stories. You enjoy them because they blur the line between the real and unreal, the possible and impossible. For instance, the ship *Titanic* really did sink. But the movie *Titanic* invented two characters, Jack and Rose, who didn't exist. But they humanized the tragedy and made viewers empathize with their plight.

You too can blur the lines in your stories. Your stories may have more reality than Hollywood's, but you'd ultimately be doing the same thing — drawing conflict into sharper focus by paring back ancillary events or people, searching for conflict, and honing its edge. Embellishments that incite incidents, escalation, or resolution are just good storytelling. Understanding your reader gives you the creative freedom to play around with your story.

I appreciate that embellishing may be a controversial suggestion, but you can draw your reader into the story without compromising its integrity. You can embellish the setting, the characters, what they were wearing, what they were feeling, and the intensity of their reactions, to name a few.

AI SPOTLIGHT

Here's a story AI created explaining why Roland was late for a meeting. In this scenario, the setting is embellished. The prompt read as follows: *Create a one-paragraph embellished story of Roland being late for a meeting because of unexpected heavy traffic.*

Roland's heart raced as he realized he was running late for the crucial meeting. With a sense of urgency, he jumped into his car and followed the familiar route. However, fate had its own plan. As Roland merged onto the highway, he was met with an unexpected sea of cars, their red taillights blazing like a symphony of frustration. Roland's mind raced, contemplating alternate routes as he anxiously watched the clock ticking away. The weight of his tardiness bore heavily on his shoulders, but he remained determined to get to the meeting, no matter how long it took.

Infusing Your Docs with a Dash of Personality

SHERYL SAYS

Bring your writing to life by infusing it with a captivating story that enthralls readers, transporting them to new worlds and evoking a range of emotions. You'll create a truly unforgettable reading experience. Here's an example.

AI SPOTLIGHT

One user manual that remains etched in my memory accomplished this by starting with an immersive scenario (somewhat like the following, which I asked AI to re-create). It not only drew me in from the get-go, but it served as a testament to the importance of protecting my technology.

In the midst of a quiet evening, Alfredo sat engrossed in his work, diligently typing away on his computer. The room was bathed in the warm glow of the screen, his sanctuary of productivity. However, dark clouds gathered ominously outside, heralding the arrival of a tempestuous lightning storm. Thunder rumbled in the distance, setting the stage for an unforeseen calamity. Suddenly, a blinding flash of lightning illuminated the room, followed by a deafening crack that shook the very foundation of his home. In an instant, the power surged, flickering momentarily before abruptly plunging the room into darkness. Alfredo's heart sank as he realized the inevitable had occurred . . . his trusty computer had succumbed to the devastating forces of nature.

WARNING

Embellishing stories by adding fanciful details isn't lying, provided it's grounding in reality. But you must know where to draw the line between adding fanciful details and outright dishonesty. Perhaps you recall Brian Williams, a once well-respected newscaster. He told a story on nationwide TV about a death-defying experience during the Iraq War in 2003, claiming he was shot down by enemy fire while on an NBC news assignment. The incident never happened, and Williams's illustrious career ended with a big Pinocchio. He was suspended for six months without pay and blemished what had been a sterling career. So use good judgment when deciding what to embellish and what not to embellish.

MY EMBELLISHED STORY WITH AN ARC

Here's a story (slightly embellished) with a beginning, middle, and end that I share at my presentation workshops. It demonstrates how you always have to be ready with Plan B in addition to keeping a sense of humor.

Beginning

My heart is racing in anticipation as I stand poised at the front of the room, ready to captivate my eagerly awaiting audience. The stage is set. My flash drive, laptop, and extra cables are meticulously arranged — each component fully tested and ready to shine. As the audience slowly trickles in, their expectant eyes fixate on me, I take a deep breath and confidently begin my opening remarks.

Oops! As I press the power button on my laptop, a surge of panic washes over me. Darkness envelopes the screen, threatening to shatter my carefully crafted presentation. In a moment of desperation, as my equipment malfunctions on stage, I attempt a series of futile attempts to fix it.

Middle

Just when all seems lost, a ray of hope emerges from the crowd in the form of Pete, a kind-hearted stranger from the audience. As Pete skillfully tinkers with the equipment, I reach into my bag of tricks and unleash Plan B: A story designed to captivate and entertain the audience while my "savior" works his magic. With Pete's expertise and my storytelling prowess, we manage to salvage the situation.

Grateful for Pete's assistance, I call upon the audience to acknowledge Pete's contribution. In a delightful display of humor, Pete bows dramatically, presses his right hand across his tummy while extending his left hand outwards. Laughter erupts, and applause thunders through the room, a testament to Pete's wit and the collective relief that washes over us all.

End

Pete turns out to be, not only my hero, but my comic relief. Then, it's on with the show.

Chapter **6**

Demystifying Writer's Block and Writing a Draft

Perhaps you're a kindred spirit who vibes with this: You're back working in the office two days a week. Your morning drive was exhausting, lasting twice as long as it usually does because of bad weather and accidents along the roadway. By the time you get to the office, the jolt from your morning espresso has worn off and your energy level has waned. (Ah, the joys of having worked at home.) You learn of a document you need to write and the deadline is looming. You have the dreaded writer's block.

Relate to that? Remember that even highly experienced writers can freeze when staring at a blank page or computer screen because they feel they need to come up with something fresh and original every time they sit down to write. This is where AI comes to the rescue.

Using AI as Your Assistant to Chop Through Writer's Block and Write a Draft

AI SPOTLIGHT

With AI-generated chatbots such as ChatGPT (https://chat.openai.com), Copilot (formerly Bing; https://copilot.microsoft.com/), and You.com (https://you.com/), you can experience the marvel of AI technology mixed with writer intelligence (WI) to get that draft started and eliminate the dreaded writer's block. Using AI for this purpose is like bouncing ideas off someone to get unstuck. Here's an example.

Sam is that guy in the opening paragraph. He needed to draft a document on health foods and was suffering from writer's block. He just couldn't think of any topics. He asked You.com to generate ten ideas. Figure 6-1 lists ten ideas the chatbot spewed out at supersonic speed.

10 ideas for a topic on health food

1. The role of superfoods in maintaining a healthy diet
2. Exploring the benefits of organic food for overall health and well-being
3. The impact of processed foods on our health and ways to reduce their consumption
4. The importance of a balanced diet and how to incorporate all essential nutrients
5. The rise of plant-based diets and their positive effects on health
6. The connection between gut health and overall well-being
7. The benefits of incorporating fermented foods into our diet for a healthy gut
8. The impact of sugar on our health and practical tips for reducing sugar intake
9. The benefits of mindful eating and its impact on our relationship with food and health
10. The role of antioxidants in preventing chronic diseases and how to include them in our diet

FIGURE 6-1: Ideas for topics on health food document.

Sam now has ten topics to choose from. He decided to write his document on superfoods for maintaining a healthy diet. Figure 6-2 is what the chatbot came up with as a first draft written in a formal style (which Sam chose).

Sam then wanted to populate his document with images. So he chose "images" from the top menu that also included videos, news, maps, social, and more. Figure 6-3 is the first page of images for a superfood diet.

Superfoods play a significant role in maintaining good health by providing essential nutrients, antioxidants, and other beneficial compounds that support various bodily functions. Here are some key roles that superfoods can play in promoting overall health:

Nutrient-Rich:

Superfoods are typically packed with vitamins, minerals, and other essential nutrients that are necessary for optimal health. These nutrients support various bodily functions, including immunity, energy production, and organ function.

Antioxidant Powerhouse:

Many superfoods are rich in antioxidants, which help protect the body against oxidative stress and damage caused by harmful free radicals. Antioxidants have been linked to a reduced risk of chronic diseases, such as heart disease, cancer, and neurodegenerative disorders.

Anti-Inflammatory Effects:

Inflammation is a natural response of the immune system, but chronic inflammation can contribute to the development of various health conditions. Some superfoods, such as berries, fatty fish, and leafy greens, have anti-inflammatory properties that can help reduce inflammation in the body.

Heart Health:

Certain superfoods, such as fatty fish (rich in omega-3 fatty acids), nuts, seeds, and whole grains, have been associated with a lower risk of heart disease. These foods can help reduce cholesterol levels, lower blood pressure, and improve overall cardiovascular health.

FIGURE 6-2: Draft for a document on superfoods in maintaining a healthy diet.

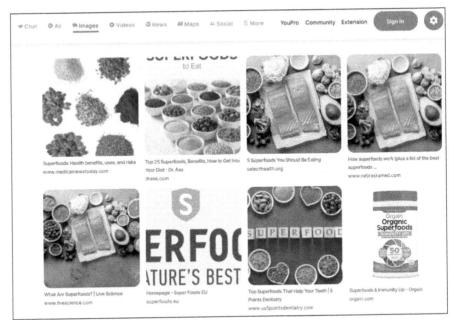

FIGURE 6-3: Images for maintaining a healthy diet.

You.com

Venturing Beyond Chatbots

AI SPOTLIGHT

Sam is now ready to move beyond chatbots, so let's take him to the next level. The following are AI tools for writing drafts:

>> Canva's Magic Write (https://www.canva.com/magic-write/)

>> Copy.ai (https://www.copy.ai/)

>> Delilah (https://www.delilah.ai/)

>> Hix.ai (https://hix.ai/)

>> HyperWrite (https://www.hyperwriteai.com)

>> Jasper (https://www.jasper.ai/)

>> Rytr (https://rytr.me)

>> You.com (https://you.com/)

Each tool will be slightly different, but there are certain fields you'll be asked to fill in:

>> **Type of document:** Email, article, summary, press release, and so on.

>> **Key points:** The key points you want addressed.

>> **Tone:** Formal, informal, joyful, sincere, sad, and so on.

>> **Length:** Number of words or pages.

Karate Chopping Through Writer's Block without AI

If Sam didn't want to use AI, there are a few other ways he could have gotten jump started. Once ideas start flowing, he could have embraced them and allowed them to guide his writing journey.

Freewriting

Freewriting is a great technique to overcome writer's block. It involves writing continuously without worrying about grammar, spelling, or punctuation. The goal is to let your thoughts flow freely and get your creative juices flowing.

Here's how you may want to get started: Set a timer for 10 or 15 minutes. Find a quiet and comfortable space where you can focus. Take a few deep breaths to relax your mind and body. Once you're ready, start writing and don't stop until the timer goes off. It can be a shopping list, a to-do list, or anything that comes to mind. Just keep writing and eventually you'll plug into your task.

Brainstorming and mind mapping

Brainstorming and mind mapping are similar and can be valuable in overcoming writer's block and stimulating creativity in business writing. Both these techniques can both be done individually or with a group.

Brainstorming is to generate a large number of ideas on a specific topic or problem. It typically involves a group of people, but you can do it on your own. Jot down a word, headline, or idea that comes to mind when you think about your topic. Extend the items in a way that makes sense to you. Look for similarities and common themes. Cut (or set) aside any ideas that don't fit into a group. Write a sentence about each. This can help to expand and explore different angles and perspectives. Just free your mind and let ideas flow. The focus is on quantity rather than quality.

Mind mapping is a visual technique that helps organize thoughts and ideas in a hierarchical and interconnected manner. Start with a main idea represented as a circle or node from which branches and sub-branches extend outward. See Figure 6-4 for an example that uses a lightbulb instead of a circle. This technique allows for non-linear thinking, making connections between ideas, and capturing the relationships between different concepts.

Outlining

Do you remember outlining from your school days? You'd have to prepare an outline before writing a report. Once finished, you'd present the outline to the teacher, and often got graded. What you learned about outlining may be valuable in business writing to get rid of writer's block. It helps you organize your thoughts, provides a roadmap or overview, breaks down the tasks, identifies and addresses issues, boosts confidence, and offers flexibility. By outlining, you may overcome the challenges of writer's block and continue the creative process.

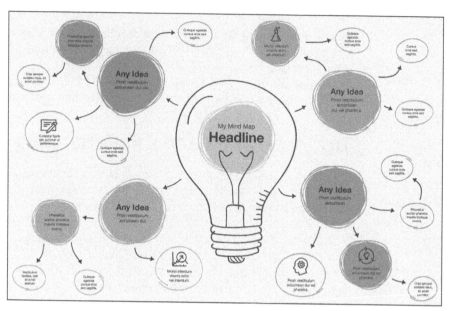

FIGURE 6-4:
Mind mapping.

© tomasknopp/Adobe Stock Photos.

A simple outline may follow these guidelines, although they're not carved in granite:

I. First point in thesis

  A. First sub-topic

    1. Support your point

    2. Add more support for your point

      a. Break it down further

      b. Another item in the breakdown

II. Second point in thesis

Unleashing the Power of WI

We live in a world where emotional language serves a purpose; hyperbole, humor, and stunning prose and stories engage people, win awards, and make a difference in people's lives. This is what separates WI from AI and here's where the real writing comes in. AI writing isn't meant to write an entire document from start to finish. It a powerful tool to help write that first draft and unleash the flood of words.

Back to Sam for a moment: Sam used the first draft as fodder for his own words and created a document in his own flavor and style. It's the "irreplaceable writer" who needs to add the human, relatable, and authentic tone in the following ways:

>> Capturing the nuances and subtleties to ensure the finished document meets the intended goals and resonates with the target readers, leading to the outcome or call to action.

>> Customizing and personalizing to the specific needs of the readers.

>> Promoting and marketing (which are very human tasks).

>> Providing the benefit of teams of writers, blending interactions, perceptions, and opinions.

>> Sharing stories to bring visions to life.

Jumping in and Writing the Draft

Sam had several options at this point. He could have taken any of the ideas the chatbot generated (as you see in Figure 6-1) and created his draft. He could have continued, using his chatbot of choice to generate a draft. Or he could have continued with a comprehensive AI tool from those mentioned earlier in this chapter. But enough about Sam . . . Let's get to your draft.

Get ready, get set . . .

Once you've cracked writer's block, you have some nuggets to work with. Gather everything you need as reference material. Get comfortable. Kick your shoes off. Grab a cup of coffee or glass of water. Use a headset (if that works for you).

REMEMBER

This is a first draft, much like a cartoonist does quick sketches to figure out what to include and where everything should go. If this is a significant document, your draft will go through several rounds of revisions. So, don't put pressure on yourself to make it perfect.

At this early stage, don't even worry about punctuation, grammar, or finding the right word. Fine-tuning will come later. Here are some tips for getting started:

>> **Set a minimum time goal for yourself.** Decide how much time to allot to this sitting. Perhaps you decide to devote 30 minutes to writing. If you're on a roll, just continue.

- >> **Start writing the part you know the most about.** There's always one part of your document you're most comfortable with or you know most about. It could be a nugget from getting rid of writer's block. It could be a section or paragraph you're most familiar with. Your reader will never know where you started, so start at the most comfortable place.

- >> **Write one paragraph at a time and then pause if you need to.** So long as you complete the assignment on time, you may choose how many paragraphs you complete in one sitting. Pace yourself. On the other hand, try not to procrastinate because you probably have to meet a deadline.

- >> **Take short breaks to refresh your mind.** It's okay and often necessary to take a mental break. Walk around. Stretch. Get a cup of coffee.

- >> **Be reasonable with your goals.** Try to stick to that goal. If you told yourself that you need more facts, commit to finding them. Holding yourself to your own goals creates successful writing assignments.

- >> **Avoid going over what you wrote:** The important thing is to keep moving. Now isn't the time to proofread or edit.

Once you're on a roll, thoughts can be like clouds, drifting and changing shape as they flow through your mind. Let WI take the lead. Let those thoughts take shape. Let the keyboard be your canvas to design the draft with the strokes of your fingertips clickety clacking.

TIP

If others will be proofreading and editing your draft, ask them to turn on track changes. Using track changes, multiple editors can make and track changes to a document.

Don't get it right — get it written

REMEMBER

A draft is work-in-progress. It provides a foundation for refinement and editing. It's an opportunity to get your ideas on paper and establish the structure and flow. Once you've gotten some ideas down, you don't need to get it absolutely right — you're still in the drafting stage. Here are some tips for moving towards completing the unpolished first draft:

- >> **Introduction:** Keeping your audience and purpose in mind, start to think about an introduction to grab the reader's attention and pique their interest so they continue reading. It should provide an overview of the topic and set the tone for the rest of the document.

GETTING LOST IN THE TRANSLATION

If your document will be printed in more than one language and you used an AI-generated language translator (most of them offer translations) be sure to have someone who's fluent in both or all the languages review the text very carefully. Every language has its unique complexities, so translation often becomes difficult for AI generators. Things often get lost in the translation and/or misinterpreted. Here's just one of many examples of a translation gone wrong:

The English version of a Pepsi commercial stated, "Pepsi brings you back to life." When it was translated into Chinese, it stated "Pepsi brings your ancestors back from the dead." This is just one example of why WI is vital.

>> **Main body:** This is the core content where you include supporting arguments or evidence for your topic. Organize your ideas into paragraphs or sections, each focusing on a specific point or subtopic. Use topic sentences that give key information at a glance to introduce each paragraph and ensure smooth transitions between paragraphs.

>> **Supporting details:** Include relevant supporting details, examples, facts, or statistics to strengthen your arguments and provide evidence for your claims. These details help to substantiate your ideas and make your writing more persuasive and informative. You don't have to include graphics at this point; merely indicate that a graphic should be included (and where).

>> **Conclusion:** End your draft by summarizing the main points discussed in the body of your writing. A conclusion should provide closure to your piece and leave a lasting impression on the reader. It can also offer final thoughts, recommendations, or a call to action.

If you come across points or facts that you're unsure about or need to research further, make notes directly in your draft using red, brackets, or other indicators. This allows you to continue writing without interrupting your flow. You can revisit those points later.

Sequencing for Maximum Impact

After completing the initial draft, shift your focus to sequencing the information. The order in which you present the flow of text can significantly influence the understanding and efficacy of your message. Chapter 15 includes more detail, but here's the short version:

>> **Sending a positive or neutral message:** When it comes to relating a positive or neutral message, remember to BLUF. This stands for "Bottom Line Up Front," stressing the importance of starting with the positive or neutral point. Unlike a joke where you save the punch line for the end, it's best to present the good news right at the beginning.

>> **Delivering a negative message:** Although negative messages are best delivered face to face, sometimes they must be delivered in written form. Delivering negative news in writing can be challenging, but there are several strategies to make them effective: build up to the news, give an explanation, or offer alternatives.

Although negative news is never easy to deliver, your AI assistant can help you create a message that will soften the blow.

AI SPOTLIGHT

Polishing the Draft

Now you're moving into the next phase of drafting! How much leeway do you have in terms of tone, organization, and style? Perhaps your draft sounds very conversational, but it needs to be more academic. Maybe you've stuck to a five-paragraph format, but there is room to expand.

After you've completed the draft there are many steps and perhaps many people who'll be involved in finalizing the document. Beyond proofreading and editing — which you'll learn about in Chapter 9 — here are several things to take into account to make sure your document is reader focused:

>> Do the headlines give key information at a glance?

>> Did you use paragraphs appropriately?

>> Did you include transitions?

>> Should you re-sequence?

>> Did you provide enough background information?

>> Did you provide closure?

>> Is it the appropriate length?

Achieving a polished document involves more than just basic proofreading and editing. It requires careful consideration of both visual appeal and tone. Chapters 7 and 8 are dedicated to guiding you through this essential process.

TIP

IN THIS CHAPTER

» **Using AI as your visual appeal assistant**

» **Generating precise prompts**

» **Peeking at infographics**

» **Using tables and charts**

» **Adding a splash of color**

» **Considering non-graphical visuals**

Chapter **7**

Designing Visuals to Enhance the Reader's Experience

ou may have spent days, weeks, or months gathering information and generating what you think is a great document. If it doesn't have visual appeal, however, readers won't read it — at least not thoroughly. Visuals are a budget-friendly, powerful way to communicate your message clearly and quickly. By visuals, I'm talking about graphics, videos, photos, graphs, charts, tables, infographics, Adobe images, memes, jpgs, white space, paragraphing, bullets and numbers . . . and just about any content that isn't text-based.

The purpose of a graphic is to grab attention, increase understanding, improve retention, convey emotion, add variety, support branding and design, and facilitate communication. This chapter walks you through ways to turn *ho-hum* documents into *smashing* documents.

Using AI as Your Assistant for Dynamic Visuals

AI SPOTLIGHT

You don't need to be a graphic designer with fancy software to create a pleasing-looking document. When it comes to visuals, this is where AI struts its stuff. It's one of the most exciting technological developments for writers in the ongoing advancement of AI. Whether you realize it or not, AI has been embedded into computer graphics, image and video editing software, 3D models, and animation apps for a while now. New tools are being developed as you're reading this. Many will thrive; others will survive; still others will take a dive. Here are some of the popular ones:

- » Adobe Photoshop (https://www.adobe.com)
- » Adobe Sensei (https://www.adobe.com/sensei)
- » Alpaca (https://www.alpacaml.com/)
- » Art Effects (https://www.deeparteffects.com/)
- » ArtDraw (https://www.autodraw.com/)
- » Dall-e: (https://openai.com/research/dall-e)
- » Designs.ai (https://designs.ai/en)
- » Fronty (https://fronty.com/)
- » Jasper.ai (https://www.jasper.ai)
- » Khroma (https://www.khroma.co/)
- » LetsEnhance (https://letsenhance.io/)
- » Midjourney (https://www.midjourney.com/)
- » Nvidia Canvas (https://www.nvidia.com/en-us/studio/canvas/)
- » Uizard (https://uizard.io/)

REMEMBER

One limitation of AI in both visuals and the written word in AI is that it lacks creativity. It can't replicate the emotional and cultural nuances that connect with readers. AI models can combine and recombine existing images, but can't come up with something actually new. Also, because it relies on vast amounts of data, there have been reports of biases in the areas of recruitment, facial recognition, policymaking, social media, education, and so on. That's why writer intelligence (WI) is essential!

Generating Precise Prompts

AI SPOTLIGHT

Writing prompts for AI artwork gives you an opportunity to blend inspiration and innovation. With each stroke of the virtual brush, AI continues to evolve, offering endless possibilities to explore. Keep pushing the boundaries. And just have fun! Here are some suggestions for creating prompts to elevate visual expression:

>> **Start by understanding what you expect the outcome to be.** Do you want to provoke thought, encourage experimentation, drive home a call to action, motivate a purchase, or something else?

>> **Be specific while keeping it simple.** Instead of simply asking AI to *Draw a flower*, be more specific by asking it to *Create a full-screen realistic illustration of a red rose with dew drops*.

>> **Use references.** This will help AI to understand your preferences and generate artwork that aligns with your vision. Perhaps you may write, *In a Picasso style, create in full color an image of a person using a [product]*.

>> **Bring in sensory language.** Describe the texture, sound, taste, or smell. An example may be, *Create a photo-looking ocean scene with dramatic waves crashing on the shoreline*.

>> **Include emotion.** Provide prompts that invite introspection or explore complex emotions. For example, *Create an abstract painting of a two-year-old child that shows the feeling of vulnerability and resilience*.

>> **Tailor prompts for specific art styles.** Do you want something surrealistic, impressionistic, minimalistic, outlandish, cartoon-like, pencil drawing, watercolor, black and white, or bright splashes of color, to name a few?

>> **Describe the composition of the image.** Photo angles such as a drone shot, lighting such as studio lighting or backlighting, photo lens effects such as fish eye lens or double exposure.

>> **Use negative prompts as a safety barrier:** For example, if you don't want AI to generate anything in a warehouse, your prompt may add, *No warehouses*.

>> **Specify output resolution:** You may say something like 1920 x 1080 pixels (16:9 aspect ratio).

>> **Create a story-like graphic.** Images can tell an entire story. Describe the character(s), setting, and key events, while also incorporating emotions and thematic elements. You may write a prompt such as, *Create a 30-something-year-old female emoji standing in front of a full-length mirror showing she's delighted with a new party dress*.

Know AI's limitations. While AI has made remarkable advancements in its artistic capabilities, it still lacks the nuanced understanding of human emotions and context. This can result in graphic images that lack depth and resonance, and may even be offensive to certain groups. Hence, humans will continue to play a vital role in the creative process, ultimately producing the final product with the artistic flair and personal touch only humans can provide. The ability of humans to infuse art with their own experiences, emotions, and perspectives ensures that art remains a deeply human expression.

WARNING

Deepfake is often used to distribute false and malicious information. While this technology is not (yet) inherently illegal, its immoral usage has faced significant criticism. Don't use it. *Deepface*, on the other hand, is a form of facial recognition technology that's been digitally altered using AI to appear genuine. It has many potential applications, one of which is in law enforcement, where it can help identify missing people or criminals based on facial recognition.

Peeking Into the World of Infographics

AI SPOTLIGHT

Humans are visual beings and infographics are a valuable way to present complex information. Think of an infographic as imagery or data visualization — an artistic representation of data and information that can tell a story. Today's popular AI generators — such as Canva (https://www.canva.com/), Venngage (https://venngage.com), Visme (https://www.visme.co/), Infogram https://infogram.com/), Snappa (https://snappa.com/), and Adobe Creative Cloud Express (https://www.adobe.com/express/) — can turn text into graphics easily. And you don't have to be a graphic designer. Check out Figures 7-1 and 7-2 to see examples.

Here are some of the advantages of infographics:

>> Delivers a quick overview of a topic.

>> Summarizes long text.

>> Compares and contrasts multiple options.

>> Shows a timeline or steps in a process.

>> Displays research outcomes or survey data.

>> Explains complex information or a process.

>> Builds brand awareness and increases brand credibility.

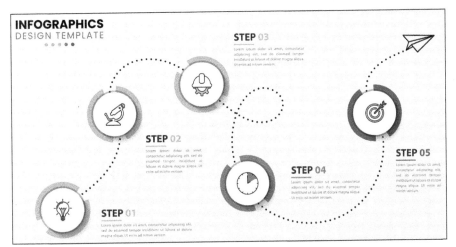

© kuliperko/Adobe Stock Photos.

© tang90246/Adobe Stock Photos.

WARNING

WHO OWNS THE COPYRIGHT?

Exploring the boundaries of ownership has opened Pandora's Box in the U.S. Copyright Office. For example, when using AI tools to create visuals replicating those of a specific artist, the copyright implications are complex. Currently copyright laws cover only materials created by people. Therefore, your AI-generated image can't be copyrighted, but may be copied by others because you don't own the rights. Stay tuned to the news because AI-generated visuals are now being addressed. Some AI tools specifically state they're allowed to reuse any of the designs you create using their program. Carefully review yours. This doesn't mean you shouldn't use AI as part of your graphic design; it just means you should ensure that people who are involved in the process make whatever tweaks will make it copyrightable.

Also note that while AI-generated work, in general, faces legal ambiguity in terms of copyright, the situation is further complicated when the AI is instructed to mimic the style of an existing artist.

Adding Tables and Charts

If a picture is worth a thousand words (now about 6,000 words with inflation), charts and tables are gold. Here's what they can do:

>> Make complex information easier to understand so readers can quickly grasp patterns, trends, and relationships.

>> Present large amounts of information in a compact space replacing long paragraphs of text.

>> Attract and sustain the interest of readers to make the information more appealing and memorable.

>> Facilitate comparison and analysis of data so readers can compare different data points, identify patterns, and draw conclusions more easily than with text alone.

>> Make information available to a wider audience by incorporating features such as color contrast, alternative text, and data labels. This helps people with visual impairments or other accessibility needs to access and understand the information.

REMEMBER

It's helpful to remember the difference between data and information. Data is the raw, unorganized detailing of facts. Information is the process of organizing data to provide meaning and context. Information is significant, structured, and useful for decision making, whereas data on its own lacks significance and structure.

Table that thought

Tables play a crucial role in transforming raw data into meaningful information. They provide structure, organization, context, and visual representation, enabling users to analyze, compare, and draw insights from the data more effectively. Key elements include:

» **Header row:** The header row is located at the top of the table and contains labels or titles for each column. It provides a quick reference for the type of data presented in each column.

» **Data rows:** Data rows are the rows that follow the header row and contain the actual data. Each row represents a separate record or observation, and each column within the row corresponds to a specific attribute or variable.

» **Columns:** Columns are vertical sections within the table that represent different categories or variables. Each column contains data related to a specific aspect of the information being presented.

The table in Figure 7-3 shows these elements. Notice that alternate lines are shaded. That's useful when people reading the table may have difficulty following horizontally. Shading makes it easier to distinguish one line from another.

<table>
<tr><td colspan="4" align="center">Table 4-5: Complexity Factors</td></tr>
<tr><td align="center">Factor</td><td align="center">Low</td><td align="center">Moderate</td><td align="center">High</td></tr>
<tr><td>Originality required</td><td></td><td>X</td><td></td></tr>
<tr><td>Processing flexibility</td><td>X</td><td></td><td></td></tr>
<tr><td>Span of operations</td><td>X</td><td></td><td></td></tr>
<tr><td>Dynamics of requirements</td><td>X</td><td></td><td>X</td></tr>
<tr><td>Equipment</td><td></td><td>X</td><td></td></tr>
<tr><td>Personnel</td><td>X</td><td></td><td></td></tr>
<tr><td>Development costs</td><td></td><td></td><td>X</td></tr>
<tr><td>Processing time</td><td></td><td>X</td><td></td></tr>
<tr><td>Communication architecture</td><td>X</td><td></td><td></td></tr>
</table>

FIGURE 7-3: Table with key elements: header row, data rows, and columns.

Chart your course

Use charts to convey information that's visually appealing, simplifies complex data, facilitates comparison and analysis, provides clarity and comprehension, saves time, and serves as a universal language. By using charts, information can be presented in a way that is easily understood, memorable, and impactful.

I was working with a client at Hanscom Air Force Base, in Massachusetts. The Electronic System Division was preparing a process improvement guide. In the guide, they were documenting the weight of officers to determine the high, low, and median weights. Their first attempt presented them in sentence form: 206, 180, 163, and so forth. When they realized that didn't work, they prepared a grid as you see in Figure 7-4. If anyone was trying to make sense of this data, the grid didn't work any better than the sentence format. To make this information easy to interpret I prepared a histogram, shown in Figure 7-5. It takes the same data and turns it into information at a glance. A *histogram* is a type of bar chart that displays the frequency or number of observations within different numerical ranges.

Weights of 80 Officers

206	180	139	163	159
155	180	165	149	127
159	171	141	190	159
153	181	180	137	161
115	156	173	165	191
159	110	179	145	144
150	206	166	188	165
127	130	172	180	147
145	150	156	171	189
190	200	208	169	139
130	128	155	185	166
165	187	159	178	169
147	150	201	128	170
189	163	150	158	180
139	149	185	129	169
175	189	150	201	175

FIGURE 7-4: "Before" grid displays the distribution of weight.

© *John Wiley & Sons, Inc.*

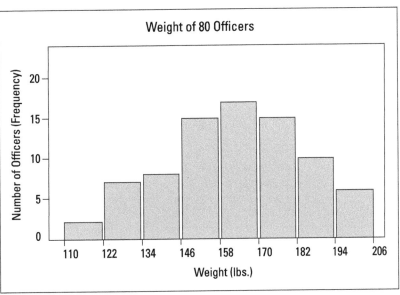

FIGURE 7-5:
"After" histogram successfully displays the distribution of weight.

© John Wiley & Sons, Inc.

In addition to histograms, there are many types of charts. These are the most commonly used:

>> **Pie chart:** As you see in Figure 7-6, a pie chart is like a wedge-shaped pizza. You may order a pizza with 50 percent pepperoni, 25 percent mushrooms, and 25 percent plain. Each section represents a percentage of the total pie (100 percent). Limit the number of items in a pie chart to avoid clutter. Some tools allow users to open wedges and examine them in more detail.

>> **Line chart:** A line chart is useful for showing the change of one or more variables over time. Line charts are plotted in relation to two axes drawn at right angles. Make the axes descriptive and use clear labels. This may be used to track trends over time and identifying pattern and anomalies, like the one shown in Figure 7-7.

>> **Flowcharts:** These display major steps in a process using flowchart symbols. They're often used for project management, process documentation, problem solving, software development, quality control, and continuous improvement. See Figure 7-8.

AI SPOTLIGHT

AI tools such as Graphmaker.ai (`https://www.graphmaker.ai/`), Creately (`https://creately.com`), Datawrapper `https://www.datawrapper.de/`), and Think Cell (`https://www.think-cell.com/en`) can assist with preparing tables and charts.

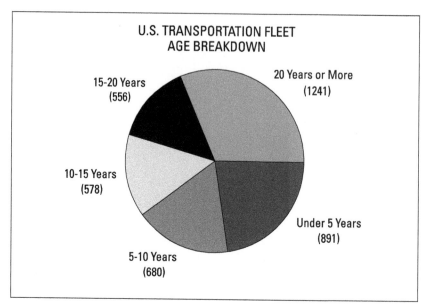

FIGURE 7-6:
Pie chart.

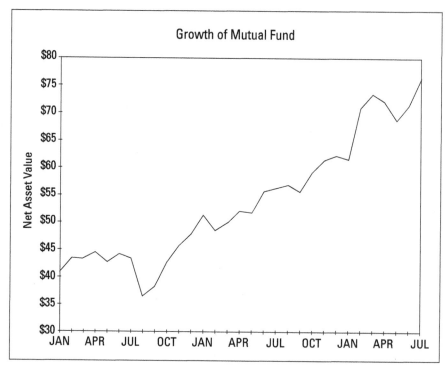

FIGURE 7-7:
Line chart.

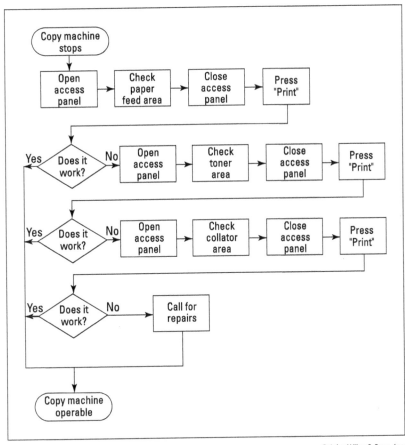

FIGURE 7-8:
Flowchart.

© John Wiley & Sons, Inc.

Coloring Your Way to Clarity

Colors have the power to elicit specific emotions and behaviors. When it comes to selecting colors for business documents, take into account the intended message, your brand identity, and the target audience. Different colors convey distinct meanings and can evoke various responses. Here are three of the commonly used colors in business documents and their associated connotations:

>> **Blue:** Often associated with trust, professionalism, and reliability, blue is a popular choice for corporate documents. It can instill a sense of confidence and dependability in your audience.

>> **Red:** Known for its boldness and energy, red can be used to capture attention and convey a sense of urgency. It is often utilized in marketing materials to create a sense of excitement and stimulation.

> » **Green:** Symbolizing growth, harmony, and prosperity, green is frequently used in documents related to sustainability, finance, and health. It can create a sense of balance and tranquility.

WARNING

Be careful not to use too many colors. They'll be distracting, lack cohesion, cause misinterpretation, and may have printing constraints . . . plus they'll make your document look like a circus poster. Also be aware that colors have different meanings across different cultures.

Digging into Visuals Beyond Graphics

Think of visuals in the broader sense. Anything the reader sees is a visual, not just a graphic. Visual impact organizes information into manageable, bite-sized chunks of information, making it easy to read. It also emphasizes what's important by separating major points from minor points. Visuals involve white space, paragraph and sentence length, strong headlines, bulleted and numbered lists, and the order in which the information is presented.

Including white space

White space is a key visual ingredient. It includes all areas on the page where there's neither text nor graphics. In other words, it's quiet space or blank space. Leave 1" to 1 ½" on the top, bottom, and sides of paper documents. For emails, default to the margins. Here's what white space does:

- » Makes the document inviting and approachable.
- » Provides a contrast and resting place for the reader's eyes.
- » Creates the impression that the document is easy to read.

Limiting paragraph and sentence length

Think of some things you've read for business or pleasure. When you have long, dense paragraphs, do you tend to skim or even slip those paragraphs (as I do)? If so, in business writing you may be missing critical information, so:

- » **Limit paragraphs to about 8 lines of text.** That's an easy-to-read, manageable chunk of information. Long, dense paragraphs are intimidating. And short, choppy paragraphs make it difficult for the reader to see the relationship between thoughts.

>> **Limit sentences to about 20–25 words.** In most cases, the shorter the sentence, the better. You can shorten sentences by breaking long sentences into two, eliminating unnecessary words, or turning a passive sentence into an active one.

Preparing strong headlines that tell a story

Given that most people don't read business documents — they scan them — creating strong headlines in a document is crucial so readers can swiftly grasp key information (just as they do in newspapers and magazines.)

Strong headlines act as signposts, guiding readers through the document so they can selectively focus on specific areas of interest and get key information at a glance, as shown in the following example:

Informative: *Findings: XYZ Machine Holds Great Promise*

Uninformative: *Findings: XYZ Machine*

Need help generating impactful headlines? Turn to your favorite chatbot to help you create them. Here's an example: I wanted to generate a headline on how to brew tea. So I turned to You.com (my chatbot of choice) and asked for six creative headlines for brewing tea. Figure 7-9 shows what it came up with.

6 creative headlines for brewing tea

1. "Steeped in Delight: Discover the Art of Brewing the Perfect Cup of Tea"
2. "From Leaves to Bliss: Unleash Your Inner Tea Connoisseur with These Brewing Techniques"
3. "Tea Brewing Magic: Unlocking the Secrets to a Flawless Infusion"
4. "Brewing Tea like a Pro: Elevate Your Tea Game with These Creative Methods"
5. "Tea Time, Elevated: Unconventional Brewing Techniques for a Memorable Sip"
6. "Tea Mastery Unleashed: Unveiling the Most Creative and Flavorful Tea Brewing Recipes"

FIGURE 7-9: Creative chatbot-generated headlines.

You can create valuable headlines in different situations, not just in business writing. I was stopped at a red light and noticed a sign posted on a pole. In large letters it said, MISSING DOG. Underneath was a small picture and some text, neither of which could be seen by passing in a car. The poster completely missed the mark. If the owner had used the headline MISSING DALMATIAN and put the dog's photo beneath it, that would have told passersby immediately the breed of dog to spot (pun intended).

Putting it on the list

If you believe in Santa Claus, you know all about making lists. When you prepare your Christmas wish list, you write the hottest item as No. 1; the second hottest, No. 2; and so on. If you don't use numbers, you won't have given Santa any visual clue as to what's most important to you. Santa may just pick a few things you ask for, and then you'll be disappointed on Christmas morning when your shiny red Jaguar isn't waiting in the driveway.

When you prepare a shopping list, you list each item but don't use numbers. The list is probably in random order. That's because once you're in the store, you just pick items off the shelf — everything has the same weight (figuratively speaking).

The following sections explain when to use a bulleted list or a numbered list.

AI SPOTLIGHT

AI can create bulleted and numbered lists. Just prompt it to do so.

Using bulleted lists

Use bulleted lists when rank and sequence aren't important. Bullets give everything on the list equal value. Always head the list with a descriptive sentence as you see below:

> *Following are the fabrication methods for stencils:*
> - *Laser cutting*
> - *Chemical etching*
> - *Electroforming*

Using numbered lists

Here are the best ways to use a numbered list:

>> **Show items in order of priority.** Doing so gives the reader a visual clue that the items on the list are in priority order. Example:

- *Please take care of these issues in the morning:*
    1. *Call the ABC Agency to arrange for a consultant for the week of May 1.*
    2. *Ask Jim to prepare his R&D report.*
    3. *Schedule a meeting with everyone involved in the Diamus project.*

>> **Describe steps in a procedure.** When you describe steps in a procedure, start each numbered item with an *action word* — something for the reader to do. Example:

- *Following are the requirements for past formulated for water printing:*

  1. *Use a squeegee action to deliver all the stencil aperture contents in the UBM surface.*

  2. *Remove any remaining solder beads with the automated wiping process.*

  3. *Remove oxides from the solder beads during the reflow process.*

  4. *Remove flux residues after the reflow with mild chemistries.*

>> **Quantify items.** If you don't number a long list, people count the listed items in their heads to make sure the number of items is correct. When you number the list, you let readers reserve their brain power for more important things. Example:

- *Following are the eight people on the team:*

  1. *Connie Burgess*

  2. *Ellen Mandel*

  3. *Joan Piergrossi*

  4. *Karen Rappaport*

  5. *Maureen Hines*

  6. *Peter Johnson*

  7. *Shari Whitcomb*

  8. *Win Treese*

Using parallel structure

Imagine gymnasts in the final tryouts for the Olympics. They gracefully dance along the parallel bars; their eyes are aglow as they look and smile at the audience. All of a sudden — oops! — the bars aren't parallel. One bar veers to the left. The poor gymnast falls to the floor. Now imagine your readers, totally absorbed in your document. All of a sudden — oops! — the list or sentence isn't parallel. One component veers off. The poor reader's expectations fall.

TIP

Whether you use a bulleted or numbered list, create items that are parallel in structure. That means all elements that function alike must be treated alike. For example, in the parallel bulleted list that follows, all the bulleted items are gerunds — they end with -*ing*. In the nonparallel bulleted list, the first two items end with *-ing*, making the last item (starting with *specify*) stick out like a wart at the end of a witch's nose:

>> **Parallel bulleted list:**

   Effective measures should involve

   ● Designing and maintaining the facility

   ● Training the operators and other people in the field

   ● Specifying security personnel and procedures

>> **Nonparallel bulleted list:**

   Effective measures should involve

   ● Designing and maintaining the facility

   ● Training the operators and other people in the field

   ● <u>Specify</u> security personnel and procedures

Punctuating a list

People often get confused as to when to use a colon to introduce a list and when to use a period to end a list. The following demystifies these pesky marks of punctuation.

>> **Colon:** Use a colon to introduce a list when the words *the following, as follows, here are,* or *here is* are stated or implied. However, don't use a colon after a verb. Example:

   ● Please consider the following ideas:

   ● Please consider these ideas: (The following is implied.)

   ● The three factors are (In this case, don't use a colon. Just follow the sentence with the bulleted or numbered list.)

>> **Periods:** Use a period after each item in a list only when the items on the list are complete sentences. When the items complete the sentence, put a period after the last item only.

Avoiding laundry lists

When you have too many items on a list, you create a laundry list and readers may just gloss over everything you worked so hard to emphasize. Instead of creating a long list of bulleted or numbered items, break the items into categories. Below on the left you see one long list. On the right you see how the list was divided into two logical chunks of information. It's easier to read and gives more information.

Our global expansion takes in the following countries:	Our global expansion takes in the following countries:
Austria	**Asia**
China	China
Hong Kong	Hong Kong
Indonesia	Indonesia
Malaysia	Malaysia
Portugal	Thailand
Spain	**Europe**
Sweden	Austria
Thailand	Portugal
	Spain
	Sweden

Chapter **8**

Honing the Tone

I magine this: You've been on the job for less than a month and get this email from your new boss: *We need to talk. Schedule an appointment.* "Yikes, what have I done wrong?" you wonder from that assertive tone? If the email had read, *What's your schedule like today? I'd love to chat when you're free,* the friendly tone would have perhaps reflected an interest in getting to know you better.

Choose your tone wisely. With the written word, there are no interpretations through nonverbal cues such as gestures, voice, inflections, eye contact, movement, and so forth. Therefore your tone must be reflected in your intent and your message. There are a wide range of tones: Formal, casual, empathetic, confident, optimistic, pessimistic, assertive, joyful, journalistic, humorous, sarcastic, scientific, sincere, philosophical, wry, hypocritical, and more. This chapter helps you hone that tone.

Using AI as Your Assistant for the Proper Tone

AI SPOTLIGHT

AI generators use natural language processing (NLP) techniques and can adapt to any tone you chose to create copy that connects with your readers at an emotional level. You can prompt AI to create a specific tone such as formal, informal, conversational, lighthearted, and more. Or you can ask a chatbot to check the tone in an existing document for professionalism and friendliness, make it more empathetic, and so on.

While many of the technologies are similar in what they offer, each has a slightly different angle and price point. Check out these popular ones:

» Anyword (https://anyword.com/)

» Copy.ai (https://www.copy.ai/)

» Grammarly (https://app.grammarly.com/)

» Jasper (https://www.jasper.ai)

» Notion AI (https://www.notion.so)

» Rytr (https://rytr.me)

» Scalenut (https://www.scalenut.com/)

» Smart Copy (https://www.smart-copy.io/)

» Writer (https://ask.writer.com/)

» Writesonic (https://writesonic.com)

» You.com (https://you.com/)

Notice the different tones in the following examples. In Figure 8-1, I asked my fave chatbot You.com to write one paragraph about molecules in a formal, scientific tone. Then I asked it to write one paragraph about molecules in an informal, simplified tone. Notice the difference in tone in Figure 8-2.

FIGURE 8-1: Formal, scientific tone delivered by chatbot.

> Molecules, the building blocks of matter, are intricate and fascinating entities that hold the key to understanding the complexities of the universe. These tiny, bound clusters of atoms dance and vibrate, constantly in motion, forming the backbone of everything we see and touch. From the elegant simplicity of water molecules to the intricacy of DNA's double helix, molecules serve as the silent architects of life, dictating the properties and behaviors of substances. With their unique arrangements and chemical bonds, molecules shape the physical and chemical properties of materials, allowing scientists to unlock the secrets of nature and harness their power for the betterment of mankind.

FIGURE 8-2:
Informal, simplified tone delivered by chatbot.

Tone: The Secret to Captivating Your Audience

You establish the atmosphere through your selection of words, arrangement of sentences, perspective, capitalization, and use of rhetorical devices such as alliterations, similes, and hyperboles. The words you choose reflect your unique voice and tone. Formal language conveys a serious and respectful attitude. Informal language projects a casual and friendly attitude.

REMEMBER

A strong, consistent voice helps you establish credibility, authority, and identity, while a suitable and appropriate tone can help you engage your readers, convey your purpose, and create the desired mood. A weak or inconsistent voice can make you sound bland, boring, or unprofessional. For instance, on its website, Grammarly offers this example: By changing "I think we should be able to solve this" to "We will be able to solve this," you'd be suggesting a more positive, reassuring tone.

Being conversational, formal, or persuasive

When deciding the tone, keep in mind your relationship with the reader and what you hope to accomplish. Although there are many forms of tone ranging from tense to humorous, this section focuses on the three most commonly used in business writing:

>> **Conversational:** This tone mimics everyday speech. The more relaxed language makes it friendly and approachable. It can include contractions, analogies, and humor (when appropriate). This is the preferred style for emails, blogs and articles, instructions and procedures, informal business communication, and more.

>> **Formal:** The formal tone is a professional and objective approach. It uses precise and concise language, avoiding contractions, slang, or colloquialisms. It's commonly used in formal business letters, reports, and academic writing.

>> **Persuasive:** The persuasive tone aims to influence the reader's beliefs or actions. It uses compelling language, appeals to emotions, and presents logical arguments to sway the reader to heed the call to action. It's frequently used in marketing materials, sales pitches, proposals, and letters appealing for contributions.

AI SPOTLIGHT

Figure 8-3 is what AI spewed out when I asked it to prepare a two-sentence example of conversational, formal, and persuasive tones.

FIGURE 8-3:
A two-sentence example in conversational, formal, and persuasive formats.

two sentence examples of conversational, formal, and persuasive writing

Conversational: "Hey, I just wanted to let you know that your presentation was fantastic! You really nailed it and the audience was captivated throughout."

Formal: "I would like to extend my sincere appreciation for the outstanding quality of your presentation. Your delivery was impeccable, and it left a lasting impression on the audience."

Persuasive: "Our new product is a game-changer. With its innovative features and unparalleled performance, it will revolutionize the way you work. Don't miss out on this opportunity to enhance your productivity and stay ahead of the competition."

Keeping it short

The shortest letter ever known was received by Victor Hugo in 1802. He sent a manuscript titled *Les Miserables* to his publisher. When Victor didn't hear back, he sent a follow-up letter asking what the publisher thought of his manuscript. What Hugo got back said it all:

!

The following "Gobbledygook" sentence is from an airline exit-seat card based on federal regulations. It's full of gobbledygook that doesn't add value and is rather confusing to read. The "To the point" gets right to the point:

Gobbledygook: *No air carrier may seat a person in a designated seat if it is likely that the person would be unable to perform one or more of the following functions under REQUIREMENTS listed below.* (34 words)

To the point: *To sit in an exit you must meet the following conditions.* (11 words)

Keeping it simple

Cornelius Vanderbilt, one of the wealthiest Americans of the nineteenth century, was a very ruthless industrialist. Here's a letter he wrote. It's short and simple with not one wasted word:

You have undertaken to cheat me. I won't sue you for the law is too slow. I'll ruin you.

Whether a sentence is long or short, it should be concise. Concise isn't the opposite of long; it's the opposite of word salad. Even a 10-word sentence may be too long. Eliminate whatever words don't add value.

> **Concise:** *Please confirm delivery of the HCE exchangers (5%/9%RD) needed by July 1, 202X. (13 words)*
>
> **Wordy:** *We wish to request that you notify us if the HCE exchangers (5%/9%RD) will be ready to be shipped no later than July 1, 202X. (25 words)*
>
> **Concise:** *Please let us know by April 15 if you plan to attend the May 2 workshop. Enrollment is light. (19 words)*
>
> **Wordy:** *Due to the lack of enrollment and interest, we might find it necessary to cancel the workshop scheduled for May 2 at 2:30. We'll regret having to do this, so please be certain that you let us know by April 15 if you're desirous of attending. (46 words)*

TIP

By incorporating a mix of sentence lengths, you can create a balanced and engaging writing style. This prevents monotony and creates overall readability.

> **Short sentences:** *The company achieved record sales. The new product launch was successful. The long-term strategy is to enter new markets.*
>
> **Medium sentences:** *The new product launch was successful, and the company yielded record sales. This should allow us to enter new markets.*
>
> **Long sentence:** *The new produce launch was very successful, the company yielded record sales, and this should allow us to enter new markets.*

AI SPOTLIGHT

AI is a wonderful way to condense a piece of writing. You can prompt your chatbot to write two sentences, three paragraphs, four pages, or whatever. I've used AI so many times — even in this book — when I had to shorten information.

Avoiding expressions on steroids

TIP

Topple the tower of babble and don't pad sentences with words that don't add value. Here are just a few examples:

Use	Instead of
agree	came to an agreement
apply	make an application
breakthrough	new breakthrough
concluded	came to the conclusion
enclosed	enclosed herewith
essential	absolutely essential
experimented	conducted an experiment
fact	true fact
opposite	completely opposite
show	give an indication
truth	honest

Choosing Positive Words

Your words have consequences. Let the reader know what you *can and will do*, not what you *can't* and *won't do*. Using positive words engages the reader's goodwill and enhances your tone. Positive words include *benefit, bonus, convenient, delighted, excellent, honest, glad, guarantee, immediately, pleasing, pleasure, safe, satisfactory, save, yes,* and many more.

> **Positive:** *Participation for January remained at 45%.*

> **Negative:** *Participation for the month of January hasn't increased. It remained at 45%.*

TIP

When you do write something negative, do it strategically. Studies show that negative word patterns result in the release of negative hormones and neurotransmitters in the brain. Unless you're doing so strategically, avoid using words such as *broken, cannot, complaint, damages, dangerous, difficult, disappoint, failure, guilt, impossible, inconvenient, problem, regret, suspicion, your inability, your refusal,* and so on.

I recently saw a user manual for an electrical appliance. On the outside of the box it read: *This is no more <u>dangerous</u> than a hair dryer.* The word *dangerous* glared like a neon sign on a dark night. Instead, it should have read: *This is as <u>safe</u> as a hair dryer.* Big difference in the tone!

Being Active or Passive

When we talk about active and passive verbs, we usually talk about voice. In the active voice, the subject (person, place, or thing) performs the action of the verb, while in the *passive voice*, the subject receives the action. Look at the difference in the following two sentences:

Active: *The cat scratched Benji.*

Passive: *Benji was scratched by the cat.*

Using the active voice

Using the active voice is a major factor in projecting a tone that's alive and interesting. Voice is the grammatical term that refers to whether the subject of the sentence or clause acts or receives the action. When you write a sentence in the active voice, you make the subject the doer (you can infer the doer when speaking directly to them).

Active: *Please turn off the lights before you leave the building in the evening.* (The doer is inferred)

Passive: *The alarm should be turned off before the building closes for the night.*

The doer doesn't need to be a person. It can be any noun including a place or thing:

The computer is being repaired by my IT person.

New business depends on up-to-date equipment.

Using the passive voice

Passive voice always includes a form of the verb to be (*is, was, were, being, has been, had been, might have been,* and so on). When you write a sentence in the passive voice, you make the subject the receiver of the action. Passive sentences are often dull and weak, but at times you can use them strategically.

AI SPOTLIGHT

AI proofreading tools will flag passive sentences. However, there are times you want to keep the passive voice. Notice that a form of the verb "to be" is underscored in each of the following sentences:

>> You want to place the focus on the action, not the doer.

Example: *The law firm was established in the early 1900s.* (You want to focus is on the action, the longevity of the firm, not the person who established the firm.)

>> You want to hide something.

Example: *The computer is broken.* (You are protecting the person who broke it.)

For decades, researchers have debated whether to use the active or passive voice for scientific writing. They're been trained to be objective in their work, and their objectivity must come through in the tone of their writing. The passive voice allows researchers to remain distant from their own work to present (what appears to be) an unbiased viewpoint. And since objectivity is important for good science, this makes good sense. On the flip side, the passive voice leaves readers with open-ended questions. Who did the counting? Who was responsible? Whichever voice you choose, do so with intent. It seems as if the jury is still out on this one.

Remembering It's Not All About You

Use *you* and *your* more than *me, I, we,* and *us.* Have you ever gone to a party and got cornered by a bore who talked incessantly about themselves? It's pretty annoying. The next time you see that bore, would you be anxious to spend more time with them? No, you'd probably find a tall plant to get behind.

We're all given two ears and one mouth and should use them in equal proportion. When appropriate, use terms that represent your reader, rather than yourself. Here's an example of using the passive voice:

Reader focus: *Your department will be getting a new accountant.*

Writer focus: *I'll be hiring a new accountant for your department.*

WARNING

If you believe that these factors are insignificant, think again. The reader is primarily interested in what you can offer them, rather than focusing on you. To illustrate this point, take a look at Figure 8-4, which showcases a letter received by one of my clients, an architectural firm. They had issued a multi-million-dollar contract for bidding, and the accompanying cover letter they received is quite telling. The sender mentioned themselves a staggering 28 times, while my client was only mentioned 3 times. My client didn't even bother reading the proposal. Rather they sent a letter to the sender that read: *28 to 3 — you lose!!!*

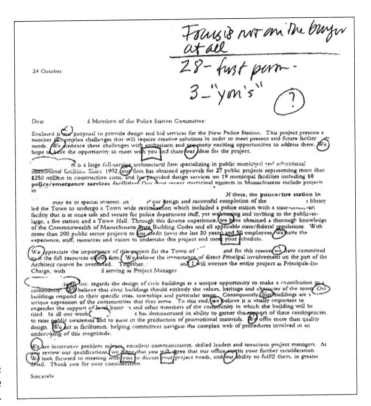

FIGURE 8-4:
It's all about the reader. Not you.

Being Consistent and Clear

Whether you're writing a technical paper, academic paper, presentation, or a social media post, consistency helps the reader understand the message without distractions. It makes the content easier to read and comprehend, and it reflects a level of professionalism and attention to detail.

TIP

Here are my guidelines for maintaining consistency and clarity:

>> **Use consistent wording.** For example, if you make reference to a *user manual*, don't later call it a *reference manual* or *user guide*. Your reader may think you refer to separate documents.

>> **Use repetition strategically.** Use repetition when you want to drive a point home.

- *See the whites get whiter.*

- *See the reds get redder.*

- *See the blues get bluer.*

>> **Avoid ambiguity.** Don't use *should* or *may* when they are not options. *Don't smoke when operating this equipment* is definite. *You shouldn't smoke when operating this equipment* expresses a hint of maybe.

>> **The words *and* and *but* aren't interchangeable.** *But* communicates a negative message, an obstacle, a hitch, or something you didn't expect. *And* communicates a positive message, something you expected.

- **Positive:** *Tom was new to consulting and outperformed expectations.* (His good performance was expected.)

- **Negative:** *Tom was new to consulting but outperformed expectations.* (His good performance was a surprise.)

Using Gender-Neutral Pronouns

REMEMBER

Language isn't static. It's constantly adapting and evolving to reflect our changing lives, experiences, technology, and cultures. Just think of new words that resulted from the recent pandemic: Covidiot, doomscrolling, super-spreader, social distancing, and so many more.

The language of genders has seen its own evolution. Many of us have become accustomed to using she/her/hers for females and he/his/him for males. As gender vocabulary continues to evolve, it's proper to address a singular person as they, them, ze, or hir. Many people now put their gender preferences in the signature blocks of their emails. Inclusive language offers respect, safety, and belonging to all people. This book uses this inclusive approach.

For Dummies books now use "they" and "their" as both singular and plural. However, *The Chicago Manual of Style* (a staple reference for writers and editors since 1906) is watching the generic use of inclusive language, stating: "They and their have become common in informal usage, but neither is considered fully acceptable in formal writing." As you go through your technical writing projects, use good judgment and always consider your audience.

When you refer to people by job descriptions, be aware of gender-neutral terms. Here are some to consider:

Use	Rather than
Cinematographer	Cameraman
Chair, moderator	Chairman, chairperson
Member of the clergy	Clergyman
Messenger	Delivery person
Firefighter	Fireman
Ancestor	Forefather
Insurance agent	Insurance man
Nonprofessional	Layman
Synthetic	Manmade
Humanity, human race	Mankind
Reporter, journalist	Newsman
Police officer	Policeman, policewoman
Letter carrier	Postman
Service technician	Repairman, repairwoman
Sales representative	Salesman, salesperson
Spokesperson	Spokesman
Flight attendant	Steward, stewardess
Meteorologist	Weatherman
Worker	Workman

Using Industry-Related Jargon Appropriately

Industry-related jargon is specialized "shop talk" unique to people in an industry. When writing to people in your industry who understand these terms, it makes no sense to water down the language. Doing so may damage the integrity of the document and insult the reader. When you write to people outside the industry, however, avoid jargon. The tone may become tangled in abstract words that the reader may view as exclusionary. When you include industry-related jargon, consider your reader as follows:

» **Explain the term at first mention.** For example, *Bob is the subject matter expert (SME).* Thereafter, SME may stand alone because you already explained it.

» **If you have many industry-related terms, include a glossary at the end of the document for easy reference.** Consider a glossary for a website or lengthy report that may have lots of industry-related terms.

We each interpret jargon and abbreviations based on our profession and personal experience. Here's an example. In her book *Visual Intelligence* (Houghton Mifflin Harcourt, 2016), author Amy E. Herman explains how people interpret the initials SOB:

Medical professionals told me SOB means 'shortness of breath,' while maintenance crews claim it's 'son of bosses.' For Texas law enforcement agents, it means 'south of the border. . .' [My favorite is] the mother of a teenage texter, who said that SOB is an acronym for 'son of a bitch.'

Thinking Seriously about Being Funny

Business writing can be dull and routine. But never trade boring for discomfort; it's an easy trap. Humor fails when it gets in the way of the message; however, when used properly, humor can break up dry content. It can even make a technical subject more enjoyable and easier to understand. Here's how Lewis Thomas handled humor in *The Lives of a Cell* (Penguin, 1978):

Ants are much like human beings as to be an embarrassment. They farm fungi, raise aphids as livestock, launch armies into wars, use chemical sprays to alarm and confuse enemies, capture slaves. The families of weaver ants engage in child labor, hold their larvae like shuttles to spin the threat that sews the leaves together for their fungus gardens. They exchange information ceaselessly. They do everything but watch television.

Will Rogers once said, "Humor is funny as long as it's happening to somebody else." What's funny to one reader may be insulting to another. Even among friends, humor can be cutting. George Bernard Shaw once sent tickets to his latest play to his good friend Winston Churchill. Mr. Shaw included this note: *Here are two tickets to my new play. One for you and one for a friend — if any.* Mr. Churchill returned the tickets with this note: *Sorry, I'm unable to attend opening night. Please send me tickets for another performance — if any.*

WARNING

Given that your readers may be culturally diverse, carefully consider avoiding humor if there's the slightest chance it may offend anyone.

AI SPOTLIGHT

Remember, while AI has made significant advancements in understanding and generating text, there are certain tones that AI can't discern. This is why WI is a must. Here are a few examples of tone that AI may have difficulty with:

>> Sarcasm and irony

>> Emotional nuances

>> Cultural references and slang

>> Subtle persuasion or manipulation

>> Context-dependent tone

USE PUNCTUATION TO CREATE A VOICE IN YOUR READER'S HEAD

One way to give your writing a voice is to invoke the music of language — punctuation. Punctuation isn't dead despite texts that read: *im on the way* or *its in the trunk.* That's okay for very casual communication such as texting (although I can't bring myself to be that casual) but it's not okay for business communication.

Here are some ways to make sentences ebb and flow like the sound of the ocean so your writing creates an unconscious voice in the minds of readers:

- Commas indicate a slight pause.
- Semicolons indicate a longer pause.
- Periods bring you to a full stop.

(continued)

(continued)

- Question marks make you stop and think.

- Slashes invite you to hold multiple ideas in the reader's head.

- Parentheses create an afterthought or added information you want to downplay.

- Em dashes (—) can be used in place of a comma, colon, or semicolon to create emphasis.

- Exclamation points indicate an *aha!* They're overused, so include them very sparingly.

Another way to give expression to your voice is through italics, bold, underscore, or capitals:

- The *goldfish* is in the tank. (As opposed to the shark being in the tank.)

- The goldfish is in the *tank*. (As opposed to it being in the sink.)

- This the best deal <u>ever</u>. (Focus is on <u>ever</u>.)

- This IS the best deal ever. (Focus is on IS).

IN THIS CHAPTER

» **Using AI as your editorial assistant**

» **Using AI translators**

» **Proofreading and editing with AI**

» **Sense-checking and double-checking your content**

» **Determining the readability of your content**

Chapter **9**

Polishing the Prose

Imagine spending days, weeks, or months writing your document only to have an error stick out like a tarantula on a piece of angel food cake. You'll be remembered for your error, not for the great document you prepared.

Proofreading and editing are akin to quality control. In manufacturing, quality control is making sure merchandise is free from defects. In writing, it means making sure your document is free from errors. Proofreading is the skill that refers to locating errors. Editing is the skill that refers to amending text by modifying words, sentences, paragraphs, and the like.

What would you do if you went to a fine restaurant and the menu included items such as

white whine

soap of the day

baked zits

turkey coffee

You'd probably run out as fast out as you could. You don't want your readers to visually run because it will impact your professionalism and credibility.

Using AI as Your Assistant for Proofreading and Editing

AI SPOTLIGHT

Fortunately, there are many AI tools to detect and fix mistakes such as grammatical, punctuation, syntax, spelling errors, and more. Here's an example of a poorly written (and that's an understatement) letter:

> I wud lyk to inform you abot a greate oppurtunity in our busines. We hav a new prodcut that can drasticaly improove yur sales and bring in lot of revenu. Our custumers hav ben raving abot it and it has ben proven to be very effactive in the market. We wud luv to partnr with you and help you grow yur busines. Plese let us no if you are intrested and we can discus furthr.
>
> Thank you for yur tim and we look forwrd to hearing from you soon.
>
> Best Regards,

I fed this into the You.com chatbot. In Figure 9-1, you see it not only fixed the errors, but it created a complete, coherent message. It even corrected the word "Regards" in the closing to have a lower case letter *r*.

Dear YouBot,

Thank you for reaching out and offering this exciting opportunity to improve our business. We appreciate your interest and enthusiasm in partnering with us to help us grow.

Before we proceed further, it would be helpful to know more details about the new product that you mentioned. Could you please provide us with information about the specific features and benefits of the product? Additionally, it would be great if you could share any market research or data that supports its effectiveness.

Once we have a better understanding of the product and its potential impact on our sales and revenue, we can discuss the possibility of a partnership in more detail. Please feel free to provide any additional information or materials that you think would be helpful for us to evaluate this opportunity.

Thank you again for considering us as a potential partner. We look forward to hearing from you soon.

Best regards,
[Your Name]

FIGURE 9-1: Cleaning up the text.

Here are some popular AI tools to assist with proofreading and editing:

>> **Grammarly** (`https://app.grammarly.com`): Delivers a complete score for the overall quality of the written work and includes recommendations for enhancing sentence structure, vocabulary, and tone. This integrates with various platforms and web browsers.

- >> **WhiteSmoke** (`https://www.whitesmoke.com/`): Enhances sentence structure, style, and readability score along with grammar suggestions. This includes a plagiarism checker.

- >> **Ginger Software** (`https://www.gingersoftware.com/`): Offers advice on enhancing sentence structure, style, and readability in addition to ideas for fixing grammar, spelling, punctuation, and syntax mistakes.

- >> **ProWritingAid** (`https://prowritingaid.com/`): Offers a variety of features such as enhancing sentence structure and readability score. This is ideal for long-form content.

- >> **Hemingway Editor** (`https://hemingwayapp.com/`): Flags adverbs, passive voice, and complicated phrases, and offers tips on how to make the writing simpler. This one is easy to use, showing a readability grade.

REMEMBER

While AI has made significant advancements, it's still prone to making mistakes. Writer intelligence (WI), on the other hand, brings invaluable expertise and contextual understanding. Humans can pick up on subtle errors, inconsistencies, and tone-related issues that AI might miss (check out the sidebar later in this chapter about Simone). Therefore, it's critical to re-read and do your own editing for anything AI generates.

Not Getting Lost in Translation

AI SPOTLIGHT

Several AI translation tools such as Google Translate (`https://translate.google.com/`), Deep Translator (`https://www.deepl.com/en/translator`), Reverso (`https://www.reverso.net/text-translation`), and others can interpret and automatically translate text and audio from one language to another. AI translators can analyze and translate large amounts of data including dictionaries and glossaries in multiple languages. This leads to improved efficiency, consistency, cost savings, and (relative) accuracy. Even a basic chatbot like You.com can translate well. Figure 9-2 shows a delicious recipe in English, and Figure 9-3 shows how You.com translated it into Spanish.

write in spanish HERB ROASTED SALMON

1 large Salmon Fillet (about 2 lbs), skinned and boned
2 TBSP freshly squeezed lemon juice (or bottled)
5 Scallions (green onions), whites and greens, minced
½ cup minced fresh parsley (2 tbsp dried)
½ cup minced dill (1tsp dried)
¼ cup dry wine (low sodium vegetable broth)

Place salmon in an oven proof non-reactive dish sprayed with a cooking oil. Drizzle lemon juice over salmon and add a dash of kosher salt and black pepper. Let sit for 15 minutes. Preheat oven to 425 degrees F. In a bowl stir together scallions, dill, parsley. Scatter the herb mixture over the salmon making sure to cover the whole salmon with mixture. Pour wine (low sodium vegetable broth) over salmon. Roast for 10-12 minutes until center is cooked. Let sit for 10 minutes. Serves 6

FIGURE 9-2: The English version of this delish dish.

SALMÓN ASADO CON HIERBAS

1 filete grande de salmón (aproximadamente 2 lbs), sin piel y deshuesado
2 cucharadas de jugo de limón recién exprimido (o envasado)
5 cebolletas (cebollas verdes), blancas y verdes, picadas finamente
½ taza de perejil fresco picado (2 cucharadas de perejil seco)
½ taza de eneldo picado (1 cucharadita de eneldo seco)
¼ de taza de vino seco (caldo vegetal bajo en sodio)

Coloca el salmón en un recipiente apto para horno previamente rociado con aceite de cocina. Rocía el jugo de limón sobre el salmón y añade una pizca de sal kosher y pimienta negra. Deja reposar durante 15 minutos. Precalienta el horno a 425 grados Fahrenheit. En un tazón, mezcla las cebolletas, el eneldo y el perejil. Esparce la mezcla de hierbas sobre el salmón asegurándote de cubrir todo el salmón con la mezcla. Vierte el vino (o caldo vegetal bajo en sodio) sobre el salmón. Asa durante 10-12 minutos hasta que el centro esté cocido. Deja reposar durante 10 minutos. Sirve para 6 personas.

FIGURE 9-3: The Spanish version of this delish dish.

WARNING

Beware, however! AI translators do make mistakes and you still need WI to ensure that the translated text is accurate and tailored to the audience. Here's why humans are necessary:

- **Context:** Understanding the context of a translation, which is essential for providing accurate translations. Interpreting idiomatic expressions and nuances may be lost in machine translation.
- **Cultural and regional understanding:** Understanding cultural and regional differences is critical for providing translations that are appropriate for the target audience. Without human intervention this opens the potential for bias that could have a significant impact on culturally or politically sensitive issues.
- **Complex content:** Handling complex content, such as legal, medical, or scientific documents, which require specialized knowledge and expertise.

TIP

Because business is conducted internationally, it's wise to show both U.S. and metric equivalents. Consider writing it this way: 1 foot (0.3048 meters). This helps promote understanding, compatibility, and flexibility whether it's for international communication, scientific standards, or personal preference. Check out sites such as `https://www.metric-conversions.org/area-conversion.htm`.

Editing for Content

Editing is an important step in the writing process. It refers to amending text by modifying words, sentences, paragraphs, or the general structure of the document — focusing on clarity, coherence, and overall quality. Here are things to look for when editing:

>> **Consider the reader:** Keep your target audience in mind while editing. Ensure that your document is clear, concise, and easy to understand for them. Are there any words that need to be explained? Is there an assumption you made?

>> **Identify patterns of error:** Look for recurring errors or issues in your writing. Knowing your common mistakes can help you be more attentive to them and make necessary revisions. Do you use the passive voice when the active would work better? Are there redundancies? Are sentences too long?

>> **Edit in stages:** Editing a large document can be overwhelming. Break it down into manageable sections and edit them one at a time so you can focus on each section more effectively.

>> **Look for omissions:** Is there something you left out? An important detail? A date? The attachment to an email?

>> **Read the document aloud:** Reading your document aloud can help you identify awkward phrasing, unclear sentences, and other issues that may not be apparent when reading silently. Are any words difficult to pronounce?

>> **Print the document and read the hard copy:** Despite the hours we spend in front of the computer, we're still more used to reading the printed word. Therefore, we tend to see errors on paper we missed on the screen. Also, on hard copy we see how the document flows from paragraph to paragraph and from page to page.

>> **Avoid jargon and unnecessary commentary:** Use clear and straightforward language in your document. Avoid using unnecessary jargon or adding commentary that does not contribute to the main message.

>> **Have someone else read it:** When a document is important, have someone else read it.

Remember, editing is an iterative process, and it may take multiple rounds of revisions to achieve the desired result. Take your time and be thorough in your editing process to ensure a polished and professional document.

TIP

If you just completed a document, take a break before editing. Resting your mind between writing and editing allows you to approach the document with a fresh perspective. This helps you spot errors and make improvements more effectively. Also read the document at different times of the day. For example, perhaps you're more alert in the mornings.

AI SPOTLIGHT

Even if you're sitting on the sidelines and learning more about AI, using editing tools such as Grammarly, ChatGPT, and Jasper are simple ways to dip your toe in the water. Find out more in Chapter 3.

Proofreading for Accuracy and Consistency

Although AI can detect many errors, it won't know if you spelled someone's name incorrectly, included the wrong date, or transposed numbers. That's where WI will always remain critical. The following are things to look for when proofreading:

>> **Confirm company designations.** Does the company use Co., Company, Inc., Incorporated?

>> **Double-check all numbers.** It's easy to transpose numbers and not realize it. This can cause serious problems.

>> **Keep an eye out for misused or misspelled *homophones* (words that sound the same but are spelled differently).** Know the difference between *principal* and *principle*, *capital* and *capitol*, *stationery* and *stationary*, and others.

>> **Be on the alert for small words that you repeat or misspell.** It's easy to write *it* instead of *is* and not realize it. It's doubtful that your computer would detect an error such as that.

>> **Check dates against the calendar to make sure the day and date coincide.** If you write Monday, May 3, be sure May 3 is a Monday.

>> **Check the accuracy of all names, including middle initials, and titles.** Do you spell the recipient's name *Carol* or *Carole*? And don't assume you know the sex of a person by the name. Carroll O'Connor was a man and Stevie Nicks is a woman.

SHERYL SAYS

And speaking of incorrect names . . . A plaque intended to honor actor James Earl Jones at a Florida celebration commemorating the life of Martin Luther King, instead paid tribute to James Earl Ray, the man who killed the civil-rights leader. The company who made the plaque blamed it on a typographical error. Shame on everyone involved!

Turning Your Brain Off when Turning Your Computer On

When people don't carefully review the essence of what they write, the results can be anything from a minor oops to major embarrassment. Sometimes they're larger than life, such as this boondoggle:

There was a Bible published in England in 1716. It was a gift to the colonies from the wife of King George II. Instead of the Bible reading, "Parables from the Vineyard," it read "Parables of the Vinegar" — thus the Bible later became known as *The Vinegar Bible.* (That was prior to the American Revolution, so perhaps there was a subtle message in there. Wink. Wink.)

There's nothing like the human eye to check, double-check, and triple-check spelling, grammar, punctuation, and subtleties. AI is a wonderful tool, but it's merely that — a tool. It's doubtful that any AI tool would pick up subtleties such as the following:

Execution: impossible to be pardoned.

Execution impossible: to be pardoned.

After I dressed and ate, my parents . . .

After I dressed and ate my parents . . .

SIMONE'S FAUX PAS

In Chapter 5, you were introduced to the importance of including stories into your writing. This gives you the ability to reinforce your messages so readers can forge a connection with the situation. Let me transport you to the story of Sally, a participant in one of my writing workshops. Simone is the Public Relations Director at the main headquarters of a renowned multinational conglomerate spanning eight diverse countries.

It was a fateful day when a catastrophic incident happened that threatened to unleash colossal financial repercussions upon the company. Simone was tasked with crafting careful talking points to the key management teams across the company's international offices. The objective was to ensure that each of them would deliver consistent messages, thereby safeguarding the company's reputation and financial stability. Here's a paraphrased version of the story as Simone told it.

In my quest to craft a captivating and persuasive email, I found myself at a loss, unsure of where to begin. So I turned to my trusted assistant — a chatbot that had never failed to amaze me. I typed in the crucial points, and the results were nothing short of extraordinary. I took the extra precaution of having AI translate the text into various languages so no cultural nuances would be lost in the translation.

With a sense of relief and accomplishment, I pasted the message into each email. With a resolute click of the send button, I believed my mission was accomplished. However, within a few seconds, the emails were returned, accompanied by an all-too-familiar reminder that I'd forgotten to include a subject line. I quickly typed in

"Important pubic relations message you must read"

and hit the send button once again. Within minutes, my inbox was inundated with a flurry of responses, all with the same unsettling news: I had inadvertently omitted the crucial letter "l" from the word "public." Reactions were as varied as the colors of a vibrant tapestry. Some people thought the blunder was humorous; others were not so generous. At the very least, I was mortified.

Consumed by the urgency to get the message out, I had neglected the simple act of proofreading *everything* and overlooked the glaring omission in the subject line. In all humility, I share this faux pas to emphasize the importance of taking the time to proofread *everything*, regardless of how inconspicuous it may seem.

(For full disclosure, I asked You.com to embellish this narrative, and I edited it down dramatically.)

Making a List and Checking It Twice

TIP

Before you send out any document — whether it was generated by humans, AI, or a combination — make sure you double-and triple-check the accuracy of everything. Use the checklist in Figure 9-4 before you send anything.

Proofreading & Editing Checklist

Before you send out any document, use the following proofreading and editing checklist:

☐ My subject line and headlines are informative to spark my reader's interest.

☐ All names are correctly spelled and all numbers are correct.

☐ My message is sequenced for the needs of my reader.

☐ My document has strong visual impact

    ☐ Ample white space throughout
    ☐ 1 to 1 ½ inch margins on the top, bottom, and sides
    ☐ Sentences limited to 20-25 words
    ☐ Paragraphs limited to 8 lines
    ☐ Bulleted and numbered lists, when appropriate
    ☐ Tables and charts, when appropriate

☐ The tone is appropriate
    ☐ Reader-focused
    ☐ Short and to the point (KISS)
    ☐ Positive words
    ☐ Active voice
    ☐ "You" approach

☐ Spelling, grammar, and punctuation are correct.

☐ I didn't lay my cup down and leave coffee stains on the paper copy.

FIGURE 9-4: Proofreading and editing checklist.

Determining the Readability of Your Documents

The concept of readability started when Edward Thorndike wrote a book titled *The Teacher's Word Book* (New York Teacher's College, Columbia University, 1921). It considered how often difficult words were found in literature and was the first publication to apply a formula to written language. Others followed and built on it — adding average syllables per word, difficulty of words, variety of language, frequency of words, and length of sentences, for example. All this calculates a grade level, or readability score.

In 2010, the *Plain Writing Act* was introduced in the United States, aiming to ensure that federal agencies produce clear and understandable communication for the general public. (Find out more at https://www.dol.gov/general/plainwriting). The intention was to make documents accessible and information easy to locate when read or heard. However, despite the diligent efforts of agencies, a significant number of technical documents, both governmental and otherwise, continue to be riddled with incomplete and incomprehensible jargon. Here are some intriguing statistics:

» Comics are written at fourth- or fifth-grade levels.

» *Readers Digest* is written at ninth-grade level.

» *The New York Times* and *The Wall Street Journal* are written at eleventh-grade levels.

» Scientific texts have been reducing readability over time to appeal to a greater audience, and levels vary widely from one publication to another.

Understanding the importance of readability

Have you ever purchased a product you needed to assemble? You pull out a user manual printed in lots of languages. There are no visuals, just small print that's difficult to read, even with 20–20 eyesight. So, you get out your magnifying glass and follow step by step. When you finish the assembly, you notice an extra part. You re-read the manual, and there's no mention of that part. What went wrong?

No one ever checked the readability, clarity, or accuracy of the manual. It was written, printed, and inserted into the package, probably in haste. Too much technical information is written in this slipshod manner by people who have no understanding of the end user.

Using AI readability tools

Consider this scenario: You're traveling in a foreign country and need directions. So you stop and ask someone. If they were to use complex language or technical terms beyond your comprehension, it would impede your ability to grasp the directions. Similarly, when creating written content, it's essential to take into account the cognitive abilities of the intended reader. This ensures that the information is conveyed effectively and comprehensibly to them.

AI SPOTLIGHT

These are some popular readability tools:

» AISEO (https://aiseo.ai/)

» Flesh-Kincaid (http://tinyurl.com/5n8wnc75)

» LongShot AI (https://www.longshot.ai/)

» Originality.AI (https://originality.ai)

» Wordtune (https://www.wordtune.com/)

These tools measure reading ease and grade level to know if you're hitting the right chords with your target audience. Use this analysis as a guide, not as the absolute. AI analytics have come under some scrutiny because this analysis can't capture the nuances of language such as figurative language, sarcasm, and irony that can impact readability. This is one more reason WI reigns supreme.

3

Writing Click-Worthy E-Content

Navigate the boundaries of emails with dynamic subject lines that grab attention and entice the recipient to open your message. Learn about email etiquette and the importance of effective replies, including promptness, clarity, and professionalism.

Reap the benefits of e-marketing. Learn the lingo, strategies for a successful campaign, and how to reach a wider audience. This includes segmenting your target audience, personalizing content, and leveraging automation tools.

Create a user-friendly, easy-to-navigate website home-page and landing pages that are engaging and interactive so people keep coming back for more.

Chapter **10**

Turning Emails from Blah to Brilliant

I n the bustling world of technology, the humble email holds its own as a gateway to an interconnected universe. Although the exact percentage varies (depending on the source) it's estimated that three-quarters of all communication is via email. And the percentage has probably increased since the COVID-19 pandemic. Some people say that email is passé and can be replaced by Google Chat, Teams, Slack, Hangouts Meet, or BlueJean Meetings; however, email isn't going away anytime soon.

Mastering the art of emails extends beyond crafting eloquent prose. Who has that luxury of time? Instead, it hinges upon the ability to strike the delicate balance between appropriateness and impact. This chapter unlocks the challenges of composing compelling emails that not only captivate the reader, but inspire a call to action (CTA).

Using AI as Your Assistant for Writing Emails

AI has significantly transformed the landscape of communication, including how we send and receive emails. Here are some ways in which AI is reshaping email:

>> **Cybersecurity:** AI is being used to improve email security. It can help identify and prevent email-based cyberattacks by detecting malicious content and attachments.

>> **Personalization:** Writing personalized emails that are tailored to the recipient's interests and preferences. This can increase the likelihood of open rates, click rates, and conversions.

>> **Systematized responses:** Responding to incoming emails automatically, which can help businesses save time and resources.

>> **Subject line optimization:** Analyzing the words, phrases, and subject lines that receive the most engagement, and using that information to generate more effective subject lines that say "read me." (This is especially helpful in e-marketing as you'll learn in Chapter 11.)

>> **Tone analysis:** Analyzing a person's writing style and tone, and suggesting changes to make the email more effective and engaging.

>> **Scheduling:** Assessing when people are most likely to open and engage with emails, and automatically scheduling emails to be sent at those optimal times.

>> **Efficiency:** Streamlining email communication by prioritizing important messages and filtering out *spam* (unsolicited and unwanted messages sent in bulk to a large number of recipients). This can save time and increase productivity.

>> **Email copywriting:** Generating high-converting email campaigns in just a few clicks to analyze customer data and write personalized emails that resonate with the target audience.

Figure 10-1 is an example of AI to the rescue: Dan has an employee who's constantly missing team meetings. Dan spoke with the employee, but he needs to capture the conversation in writing in case this needs to escalate to the next level. Dan hopes this employee will change their behavior. He's laid out some strategies. The figure shows the input given to You.com and how the chatbot responded. Pay special attention to the strong subject line the chatbot created.

Subject: Follow-up to Verbal Reprimand - Importance of Attendance and Performance Improvement

Dear [Employee's Name],

I hope this email finds you well. I am writing to follow up on our recent conversation regarding your attendance record and the concerns raised about your consistent absence from team meetings.

As you may recall, during our meeting on [date], we discussed the impact that your missed meetings have had on the team's productivity and overall performance. It was emphasized that attendance at these meetings is crucial for effective collaboration, decision-making, and the successful completion of our collective goals.

I want to reiterate that attendance is an essential aspect of your role as a valuable member of our team. Consistently missing meetings not only disrupts the workflow but also hinders your ability to contribute to important discussions and stay updated on project developments. It is essential that we address this issue promptly to ensure that we maintain a high level of efficiency and cohesion within our team.

I understand that there may be valid reasons for missing a meeting occasionally, such as illness or unforeseen circumstances. However, it is imperative that you communicate any absences well in advance and provide a valid justification when necessary. This will enable us to make alternative arrangements and ensure that your absence does not impede the progress of our team.

Moving forward, I would like to propose the following steps to address this issue and help you improve your attendance:

1. Prioritize Attendance: Make a conscious effort to prioritize attending all scheduled meetings. Plan your workload and personal commitments accordingly to ensure your availability.
2. Proactive Communication: If you anticipate a potential conflict or an unavoidable absence, inform your supervisor or the relevant team members as soon as possible, providing a valid reason for your absence.
3. Performance Improvement: Take this opportunity to reflect on the impact of your absences and identify any underlying issues that may be contributing to this behavior. If there are any challenges that you are facing, please let me know so that we can work together to find a solution.

Please be aware that failure to adhere to these expectations and missing another meeting without a valid reason may result in more serious consequences, such as suspension or termination. However, I genuinely believe that with your commitment to improvement, we can resolve this issue and move forward positively.

I am confident in your abilities and the value you bring to our team, and I want to see you succeed. If you have any questions or require any support, please do not hesitate to reach out. Let's work together to ensure that we maintain a consistent level of attendance and foster a collaborative environment.

Thank you for your attention to this matter, and I look forward to seeing the positive changes in your attendance record.

Best regards,

FIGURE 10-1:
AI to the rescue.

Here are just a few of the many AI email assistants that can boost your email productivity:

>> Capterra (https://www.capterra.com/)

>> ChatGPT (https://chat.openai.com/auth/login)

- » EmailTree (`https://emailtree.ai/`)
- » Google Workspace (`https://workspace.google.com/`)
- » Grammarly (`https://app.grammarly.com/`)
- » HubSpot (`https://www.hubspot.com/`)
- » Mailbutler (`https://www.mailbutler.io/`)
- » QuickMail (`https://quickmail.com/`)
- » Sanebox (`https://www.sanebox.com/`)
- » YAMM (`https://yamm.com/`)

REMEMBER

When writing an important email it's important to fill out the Kick-Start Brief in Chapter 4 to understand your reader, purpose, key issue, and the questions your reader will need answered. This Brief provides a foundation for you to customize your content to precisely meet the needs of your reader and drive the CTA.

Generating Precise Prompts

AI SPOTLIGHT

Here are some suggestions for creating effective AI prompts, with a particular emphasis on emails:

- » Include the recipient's information and your relationship (client, a business partner, colleague, for example) as this will influence the tone and formality.
- » State the purpose of the message.
- » Outline of the main points or information you want to include.
- » Incorporate the call to action.
- » Request a descriptive subject line.

Navigating Email Boundaries

Before delving into ways to turn emails from blah to brilliant, it's important to know if email is the best way to deliver the message. Remember that email is one-way messaging, unlike a two-way conversation by phone, video conference, or in person where people can get "messages" from intonation and body language and respond immediately. Also, emails are sometimes thought of as cold and impersonal.

**SHERYL
SAYS**

I was having trouble coming up with a title to open this section, so I turned to my AI assistant You.com. I asked it for six title options for when email is and isn't appropriate. Figure 10-2 shows the options listed. I opted for an abbreviated version of number 4.

---

6 titles for knowing when email is and isn't appropriate

1. "Understanding Email Etiquette: Knowing When to Email and When Not to"

2. "Email Communication: Appropriate and Inappropriate Times to Send Emails"

3. "Mastering Email Timing: When to Hit Send and When to Hold Off"

4. "Navigating Email Boundaries: Recognizing the Right Moments for Email Communication"

5. "Email Dos and Don'ts: Knowing the Right Situations to Send Emails"

6. "Email Etiquette: Determining the Appropriate Times to Use Email Communication"

FIGURE 10-2:
Title options
generated by AI.

Knowing when email is appropriate

It's important to consider the goals, urgency, sensitivity, and complexity of the communication when deciding whether to send an email. Email is appropriate to

>> Share detailed information or data

>> Ensure there's a record of your message

>> Document an important conversation

>> Direct the recipient to resources for additional information

>> Provide updates

>> Communicate a decision

>> Confirm appointments

>> Send a company-wide announcement all need to see

>> Inform of meetings or meeting changes

Knowing when email isn't appropriate

Because email is so quick and easy, people just pop out messages at the speed of thoughtlessness. Consider the specific circumstances and choose the most appropriate channel for effective communication, which may be two-way communication. These are situations where two-way communication would be more appropriate:

>> Bad or negative news

>> Change an agreed-upon plan

>> Deliver time-sensitive information

>> Sensitive or confidential information

>> Complex or nuanced discussions

>> Emotional or sensitive topics

>> Urgent or time-sensitive matters

>> Building relationships and trust

>> Conflict resolution

>> Collaborative or brainstorming sessions

>> Cultural or language barriers

>> Need an immediate response

WARNING

Never vent in an email. An email sent in anger is there forever. Once you send it, you can't hit the delete key and watch the letters march backwards into oblivion. It's too late. If you must vent, do so in your word processor and write whatever you want! In that way, you won't accidentally hit the send button. You can revisit your words the following day and see if what you wrote is still appropriate. Chances are, you won't think so.

Timing is everything

Know the best time to deliver your message. When is it too early? When is it too late? For example, if it's noon and you need to let people know about a one o'clock meeting, an email won't do. Phone the people and/or a leave a note on their computer screens if they work in your office. Although there's no one-size-fits-all approach, you can optimize the timing of your emails by understanding your audience, analyzing their behavior and engagement patterns, testing different send times, and considering industry and content relevance. This will lead to higher deliverability, open rates, and engagement.

REMEMBER

Studies show that Thursdays are the best day to send important emails, followed by Tuesday, and Wednesday. On Mondays, people are back from the weekend and playing catch-up. On Fridays, they're mentally thinking about their weekend.

DON'T ASSUME THE RECIPIENT ACTUALLY RECEIVED YOUR MESSAGE

SHERYL SAYS

Several months ago I received an email that sent shudders up my spine. It was from my dear friend Pam, requesting to meet up for lunch the following week. The reason this message left me reeling was because Pam had passed away six months earlier. I checked the date on the email, only to discover that it had been sent a week before her untimely death. It seemed that this message had been floating around in cyberspace for more than six months, and I couldn't help but think that Pam wondered why I didn't respond.

This incident taught me a valuable lesson: If you don't receive a timely response from someone, it's important to follow up with another email or phone call. There can be various reasons for not getting a response, including:

- They never got the message.

- It landed in their junk or spam folder.

- You unintentionally sent it to the wrong person.

- They just overlooked it amidst the massive amounts of messages they receive each day.

TIP

Avoid using *yesterday*, *today*, or *tomorrow*. These terms are relative when the recipient reads the message, rather than when you send it. This can potentially cause confusion or miscommunication if the message isn't read immediately or there's a delay in its delivery. To ensure clarity, use specific dates and time references.

SHERYL SAYS

Barb, a participant in one of my workshops, worked for a major university. It was her responsibility to contact incoming students to let them know about check-in procedures, parking policies, and more for the fall term. She sent all this information via email in May. In August, she was barraged with emails and phone calls from these incoming students asking about check-in procedures, parking policies, and so on. She had already sent that information and wondered why the throngs of inquiries. It's because the timing of her email was way off. Students who haven't yet graduated from high school, and have a whole summer ahead of them, aren't thinking about check-in procedures and parking policies for college the following fall. If she had sent the emails closer to the time students needed the information, they would have paid attention. Timing is everything!

Crafting Seductive Subject Lines

REMEMBER

The subject line is the most important piece of information in an email message. It stands alone to pull in the reader without the benefit of context. Your words are trapped inside a field with competing subject lines, unable to set itself apart with bold, italics, or underscore.

There are people who get hundreds of emails a day, and they can't possibly read them all. So, if your subject line doesn't seduce them, they may never open your message — however important it may be. If you look down the subject line column of your inbox, perhaps you see subject lines such as these that give you absolutely no information and no reason to click:

- » One more thing. . .
- » Friday
- » Follow up
- » Please do me a favor
- » Meeting

Including key information at a glance

Always include in your subject line a key piece of information so your reader can get the gist of your message at a glance. Notice the following sets of subject lines and how much more information can be garnered from the informative version.

Informative: *15% profit expected for Q2*

Uninformative: *Profit report*

Informative: *MIS: Urgent meeting May 6 @ 9:15 in Blue Rm*

Uninformative: *MIS Meeting*

Informative: *Brad Jones joining Mktg. Grp. April 12*

Uninformative: *New hire*

Informative: *Contact you requested is Jane Brown at Mellows Co.*

Uninformative: *Contact info*

Be sensitive to the fact that we live in a global world and people outside the United States refer to times and dates differently. Most countries use a 24-hour clock format. So, instead of saying 2:15 p.m., the time would be expressed as 14:15.

Similarly, most countries use different conventions for representing dates. In the United States, the common format is to write the month first, followed by the day, then the year. For example, May 6, 202X would be written as 5/6/202X. However, in other countries, the day is written before the month. So, in those countries, June 5, 202X would be written as 5/6/202X.

Delivering the message in the subject line

If you're emailing someone you know well, consider delivering the message as the subject line and putting your initials at the end, indicating that's all there is. When you deliver the message in the subject line, the recipient gets your message at a glance. If they don't have a chance to read your entire message, at least they'll get the gist. Then use the text box to fill the message out with more information. Here's how that can work:

To someone you know: *I'll finish the report tomorrow morning — Jen*

To others: *I'll finish the report tomorrow morning* [then continue the message in the text box]

Following is a series of email subject lines I exchanged with a colleague. We rescheduled a meeting, and neither of us needed to write text beyond the subject line. Usually I don't recommend scheduling appointments via email because it's more efficient to schedule appointments when you're both looking at your calendars, and it's not appropriate in all professional settings. However, I knew my audience. This woman lives and breathes email and doesn't return phone calls:

Mon doesn't work. How's Tues? — SLR

Tues is NG. How's Wed? — MN

Wed is fine. — SLR

See you Wed at 3:15 — MN

When you first start sending subject lines without a text box, most people understand right away and will respond in the same manner when appropriate. A few, however, let you know that they "didn't get your message." When you tell them you tried to save them time and delivered the message in the subject line, they too may start responding with this electronic shorthand.

SUBJECT LINE GONE AWRY

I'm a member of a Patient Advocate Committee (PAC) group for my healthcare association. We have online meetings on the first Wednesday, every other month. The organizer sends out an email a week before the meeting with a standard subject line that reads: *[Month] PAC meeting*. In July, we received our typical email reading: *July PAC meeting*. Most of us don't get into the weeds of the message because they're the same each time. We merely look at the login — which is all we really need. Many of us logged as expected on July 5 (the first Wednesday of the month). There was no meeting. What went wrong?

Because the 4th of July fell on Tuesday, the organizer thought many people may have taken the week off, and she postponed the meeting to the second Wednesday, July 12. She didn't stop to think of the readers and what we needed to know. She merely performed a mental spewing and expected each of us to read her entire message. Had she simply prepared a subject line that read: *July PAC meeting on July 12*, there would have been no confusion, and we all would have noted the changed date.

Here's another example: I was recently in contract negotiations with a client. When I sent my final offer the client put one word in the subject line: *Agreed!* I answered with one-word subject line: *Deal!* Nothing more was needed for either of these exchanges.

Changing the subject line when replying

Striving to be more efficient, people have started changing subject lines when replying a reply to a message. There are pros and cons to this. Do change the subject line in the following circumstances:

» The original subject line doesn't reflect your response. For example, someone may have sent you a message: *Please send [XX] report.* Rather than shooting back the same subject line, change it to read: *Attaching the [XX] report you requested.*

» When the conversation takes a different direction and the initial subject line no longer reflects the current content. I recently received a message with the subject line *Confirming our meeting for Monday*, but I didn't have any meeting scheduled with that person. After reading the message, I realized that it was actually a message I had sent her months ago. She must have seen the message, clicked on reply, and asked me a completely unrelated question.

» If you're continuing a long email thread, modify the subject line. For example: *ABC Contract: New signing date March 1*. This allows the recipient to easily identify the topic and "get" your message.

DON'T MUDDLE THE CONTENT

Stick to one topic per email. If you're sending a follow-up email, stay on topic. Don't introduce another topic. Here are a few reasons why:

- The subject line should reflect the content of the message. If the subject line is misleading or unrelated to the actual content, it can create confusion and make it harder for the recipient to locate specific information in their inbox later on.

- Introducing unrelated content in an email can make it difficult for the recipient to understand the main purpose of the message. This can lead to confusion.

- Including unrelated content in an email can waste the recipient's time. They may need to spend extra time searching for relevant information or trying to understand the purpose of the email.

Staying on topic and avoiding unrelated content demonstrates professionalism in your communication and shows that you respect the recipient's time and value clear and concise communication.

TIP

Remember that not everyone will read your entire message, especially if it reads beyond the opening screen. Consider using *Action Requested* or *Action Needed* in the subject line. In that way, the recipient knows immediately there's something they're required to do. Here's an example:

Action Required: Delta contract needed before noon on June 10

Using Cc and Bcc Appropriately

When it comes to sending emails, it's important to understand how to use Cc and Bcc fields. *Cc* stands for carbon copy, which is a throwback from the days people made carbon copies on typewriters; *Bcc* stands for blind carbon copy, which includes recipients without the knowledge of other recipients. These fields allow you to include additional recipients in your email, but there are some differences in their usage.

Cc:

There's a difference between putting someone's name in the To field and the Cc Field. The person in the To field is the main recipient and should be directly involved in the conversation. When you include someone in the Cc field, you're keeping them in the loop but don't need or expect a reply.

An example might be if you're part of a project team, and you want to keep your manager informed about the progress. In this case, you can include your manager in the Cc field when sending project-related emails to other team members. They're all aware the manager is included. This allows your manager to stay informed about the project's status and any updates without being directly involved in the conversation or feeling they need to reply.

Bcc:

Use Bcc responsibly and consider the privacy and expectations of your recipients. Here are some appropriate uses of Bcc:

>> **Protecting privacy:** Use Bcc when you want to keep recipients' email addresses private. For example, when informing suppliers or clients about a change or update, this feature ensures that their email addresses are not visible to other recipients.

>> **Mass emails:** This is very appropriate (and recommended) for sending mass emails that don't require a response. It helps protect the privacy of recipients' addresses by hiding their addresses from each other.

>> **Impersonal emails:** This is suitable for business announcements or updates. For instance, if you're sending a company-wide email with updated information or a new policy, Bcc will prevent unnecessary reply-all responses.

Here are some reasons to avoid using Bcc:

>> **It can be seen as deceitful or misleading, as it hides the fact that other recipients are included in the email.** It may give the impression that the email is intended for the primary recipient only, when in reality, others are also receiving it.

>> **Although it hides the email addresses of recipients from each other, it doesn't guarantee complete privacy.** The primary recipient can still see that others have been included. If privacy is a concern, it may be better to use a more secure method, such as an encrypted email service or a secure file-sharing platform.

>> **Some recipients may feel left out of the conversation or question why they weren't included as direct recipients.** This can potentially strain relationships or create misunderstandings.

>> **Some email filters and spam detection systems may flag or block emails that contain a large number of Bcc recipients.** Using Bcc excessively or inappropriately can inadvertently trigger spam filters and affect the deliverability of your emails.

Creating Visual Appeal

How often have you received a message of one paragraph that goes on from one screen to the next? Probably too often. It's hard to read. You may just skim it or skip it. So make sure your message has strong visual impact. Remember, this is a business document and you should treat it with the same respect as any other business document you generate.

AI SPOTLIGHT

AI tools are handy for structuring emails for better visual appeal by suggesting paragraph breaks, summarizing long content, and recommending headlines so key information jumps out at a glance.

Including informative headlines

Strong headlines draw attention to key information at a glance — not only in the subject line but in the body of the message as well. Take a look at the "Before" email in Figure 10-3. If you were asked to scan it quickly, could you answer the following questions at a glance?

>> When is the meeting?

>> How many items are on the agenda?

>> Who is the new EEO coordinator?

You probably couldn't. The subject line — which is the main headline — doesn't give key information at a glance. It says: Reaffirming EEO policy. What about it? This is what you'd typically see as an email message, although not all senders bother to use paragraphs.

Date: October 6, XXXX

To: All Employees

From: Sy Burnett, Human Relations Director

Re: Reaffirming EEO policy

_____

As you know, it is illegal to discriminate against any employee or applicant for employment because of race, color, religion, sex, national origin, handicap, or veteran status. I've scheduled a meeting because we need to discuss these critical issues. It'll be in the new cafeteria on October 13 from 10:30 to 11:30, and everyone must attend. There are several questionable issues that have come to my attention, and we need to reaffirm our company's policy.

Here are some of the issues we need to discuss: We must ensure opportunities for all employees and applicants for employment in accordance with all applicable Equal Employment Opportunity/Affirmative Action laws, directives and regulations of federal, state, and local governing bodies or agencies. Promotion decisions must be in accord with the principles of equal employment opportunity. And we must ensure that all personnel actions such as compensation, benefits, transfers, layoffs, return from layoff, company-sponsored training, education, tuition assistance, and social and recreational programs will be administered fairly.

Because we've added so many members to our staff in recent months, I've hired Di Hartt as a new assistant. She will be responsible for equal employment opportunity issues. I'll be introducing Di to you at the meeting. Employees with suggestions, problems, or complaints with regard to equal employment opportunities should report their claims to their managers. If this is not comfortable for any reason, see Di. She will monitor the program and be responsible for making quarterly reports to us on the effectiveness of the program.

FIGURE 10-3: "Before" email where nothing stands out.

Now take a look at the "After" document in Figure 10-4. Notice how the subject line gives key information at a glance. It lets you know there's a meeting and when. All the important information in the body had headlines (and bullets) that give key information at a glance.

TIP

Think of newspapers and magazines using strong headlines as guideposts for visual impact. You can do the same in your emails. Here are just a few to consider:

Action requested

Action required

Next step

Meeting information:

Date:

Time:

Place:

Deadline: [date]

Effective date: [date]

Including graphics

You can safely include graphics in your emails while minimizing potential risks and ensuring a positive user experience by using trusted sources only, optimizing image sizes, considering image formats (such as png or gif), testing across email clients, and using alternative text that describes the image for people who use screen readers.

Date: April 6, XXXX

To: All Employees

From: Sy Burnett, Human Relations Director

Re: Mandatory Meeting on October 13 to reaffirm EEO policy

There are several issues regarding potential Equal Employment Opportunity (EEO)/Affirmative Action violations that have come to my attention. I've scheduled a meeting for the entire staff.

Date: October 13
Time: 10:30–11.30 AM
Place: Cafeteria

Agenda Issues

1. We must ensure opportunities for all employees and applicants in accordance with all applicable laws, directives and regulations of federal, state, and local governing bodies or agencies.

2. Promotion decisions must be in accord with the principles of equal employment opportunity.

3. We must ensure that all personnel actions such as compensation, benefits, transfers, layoffs, return from layoff, company-sponsored training, education, tuition assistance, and social and recreational programs will be administered fairly.

New EEO Coordinator: Di Hartt

I'll be introducing Di at the meeting. Employees with suggestions, problems, or complaints with regard to equal employment opportunities should report their claims to their managers first. If this is not comfortable for any reason, see Di. She will monitor the program and be responsible for making quarterly reports to us on the effectiveness of the program.

FIGURE 10-4: "After" email with a subject line and headlines that tell the story.

AI SPOTLIGHT

AI generators such as TargetBay (`https://targetbay.com/`), Zapier (`https://zapier.com/`), and Adobe Photoshop (`https://www.adobe.com/products/photoshop.html`) can edit images and optimize them before sending them out.

Using other visual cues

Here are some more visual cues to make your emails more readable:

- » Use bulleted and numbered lists, when appropriate.
- » Limit paragraphs to eight lines of text.
- » Double space between paragraphs.
- » Upper and lower case. (ALL CAPS ARE LIKE SHOUTING).
- » Correct your grammar and punctuation.

Starting and Ending your Message Professionally

It's important to keep in mind that there's a real person on the other end who'll be reading your message. Similar to how you wouldn't answer the phone without a greeting or abruptly hang up to end a conversation, start and end your messages with the same considerations.

Including a salutation and closing

Start each message with a salutation and end with a closing. Unlike the salutations and closings in letters, email salutations and closings can be less formal. Following are a few examples:

Salutations	Closings
Hi Ken,	Regards,
Hello everyone,	See you later,
Hi,	Best,
Ken,	Thanks,

Creating a signature block

Prepare an electronic signature file that will populate the end of each message. (If you don't know how, check your help screen.) This gives contact information much like letterhead on stationery. At the very least, it should include your name, title, phone number, and a tag line if you have one. Your signature block may look something like this:

Alan Wright

Wright Brothers Financial Advisors

508-000-0000 (office)

508-000-0000 (cell)

Some people include gender pronouns as a sign of inclusivity. If you use them, put the pronouns under your contact information, but before the tag line. Here are the pronouns commonly used:

>> He/Him/His (for a person identifying as a male)

>> She/Her/Hers (for a person identifying as a female)

>> They/Them/Their (for a person identifying as gender-neutral)

Replying to Messages

When you receive a message, the common courtesy is to respond within 24 hours. Even if you don't have an answer, reply with *On it* or *Thanks*. A prompt response shows that you're on top of things.

Replying to all is the most efficient option when you have important information for the majority of the people included in the To or Cc message. So ask yourself if the majority of the recipients need to see your reply. If not, reply only to the sender or to those who need a reply. Here are two examples of reply to all gone awry:

>> **Example 1:** A branch of the U.S. government had sent out a request for proposal (RFP) to three specific companies, one of which was a client of mine. To maintain confidentiality, I'll refer to them as Companies A, B, and C. Unfortunately for Companies B and C, they unintentionally replied to all when submitting their proposals.

Consequently, Company A had access to their proposals and gained insight into their pricing strategies. Being aware that the government typically selects the lowest bidder for contracts, my client from Company A was able to slightly undercut the other two. As a result, my client was awarded the contract.

>> **Example 2:** James, my colleague, shares an amusing incident from a foggy morning. When he entered his workplace's parking lot, he noticed that someone had left their car lights on. He decided to notify everyone by sending an email to the entire distribution list, which consisted of 30+ people. James used the subject line *Lic. #234 ADB car lights on* to draw attention to the issue.

Since James' colleagues knew he was in the office, about half of them took advantage of the situation to send him their own unrelated messages. One person asked him to meet for lunch, another wanted information about an upcoming seminar, and yet another sought some other information. Interestingly, none of these people bothered to change the subject line from *Lic. #234 ADB car lights on,* even though their messages had nothing to do with the car lights.

Eliminating Spam

While spam may seem like a mere annoyance and overwhelm inboxes, it can pose several dangers:

>> **Malware and phishing attempts:** Spam emails often contain malicious attachments or links that can infect your computer or device with malware. Additionally, some spam emails are designed to trick recipients into revealing sensitive information through phishing techniques, posing a risk to personal and financial security.

>> **Financial scams:** Spam emails frequently include fraudulent schemes such as lottery scams, investment scams, or requests for financial assistance. These scams aim to deceive recipients into providing money or personal information, leading to financial loss. Many people, especially seniors, fall victim.

>> **Identity theft:** Some spam emails attempt to gather personal information, such as usernames, passwords, or social security numbers, with the intention of committing identity theft. This stolen information can be used for various fraudulent activities, including opening accounts in your name or accessing your existing accounts.

AI
SPOTLIGHT

AI spam filters have become an essential component of email services, helping users manage their inboxes by reducing the influx of unwanted and potentially harmful emails. Through the use of AI-driven techniques, these filters aim to provide a safer and more efficient email experience for users. Most of the major email providers have built-in spam filters that analyze text at a deeper level and help win the war against spamming. Spammers are becoming more sophisticated, but so are email providers.

Applying the Art of Email Finesse

Email finesse (or etiquette) refers to the guidelines and best practices that govern how people interact with each other. Follow proper protocol in order to communicate clearly and respectfully, whether you're emailing a prospective customer, business partner, coworker, manager, or acquaintance. This will help you establish your professionalism, communicate better, and build strong relationships. Here are some of the do's and taboos.

>> Do's:

- Respond within 24 hours. (If not possible, arrange for an "out of office" reply.)
- Use a professional tone.
- Practice good grammar and punctuation.
- Include a salutation, closing, and signature block.
- Provide ample white space.
- Use Cc and Bcc appropriately.
- Think before forwarding.
- Resist emojis unless you know the person well.
- Praise through email but give constructive feedback verbally.
- Be mindful of abbreviations.
- If you say you're sending an attachment, be sure to send it.
- Proofread very carefully before pressing send.

CHAPTER 10 **Turning Emails from Blah to Brilliant** 149

» Taboos:

- Sending an irrelevant or unnecessary message.

- Sending sensitive or confidential information.

- Using inappropriate or insensitive language.

- Responding to all unless everyone on the list needs to see your response.

- Rambling.

- Overusing exclamation points!!!

- Sending emotional messages.

- Putting too many disparate thoughts into one message.

- Adding humor without considering your audience.

- Assuming the recipient actually received your email.

Chapter **11**

Unlocking the Power of E-Marketing

I n the vast landscape of business activities, fostering robust connections with customers reigns supreme. It's the backbone of any business. For this reason, it's super important to have a way to effectively communicate with your customers, clients, and potential prospects. That's where e-marketing comes in! It's this awesome tool that helps to stay on top of their minds and keep them engaged. Whether you're in the middle of your busy season, experiencing slower times, or just want to keep in touch regularly, e-marketing is the vehicle for doing that.

The world of e-marketing has undergone a remarkable transformation from its origins in email marketing. It now encompasses a vast array of digital marketing strategies that include text marketing, web marketing, and social media marketing (more about each later in this chapter). This expansive horizon of e-marketing offers businesses boundless opportunities to establish connections with customers, cultivate brand recognition, and enhance conversion rates. By embracing these digital strategies, businesses can confidently navigate the ever-evolving digital landscape and meaningfully engage with customers.

Using AI as Your Assistant for Email Campaigns

AI SPOTLIGHT

AI-powered e-marketing can optimize the customer experience, increase engagement rates, and save time for companies. With the help of AI tools such as these and others, e-marketing is becoming more effective, and conversations are higher than ever before. These tools offer different advantages and price points, so check them out before making a decision:

>> Brevo (https://landing.brevo.com/)

>> Constant Contact (https://www.constantcontact.com/)

>> Copy.ai (https://www.copy.ai/)

>> Darktrace (https://darktrace.com/)

>> GetResponse (https://www.getresponse.com)

>> HubSpot (https://www.hubspot.com/)

>> Knowmail (https://www.knowmail.me/)

>> Mailchimp (https://mailchimp.com/)

>> Mailmodo (https://www.mailmodo.com/)

>> Phrasee (https://phrasee.co/)

REMEMBER

Here's how AI can help:

>> **Personalization:** Analyzing customer data and behavior to personalize content. This includes subject lines, recommendations, and offers. By delivering relevant and tailored content to each recipient, AI-powered email campaigns can increase engagement and click-through rates. Also, they can segment by a customer's location, age, purchase history, and interests. This enables marketers to send more targeted emails and increase open rates and conversions.

>> **Predictive analytics:** Assessing past customer interactions and behaviors to predict future actions. By leveraging predictive analytics, you can identify the best time to send emails, the most effective content, and the optimal frequency for each recipient.

>> **A/B testing:** Automating *A/B testing* (testing two different versions) to try different subject lines, images, layouts, and calls to action to see which variations perform best. By continuously optimizing email elements, AI can improve click-through rates over time.

>> **Templates and follow ups:** Creating templates, sending follow-up messages, and tracking the performance of email campaigns.

It's important to use AI tools ethically to enhance the customer experience without compromising their privacy or trust. *Spam* (junk email) is on the minds of most recipients. While many have learned to identify spam based on certain characteristics such as spelling mistakes, poor grammar, and suspicious links, many harmful spams still get through. It's AI to the rescue! Knowmail (https://www.knowmail.me/) is a tool to keep email as efficient and relevant as possible by filtering the most important messages and summarizing actionable conversations. And new companies are joining the battle to regularly increase the efficiency of e-marketing campaigns on the parts of both senders and recipients. AI can be used to create convincing phishing emails that can evade traditional email security systems. However, companies such as Darktrace (https://darktrace.com/) are using AI to tackle novel email attacks and increasingly complex malicious communication.

SHERYL
SAYS

I'm not recommending one AI generator over another, but Mailmodo has a good article on AI and email marketing: https://www.mailmodo.com/guides/ai-in-email-marketing/.

REMEMBER

When unlocking the power of e-marketing it's important to fill out the Kick-Start Brief in Chapter 4 to understand your reader, purpose, key issue, and the questions your reader will need answered. This Brief provides a foundation for you to customize your content to precisely meet the needs of your reader and drive your call to action (CTA).

Generating Precise Prompts

Here are some suggestions for creating effective AI prompts, with a particular emphasis on e-marketing:

>> Identify the target audience.

>> State the purpose of the campaign.

>> Ask for help with a strong subject line or headline.

>> Outline the main points or information you want to include.

>> Provide guidance regarding the tone which can be formal, casual, friendly, professional, humorous, or more.

>> Choose marketing channels such as Internet marketing, social media marketing, email marketing, ads, influencer marketing, and more.

>> Include any incentives you may be offering.

>> Request a strong CTA.

Leveraging the Benefits of E-Marketing

The overall purpose of e-marketing campaigns is to promote a company's products or services, build customer loyalty, solidify relationships, and convert prospects to customers. In Figure 11-1 you see the cycle of e-marketing. It can help in the following ways and more:

>> Craft impactful subject lines

>> Allow hyper-personalization

>> Build, clean up, and manage mailing lists

>> Track performance

>> Integrate e-commerce platforms

>> Structure your campaign for maximum effectiveness

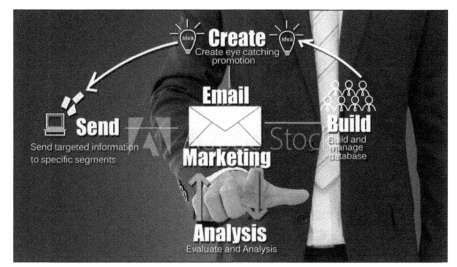

FIGURE 11-1:
The e-marketing
cycle.

TIP

A DOZEN REASONS TO USE E-MARKETING CAMPAIGNS

Unlock the power of e-marketing campaigns and revolutionize your business growth for these 12 compelling reasons:

1. **Promoting products or services:** Inform customers about new product launches, special offers, discounts, or exclusive deals. By highlighting the value and benefits of their offerings, businesses can encourage recipients to make a purchase and return to the site to find out what's new.

2. **Building customer loyalty:** Help businesses stay connected with their existing customers and build strong relationships. By sending newsletters, updates, specials, tips, tutorials, and personalized content, companies can nurture customer loyalty and encourage repeat purchases.

3. **Educating and informing:** Educate customers about the brand, its values, and the benefits of its products or services. By providing valuable information, companies can position themselves as industry experts and build trust with their audience.

4. **Building brand recognition:** Brand recognition extends beyond design. If you consistently provide valuable content to your readers, they'll begin to recognize your emails and even anticipate them.

(continued)

(continued)

5. **Improving sales:** Promoting your business through e-marketing gives readers immediacy. They can make purchases right from their computers or phones.

6. **Optimizing time and budget:** While businesses often spend large amounts of money on advertising, marketing, and PR campaigns, e-marketing is low cost. Aided by AI technology, enticing subject lines and copy require less time and money than ever before.

7. **Establishing authority:** Show yourself as a leader in your industry by letting recipients know of your accomplishments, new offerings, and more.

8. **Engaging and re-engaging:** Engage with customers and prospects, keeping them interested and involved with the brand. They can send interactive content, surveys, quizzes, or invitations to events, encouraging recipients to interact and respond.

9. **Driving traffic and conversions:** Drive traffic to the company's website, blog, or social media channels. Calls to action can link to relevant content and encourage viewers to make a purchase or sign up for a service.

10. **Segmenting and personalizing:** Segment their audience based on various criteria, such as demographics, past purchase behavior, or engagement level. By tailoring the content and offers to specific segments, businesses can deliver highly relevant and personalized messages that resonate with recipients, increasing the chances of conversion.

11. **Strengthening customer service:** Show your readers you care with special product offerings, special coupons, one-day discounts, or even just a "happy birthday" gift coupon.

12. **Providing better customer service:** AI-enabled live chats are a cost-effective way to enhance customer satisfaction.

Delving into the Different Types of E-Marketing

E-marketing, when used properly, is like sending a personalized message to each recipient. But are you sending the right messages to the right people at the right time? You want them to be interested in all things your organization brings to the table and look forward to hearing the latest and greatest of what you have to offer. By sending a few specific types of e-marketing messages you'll be able to reach the right people with the right content at the right time. On the following list, put a checkmark next to those that would work best for your business:

- ❑ **Abandoned cart:** These are sent to customers who've added products to an online shopping cart but haven't completed the checkout process. These emails act as reminders to encourage people to return to your site and complete their purchase.

- ❑ **Behavioral:** These are messages based on a recipient's behavior, which boils down to personalization. It takes getting to know your customers, creating a buyer persona, and tailoring your messages so they're relevant to where customers are in the buying cycle.

- ❑ **Co-marketing:** This is where two or more companies team up to market a mutually beneficial event or promotion.

- ❑ **Event evites:** Events cost money and you want to populate them with as many people as possible. Evites are a great way to attract registrants. AI can help you tell why the event will be awesome and can create a subject line that's enticing.

- ❑ **Informational:** One-to-many emails you can send only to people who've opted in. Your emails can bring them up to speed on your latest content, product announcements, and more.

- ❑ **Internal updates:** Don't forget about important announcements for people who work at your company. This can include internal newsletters, updates, awards and recognition, product and service updates, events, and more.

- ❑ **Kick-back emails:** When a customer, lead, or prospect fills out a form on your landing page, you should have an automatic kick-back email ready to acknowledge their message.

- ❑ **Milestones:** Take advantage of the chance to connect with your customers to highlight milestones such as the customer's birthday, a full year of being a customer, or whatever.

- ❑ **New content announcement:** You may be announcing the next sale, an e-book, webinar, coupon, free trial . . . and the list goes on. This usually has a CTA that links to a targeted landing page. (Learn more about landing pages in Chapter 12.)

- ❑ **Newsletters:** With assistance from AI, you can generate interesting newsletters and subject lines that shout "open me."

- ❑ **Post-purchase drip campaign:** This isn't to sell something new (at least not on the surface) but to follow up with a customer who's made a purchase. You can ask for feedback or encourage a review.

- ❑ **Re-engagement:** You haven't heard back from the customer in a while and want to subtly remind them of your brand. Share promotions, company announcements, newsletter content, and more.

- ❏ **Referrals:** Even the most successful sales team can use help in reaching new leads. Referral emails can bring in major sales and expand your reach.

- ❏ **Seasonal campaigns:** 'Tis the season to send a special offer for Christmas, Valentine's Day, Fourth of July, Thanksgiving, the start of summer, or for any season or time of the year.

- ❏ **Social media:** What does social media have to do with email? Lots. Use e-marketing to make use of LinkedIn Groups, LinkedIn Announcements, Google+ Events, and more.

- ❏ **Surveys:** These can ask customers to rate and review a recent purchase or complete to gauge their interest and guide future products. Or it can be an assessment of customer service to see where you may need to improve.

- ❏ **Welcomes:** This is usually the first email with a potential or current customer. You can send a welcome email after a customer's initial action with your company — like signing up for an email list or creating an account.

Learning the Lingo

TIP

If you're new to e-marketing, it's helpful to familiarize yourself with some key terms:

- » **Accessibility:** Ensuring that emails and documents are designed in a way that accommodates different accessibility needs.

- » **Blacklist:** A list of IP addresses that shout *spammers*.

- » **Bounce rate:** The percentage of emails that are returned to the sender because they can't reach the intended recipient.

- » **Call to Action (CTA):** What you request the recipient to do. It can direct them to a landing page, click to take advantage of an offer, and so on.

- » **Click-Through Rate (CTR):** The number of clicks divided by the number of recipients who opened the message.

- » **Conversion rate:** The percentage of recipients who responded to the CTA by filling out a form, making a purchase, signing up for the service, or something else.

- » **Engagement rate:** A measure of the level of interaction and response that a piece of content receives from the reader.

- » **Email filter:** A technique that blocks email based on the sender, subject line, or content.

- **House List (or Retention List):** It's a permissions-only list built on subscribers who've opted in.

- **Landing page:** A page that recipients can link to from an email to provide additional information directly related to products or services promoted in the email's CTA.

- **Lead generation:** Collecting contact information from potential customers or leads who have shown interest in a product or service.

- **Mobile optimization:** Making sure that emails have the design and formatting to display properly on smartphones and tablets.

- **Open rate:** The percentage of people who open and read an email out of the total number of people who received it.

- **Opt-in (subscribe) or opt-out (unsubscribe):** Recipients can choose whether or not to continue receiving your messages.

- **Scrubbing the list:** Removing inactive or unengaged subscribers from the list.

- **Segmentation:** Automatically placing subscribers into groups based on their activity, such as signup date, time zone, sales history, and other factors.

- **Soft bounce:** A failed delivery due to a temporary issue such as a full mailbox or unavailable server.

- **Split testing (or A/B testing):** Creating two or more versions of an email with slight variations in elements such as subject lines or placement of CTA to see which version yields better results.

- **Whitelist:** A list of IP addresses that have been approved to deliver email to a recipient.

NEWSLETTERS UNLEASHED

E-newsletters are an effective marketing tool, and it seems everyone is sending one these days. They can highlight sales, promote products or events, or provide useful content related to services or industries. They're typically sent out as necessary, weekly, bi-monthly, monthly, or quarterly and are written by an e-marketing specialist within a company, a freelance writer, or an agency that specializes in e-marketing.

AI can revolutionize newsletters by creating content in different tones and moods and injecting freshness into stale newsletters. By leveraging consumer data, AI can personalize newsletters, resulting in higher engagement and conversion rates. Analyzing user preferences and behaviors, AI delivers tailored content, making newsletters more

(continued)

(continued)

relevant and captivating. This is a form of journalistic writing that needs a personal touch. Whether you volunteer or you're assigned this project, here are some things to consider:

- **Define your goals:** Are you looking to drive sales, increase website traffic, or build brand awareness?

- **Know your audience:** Understand who your target audience is and what they're interested in. (Check out Chapter 4.)

- **Select the right marketing platform:** Choose a platform that offers the features you need, such as customizable templates, automation, and analytics.

- **Provide valuable content:** Include informative articles, helpful tips, or exclusive offers that are relevant to the reader's interests.

- **Use a clean and visually appealing design:** Use a consistent color scheme, include high-quality images, and make sure the layout is easy to read and navigate.

- **Include a clear CTA:** Every newsletter should have a clear CTA that tells your subscribers what you want them to do next.

- **Test and optimize:** Use analytics to track your performance and make data-driven decisions to optimize your newsletter over time.

- **Respect privacy and provide an easy unsubscribe option:** Ensure that you comply with privacy regulations and provide an easy way for subscribers to unsubscribe if they no longer wish to receive your newsletter.

Remember, creating an effective e-newsletter takes time and effort. By following these tips and continuously improving your strategy, you can create a newsletter that engages your audience and drives results. In addition, popular newsletter generators such as Constant Contact (https://www.constantcontact.com/) and Mailchimp (https://mailchimp.com/) offer interfaces and a wide range of customization options to create newsletters that match your brand or personal style.

Newsletter creation platforms often offer a range of useful features that can include color palette generators, image libraries, content management systems, and advanced functionalities. Many can handle every aspect of the newsletter creation process from conception to distribution. They may even provide tools for monitoring and analyzing the results of newsletter campaigns. This comprehensive approach allows you to have a seamless experience and achieve better results with your campaigns.

How many times have you received a newsletter with a one-word subject line that reads, *Newsletter*? Too many times. It lacks specificity and dramatically decreases the open rate. You probably saw that same subject line the month before and the month before that. Let AI assist you in making the subject line compelling.

Strategizing a Successful Campaign

To create a successful e-marketing campaign, consider implementing the following strategies, all designed to increase open rates and boost revenue:

>> **Scrub your list:** Update your email list regularly to remove inactive or unengaged subscribers. You want to reach recipients who are interested in your content.

>> **Personalize each message:** Use customer data to create personalized messages. Address subscribers by name and tailor the content to their interests and preferences.

>> **Segment your campaigns:** This is based on criteria such as demographics, purchase history, or engagement level, geographic location, and more.

>> **Conduct split tests:** Experiment with new approaches and determine what resonates best with your audience.

Knowing what's hot

AI SPOTLIGHT

Hyper-personalization is the new buzzword in e-marketing. This means tailoring messages and recommending products by audience segment, sending triggered emails based on the recipient's behavior. This increases engagement, improves conversion rates, enhances the customer experience, and increases customer loyalty. AI tools such as Amplitude (`https://amplitude.com`), Bloomreach (`https://www.bloomreach.com`), and others can step in and hyper-personalize.

Another hot trend is *interactive emails*. They've been around for a while, but are gaining momentum. This means automated buttons and CTAs; rollover effects to show product offerings, accordion features to make long-form emails more compact, and surveys, polls, and user-generated interactive content. Constant Contact and Mailchimp are key players in this arena.

WARNING

The *CAN-SPAM Act* in the United States imposes certain requirements on businesses that send commercial emails. Failure to comply with these requirements can result in penalties and legal consequences. Here are some of the regulations:

>> You must provide recipients with a functional opt-out link.

>> You're obligated to honor their opt-out request within ten business days.

>> You can't charge a fee or require recipients to provide any personal identifying information beyond their email address in order to opt out.

>> You're prohibited from selling or transferring their email address to any third parties.

Timing it right

Timing is critical. Optimize your send time to maximize open rates. As mentioned in Chapter 10, studies show that Thursdays are the best day to send important emails, followed by Tuesday and Wednesday.

The morning hours — especially between 9 a.m. and 11 a.m. — are often highlighted as peak times for email engagement. This aligns with the start of the workday for many professionals. However, the best day and time can vary depending on your industry and audience.

Getting the Writing Right

Writing effective marketing emails is essential for engaging your audience and driving the desired CTA. Here are some tips to help you craft compelling email marketing content and beyond:

>> **Segment your audience:** Segmenting your email list based on demographics, interests, or past interactions allows you to send targeted and relevant content to specific groups.

>> **Write attention-grabbing subject lines:** The subject line is the first thing recipients see, so make it compelling and relevant to encourage them to open the email. Use concise and engaging language that piques their curiosity or offers value. (More about subject lines later in this chapter.)

>> **Personalize the content:** This means segmenting the recipients into their preferences and behavior and addressing them by name. This creates a sense of connection and increases engagement.

>> **Keep the message concise:** Use clear and straightforward language to convey your message effectively.

>> **Maintain the brand's voice:** Your message must reflect your brand's voice and personality. Consistency in tone and style helps build brand recognition and trust.

>> **Use a CTA:** Use persuasive language and make the CTA stand out visually to encourage click-throughs.

>> **Mobile optimization:** Most people access emails on their smartphones or tablets, so optimizing for multiple devices is crucial.

>> **Proofread and edit:** A well-written and error-free email enhances your professionalism and credibility.

>> **Test and optimize:** A/B testing can help you identify what works best for your audience. Test different subject lines, email layouts, CTAs, and content variations to optimize your email campaigns.

Creating an incentive-focused subject line

You must entice each recipient with a focused subject line that attracts their interest and encourages them to click. Here are a few suggestions:

Only 24 hours left before this expires (Leave the "this" to their imagination)

Learn to get paid for creative ideas

[Name], check out the name of the winner

By analyzing data and using predictive models, AI can generate subject lines that are catchy, compelling, and tailored to your target audience and your campaign.

Finding the right balance between an engaging subject line and avoiding clickbait is crucial. *Clickbait*, known for its sensationalized nature, lures you into clicking on links for articles, images, or videos. However, instead of providing factual information, clickbait thrives on exploiting your emotions and curiosity, ultimately wasting your time.

Avoiding being dumped into spam

Here are some steps you can take that may prevent your messages from going into the recipient's spam/junk folders:

>> **Avoid spam-triggers:** They may include words such as bargain, bad credit, best price, extra income, double your income, eliminate debt, FREE, $$, profit, money, back, and others that will be caught by spam filters. Also avoid excessive capitalizations, explanation marks, or spammy language.

>> **Use a reputable email provider:** Reputable providers take steps to prevent spammers from using their platforms, which helps ensure the deliverability of your emails.

>> **Build a solid sender reputation:** You earn a positive reputation by sending quality messages that recipients see as valuable.

>> **Monitor your sending domain and IP address:** If you're sharing an IP address with other senders whose actions have tarnished its reputation, your emails may suffer as a result.

>> **Test your emails:** Before sending out your emails, consider tools such as Mail Tester (`https://www.mail-tester.com/`) or Mailmeteor (`https://mailmeteor.com/email-subject-line-tester`) to check the quality and spamminess of your emails. These tools mimic spam filters and provide insights into how your emails may be perceived.

Including a salutation and closing

You'd never answer the phone without saying *hello* or end a conversation without saying *goodbye*. Personalize the greeting: Even if you're sending a newsletter, add a personal touch with *Dear Member, Dear Subscriber, Dear Jerry,* and the like. HubSpot (`https://www.hubspot.com/`) reports that this type of personalization can elevate the conversion rate by nearly 50 percent.

Another personal touch is a signature line. People are more inclined to take your message seriously when it appears to come from a human being, not just a collective marketing team or AI generation. Your email signature is your ticket to attention. More about that in Chapter 10.

Keeping the CTA above the fold

The term *above the fold* originated in the newspaper industry. It refers to the upper half of the front page of a newspaper or tabloid where an important news story or photograph is often found. Use this valuable real estate in your e-marketing messages so your CTA is immediately visible. Placing the CTA above the fold has several benefits:

>> **Immediate visibility:** Ensures the CTA is immediately visible on the opening screen without the need to scroll. This catches the viewer's attention and makes it easy to take action.

>> **Reduced distractions:** Minimizes distractions from other links, images, or buttons. Helps to maintain focus on the primary CTA to increase the likelihood of conversion.

>> **Limited choices:** Keep the number of CTAs to a minimum because people get confused by too many choices.

Your CTA may be *shop now, learn more, enroll now, subscribe, get started, book now, download now, claim your discount, request a demo, join now,* or anything else that's appropriate. Words such as *limited time only* or *offer ends soon* engender a sense of urgency to act immediately.

TIP

Place the CTA button toward the bottom or to the right of the content so it aligns with people's natural reading pattern and increases the chances of it being noticed and clicked. People typically read from top to bottom and from left to right.

Using some of the AI testing and tracking mentioned earlier in this chapter will help you determine the most effective placement of your CTA. For more information, check out these sites:

» `https://blog.hubspot.com/insiders/inbound-marketing-tips`

» `https://www.constantcontact.com/blog/marketing-tips/`

» `https://www.indeed.com/career-advice/career-development/marketing-tips`

RETURN ON INVESTMENT (ROI)

Deciding where to invest marketing dollars isn't a decision that companies take lightly. E-marketing has proven to have the highest ROI of all forms of marketing. HubSpot reports that ROI for companies is about $36 in return for every $1 spent. Not only does e-marketing keep you in touch with those who want to hear from you — keeping you at the top of their mind — it also allows you to educate your customers, clients, and prospects on new or updated products and services, drive traffic to your site, conduct surveys, make announcements, hold contests, and anything that works for your type of business.

A/B testing, or split testing, is a way to compare two versions of something to figure out which performs better. Split your recipients into two to test variations on each campaign and determine which performs better. In other words, you can show version A of a piece of marketing content to one half of your audience and version B to another and learn which is more appropriate and will give you the highest ROI. AI tools such as these can facilitate the process:

- Optimizely (`https://www.optimizely.com/`)
- Oracle Maxymizer (`https://www.oracle.com/vn/cx/marketing/personalization-testing/`)
- Qualaroo (`https://qualaroo.com/`)
- VWO (`https://vwo.com/`)

Using Digital Marketing

Digital marketing offers a wide array of benefits that revolutionize the way businesses promote their products and services. When you combine text marketing, web marketing, and social media marketing, you can propel your business towards increased profitability.

Text marketing (SMS marketing)

Today, cellphones are an extra limb for people that's always attached to their hand. People use their cellphones to make phone calls, check emails, text, search the web, and more. Studies have shown that nearly 70 percent of all cellphone users read every text they receive — even spam. That's why lots of companies have turned to text marketing (also known as *SMS marketing*, an abbreviation for short message service) to remind customers about appointments, flash sales, paying bills, confirming updates, informing of special online-only offers, conducting customer preference polls and contests, sending inspirational and motivational messages, and so much more.

WARNING

In the United States, similar legal standards to the *Telephone Consumer Protection Act* (http://tinyurl.com/5pktkwpm) that govern commercial text messages include the requirement for express written consent before sending promotional texts, restrictions on telemarketing calls, and oversight by the Federal Communications Commission (FCC). Non-compliance can result in significant penalties, making it crucial for businesses to obtain explicit consent and adhere to the regulations to protect consumer privacy.

AI SPOTLIGHT

Popular AI tools include:

>> Copy.ai (https://www.copy.ai/)

>> Jasper (https://www.jasper.ai/)

>> SlickText (https://www.slicktext.com/)

>> Textback (https://textback.ai/)

According to the Data & Marketing Association (https://www.business.com/articles/text-message-marketing-benefits/), marketing-related texts have an amazing open rate of about 99 percent. That's compared to a 30 percent open rate of emails. Millennials prefer texting over emails, and the trend has been accelerated by Gen Zs. Here's why people are jumping aboard:

>> **Convenience and automation:** It provides convenience for both businesses and customers. Customers can opt in or opt out of receiving messages, giving them control over their communication preferences, just as with email. However, text messaging streamlines communication because of its immediacy.

>> **Built-in subscriber list:** Start by building a list of subscribers who have explicitly consented to receive SMS messages from your business.

>> **Customer loyalty:** A growing number of consumers prefer accessing rewards information from a link in a text message rather than through an app or email. Evidence consistently suggests that many companies use apps for mobile loyalty but more members prefer text engagement over apps.

>> **Cost effectiveness:** It offers a low-cost service with high reachability to the right audience, making it an attractive option for businesses of all sizes. The only costs associated with text marketing involves using a text message service, which most companies already have.

>> **Integration with other channels:** Although it can work as a standalone marketing method, it can also support other marketing methods. For instance, you can use text message marketing to alert your customers to offerings that may be advertised on a social media platform.

>> **Enhanced brand awareness:** Allowing businesses to connect with their target audience directly helps businesses build a brand around the world, provided consumer privacy is protected through legal requirements for opt-in.

WARNING

In the United States, according to the *Telephone Consumer Protection Act* (http://tinyurl.com/5pktkwpm), companies are required to get a customer's written permission to send text messages to their phones and mobile devices. Written consent can involve signing a physical document or using a digital signature. Just as with email, make it easy to unsubscribe.

TIP

When it comes to writing text marketing messages, you can create effective and engaging content in the following ways:

>> **Keep it concise:** Text messages have a character limit, typically around 160 characters. Avoid unnecessary words or information that may distract from the main message.

>> **Use clear and compelling language:** You can grab the reader's attention with concise phrases and strong verbs such as increase, engage, and transform.

>> **Highlight important information:** Use capital letters (sparingly) or other formatting techniques (such as bullets) to highlight important words or phrases in your message.

>> **Personalize when possible:** Use the recipient's name or include personalized offers or recommendations based on their preferences or past interactions.

>> **Include a clear CTA:** Place the CTA as close to the top as possible to reduce the need for excessive scrolling.

>> **Test your messages:** Before sending out your text marketing messages, test them to ensure they're error-free and deliver the intended message. This can help you avoid embarrassing typos or mistakes that may impact the effectiveness of your campaign.

>> **Use emojis:** These little icons can add a visual component and help convey emotions that enhance the message. However, use them sparingly and make sure they align with your brand and the context of your message.

AI SPOTLIGHT

AI tools such as the following are some of the top choices for text marketing:

>> EZTesting (https://www.eztexting.com/)

>> Podium (https://www.podium.com/)

>> ProTexting, (https://blog.protexting.com/)

>> Textedly (https://www.textedly.com/)

>> Twilio (https://www.twilio.com/)

Web marketing

Web marketing is a subset of e-marketing that focuses specifically on marketing efforts conducted through the Internet and web-based platforms. It encompasses a range of strategies and tactics aimed at promoting products or services online. Here are some key features:

>> **Scope and focus:** Web marketing primarily revolves around online channels and platforms, such as websites and search engines.

>> **Versatile and flexible:** It provides nearly limitless options for original concepts and digital marketing strategies with a wide range of tools.

>> **Tracking and analytics:** Marketers can use analytics tools to track user behavior, such as clicks, time spent on web pages, email open rates, and more. This aids marketing strategies and optimizes campaigns for better results.

>> **Display advertising:** It allows for sales and brand awareness with targeted ads.

TIP

When it comes to writing web marketing campaigns, create compelling and effective content in the following ways:

>> **Write concise, targeted copy:** Keep your copy concise and focused, addressing the needs and pain points of your audience. Use clear and persuasive language to convey your value proposition.

>> **Use persuasive storytelling:** Storytelling is a powerful tool in marketing. Use this technique to engage your viewer and create an emotional connection with your brand. Craft narratives that highlight the benefits and solutions your product or service offers, and don't forget stories about how customers have successfully used your product, made more money, or whatever their takeaway has been. (Check out Chapter 5 to learn more.)

>> **Incorporate social proof:** *Social proof* is evidence that other people have purchased and found value in your product or service. Including social proof in your web marketing campaigns can help build trust and credibility. Use testimonials, case studies, stories, and statistics to demonstrate the value and success of your product or service. Be sure to get written permission before including anything that can identify a person or company.

>> **Fold in videos:** They can be of a delighted customer using your product or one bragging about how it helped increase revenue. A video is a powerful way to obtain leads and earn conversions. With the growth of sites such as YouTube (www.youtube.com), videos are easy to post and are becoming a powerful way to engage viewers.

AI SPOTLIGHT

Here are some AI tools that can help with web marketing:

>> Adzooma (https://www.adzooma.com/)

>> Browse AI (https://www.browse.ai/)

>> Chatfuel (https://chatfuel.com/)

>> Hemingway App (https://hemingwayapp.com/)

>> Surfer SEO (https://surferseo.com/)

» Tidio (`https://www.tidio.com/`)

» Writer.com (`https://writer.com/`)

» Zapier (`https://zapier.com/`)

Social media marketing

The power of social media platforms has revolutionized the way businesses interact with customers. From Facebook and Instagram to X (formerly Twitter) and LinkedIn, social media marketing allows businesses to create a strong brand presence, engage with customers, and foster meaningful relationships. Through compelling content, targeted ads, and influencer partnerships, businesses can tap into the vast potential of social media to amplify their reach and drive conversions.

That's why a social media campaign should become an essential part of your customer's journey. Social media platforms provide opportunities for brands to engage with their target audience, build brand awareness, and influence purchase decisions.

REMEMBER

Social media marketing is about building relationships, engaging your readers, and providing value. First you must define your goals, whether it's increasing brand awareness, driving traffic to your website, generating leads, boosting sales, or whatever. Also target your audience in terms of demographics, interests, and pain points.

TIP

Armed with this knowledge, you'll be able to create content that speaks directly to reader's needs and desires, increasing the chances of engagement and conversion:

» **Be genuine:** This means creating authentic connections by delivering honest, transparent, and valuable content that resonates with readers' needs and cultivates trust. Otherwise, you come across as sales-y.

» **Craft captivating headlines and captions:** With the short attention spans on social media, grabbing your reader's attention quickly is a must. Create catchy headlines and captions that pique curiosity, evoke emotions, or promise value. Use compelling language, selective humor, or intriguing questions to entice them to click, like, or share.

» **Use visuals effectively:** Visual content is highly engaging on social media. Incorporate eye-catching images, videos, infographics, or memes to grab attention and convey your message effectively. Your visuals should be high-quality, relevant, and aligned with your brand's style and tone. (Check out Chapter 7 to learn more about visuals.)

>> **Share stories:** As discussed in Chapter 5, people relate to stories. Share personal narratives, customer success stories, or behind-the-scenes glimpses to create an emotional connection. Showcasing your brand values and humanizing your content can help build trust and loyalty.

>> **Encourage user-generated content:** This is a great way to demonstrate social proof. Encourage your followers to share their experiences, reviews, or creative content related to your brand. Run contests or campaigns that encourage user participation and amplify your reach.

>> **Use social listening:** Monitor conversations and trends related to your brand or industry using social listening tools. This will help you understand what your audience is talking about and what topics interest them. Use this information to tailor your content and engage in meaningful conversations.

>> **Show appreciation:** Building true connections can foster brand loyalty and advocacy. Always be genuine in your interactions, respond to comments and messages, and show appreciation for your reader's support.

AI SPOTLIGHT

When it comes to social media marketing, several AI tools can help streamline your strategy and improve your marketing efforts. Here are a few:

>> Buffer (https://buffer.com Copy.ai (https://www.copy.ai/)

>> Digital First AI (https://www.digitalfirst.ai/)

>> Emplifi (https://emplifi.io/)

>> FeedHive (https://www.feedhive.com/)

>> Hootsuite Insights (https://www.hootsuite.com/products/infights)

>> Predis (https://predis.ai/)

Chapter **12**

Enhancing Web Content

The World Wide Web is akin to Times Square, the bustling heart of New York City. It dazzles visitors with its vibrant lights, towering billboards, and an array of enticing offerings, all aimed at drawing people into specific destinations. But once these visitors are lured in, the question remains: Are the destinations compelling enough to keep them engaged? And will they keep coming back for more?

Much like the bustling streets of Times Square, websites employ the same attributes to captivate and retain visitors. They strive to pique their curiosity, lure visitors in with irresistible content, and create an immersive experience that leaves a lasting impression. Just as the bright lights of Times Square mesmerize passersby, websites rely on stunning visuals, captivating designs, and eye-catching elements to capture attention.

However, luring visitors in is only half the battle. To keep them coming back for more, websites must deliver on their promises and provide an exceptional user experience. Just as Times Square offers an array of entertainment options to cater to different tastes, websites need to provide valuable and relevant content that resonates with their target audience. Whether it's engaging articles, informative videos, or interactive features, websites must continuously deliver fresh and captivating experiences to keep users engaged and returning again and again.

Being Web Word Wise (WWW)

The web has been around for so long, you're probably familiar with most of the terminology, but people are at all different levels of understanding, so here are a few terms that may trip people up:

WARNING

>> **Captcha:** A security measure aimed at preventing bots from accessing sensitive information or performing malicious activities on a website.

>> **Cookies:** A small text file created by a website or application that's stored on a visitor's computer.

>> **Dark web:** A hidden part of the Internet where anonymous users can access illicit and illegal activities and content. (I mention this term to only provide awareness and understanding, but it's advisable to steer clear of it.)

>> **DNS (Domain Name System):** The equivalent of a phone book or directory. It keeps an updated list of domain names and translates them back into IP addresses.

>> **Homepage:** The main page of a website that's often the entry point for visitors from which they can navigate through the site.

>> **Landing page:** A standalone web page designed for a specific campaign or purpose. It's typically created to drive conversions and encourage visitors to take a specific action.

>> **Metadata:** This provides information about one or more aspects of the data. It's used to summarize basic information about data that can make tracking and working with specific data easier.

>> **Permalink:** Somewhat like a bookmark that allows users to retrieve resources for future use, such as an e-book, article, record in the catalog, video, database, and such.

>> **SEO (Search Engine Optimization):** The process of improving the rankings of a web page (or website) in a search engine.

>> **Sitemap:** A file that provides information about the pages, videos, and other files on a site, and the relationships between them. Search engines read this file to crawl your site more efficiently.

>> **USP (Unique Selling Proposition):** The sizzle that differentiates your product or service. It answers the niggling question, "What makes you so special?"

Using AI as Your Assistant for Writing Web Content

AI SPOTLIGHT

AI tools can assist with content generation and optimization, personalization, content curation, SEO, and other aspects of the content. Here are a few of the key players:

>> Copy.ai (https://www.copy.ai/)

>> Grammarly (https://www.grammarly.com/)

>> Hostinger AI Website Builder (https://www.hostinger.com/)

>> Jimdo (https://www.jimdo.com/)

>> Unbounce (https://unbounce.com/)

>> Wix (https://www.wix.com/)

REMEMBER

When writing for the web it's important to fill out the Kick-Start Brief in Chapter 4 to understand your reader (actually online, visitors), purpose, key issue, and the questions your visitor will need answered. This Brief provides a foundation for you to customize your content to precisely meet the needs of your visitor and drive the call to action (CTA).

Generating Precise Prompts

AI SPOTLIGHT

Here are some suggestions for creating effective AI prompts, with a particular emphasis on developing web content:

>> Identify the target audience in terms of demographics, interests, knowledge level, and any other relevant details.

>> Indicate the desired tone such as formal, casual, informative, persuasive, humorous, or whatever is appropriate.

>> Provide a clear outline or bullet points of the main ideas, key points, and structure you want the content to follow.

>> Mention specific examples, references, or sources you want the AI to include.

>> Include relevant keywords, meta tags, or SEO guidelines you want the AI tool to follow.

>> Specify the length of the content, whether it should be in paragraphs, bullet points, or any other specific format.

>> Determine the landing pages.

>> Request a strong CTA.

Fashioning a Homepage

A *homepage* (also home page, front page, or main page) is typically the entry point to your website. It's often the entry point from which visitors can navigate through the site. Think of it as a giant magazine rack where viewers can scan the front covers of the magazine.

Keep it engaging and interactive

When someone visits your site, they decide within milliseconds whether to explore it or leave. It's the central hub that welcomes visitors, explains key benefits, and serves as a gateway to other sections or pages. Creating effective content for your homepage takes lots of time, effort, and testing to get right. Think of this page as a work-in-progress that you can always tweak and improve upon. Some key things to remember:

>> Have a design that compliments your business.

>> Make it concise.

>> Use keywords.

>> Write copy from the visitor's perspective.

>> Focus on benefits, not features.

>> Provide simple navigation.

>> Add a personal touch.

>> Use headlines and subheads.

>> Sound enthusiastic without going overboard.

>> Proofread carefully.

Visuals can be more persuasive than words

Including visuals on a website homepage can help create a visually appealing, engaging, and informative experience for visitors, ultimately leading to increased user engagement, brand recognition, and conversions. It grabs attention more quickly than words, evokes emotion, and can improve SEO by making the website more visually appealing and shareable.

Putting your best face forward

Including personal photos on the web depends on circumstances, goals, and the nature of the business. This practice isn't limited to small business owners. Many large corporations showcase their corporate officers with photos. This aims to humanize the company and establish a sense of familiarity. By creating a personal connection, it becomes easier to build trust and make the leaders more relatable to the public. Ultimately, the inclusion of personal photos can contribute to fostering a positive perception of the leadership team and the organization as a whole.

Authenticity is critical in marketing. In a world where people find random businesses online, a photo lets visitors know there's a real person. A photo, such as the one in Figure 12-1, increases your ability to connect with people and be remembered long after they've clicked out. However, for many people this is a privacy issue, they don't like the way they look in photos, or they don't want to reveal their ages. Also, slow-loading websites can lead to a poor user experience and increased bounce rates. Although these are valid reasons, the advantages outweigh the disadvantages. If a visitor has been able to connect with and trust your business from the moment they land on your homepage, you're golden.

WARNING

It's important to consider privacy, security, legal considerations, and the overall purpose and context of sharing the photos. If you do decide to share photos, be sure to take necessary precautions to protect your privacy and respect copyright laws.

Highlighting a knockout project

If you're in a creative field, showcase a smashing project to tell your story. Figure 12-2 sets itself above the competition by grabbing attention with an incredible home that evokes emotion . . . reinforcing that a picture is worth a million words.

FIGURE 12-1:
A photo can
create a sense
of trust.

www.guidedinsights.com.

FIGURE 12-2:
Homepage of
2M Architecture
showcasing an
astounding
home.

Courtesy of 2M Architecture.

SHOULD YOU INCLUDE YOUR MISSION STATEMENT?

You worked hard to develop your mission statement. It means something to you and your employees. But should you put it on your website? Weigh the pros and cons and decide what works best for your company.

Pros:

- A mission (or vision) and set of core values are crucial to a successful company and culture that can give your company a unique identify.

- If you're a non-profit, articulating what you do and why you do it goes a long way to show visitors how you're making the world a better place.

- It gives employees a more significant purpose beyond just the general task or duty.

Cons:

- It means something to you and your team, but in most cases your customers/clients don't care. They want answers to help them solve their problems and to find good products and services.

- Because your mission statement is about you, you've used the words *we, our, us*. Your website should reflect the words *you* and *yours*.

As an option, consider telling a story, displaying a customer testimonial, or sending visitors to an About Us page.

Knowing the Anatomy of a Landing Page

A *landing page*, as shown in Figure 12-3, is a standalone web page specifically designed to convert visitors into leads or new patients. Landing pages are often created for a specific offer or marketing campaign with the primary goal of having visitors make a purchase, schedule an appointment, sign up for a newsletter, fill out a form, or whatever. Here are some key characteristics:

>> **Focused message:** Focus on the campaign or offer the page is promoting and eliminate all distractions.

>> **Social proof:** Testimonials, videos, customer reviews, user-generated content, and logos of prominent customers add to your credibility and convince prospective viewers to trust you.

>> **Limited navigation:** This keeps visitors focused on the desired action and prevents them from getting distracted by other content.

>> **Call to action (CTA):** A landing page prominently features a CTA button or form that encourages visitors to take the desired action. Place the CTA button above the *fold* (that means opening screen) so it's highly visible and compelling.

As you surf the net, notice the sites that lure you in and those you leave immediately. Pay attention to the pros and woes of each one.

TIP

Optimizing for SEO

Search engine optimization (SEO) is the powerful force behind boosting websites to the forefront of search engine rankings. Simply creating a website isn't enough to attract visitors.

Optimizing a website for SEO is crucial because it enhances the visibility and discoverability of the website in search engine results pages. By implementing SEO strategies such as keyword research, on-page optimization, and link building, a website can rank higher in search engine rankings, attract more traffic, and ultimately increase its online presence and potential for conversions. In today's competitive digital landscape, optimizing a website for SEO is essential for businesses to stand out, reach their target audience, and achieve long-term success.

REMEMBER

Check out `https://top10seosoftware.com/` to learn about sites that can help boost SEO rankings. They'll analyze a website's performance and provide solutions to areas that need improvement, such as page load times, keyword optimization, content quality, and more.

Using keywords and phrases

Many resources can help with keywords and phrases. Semrush (`https://www.semrush.com/`) is one of several AI generators that can boost your marketing and top your rivals in less time with powerful keyword research tools. There are others. Search for *ai generators to identify keywords for a website*. Once you identify the keywords and phrases, pepper your site with them.

TIP

Understand what *sponsored ads* are. Also called advertorials, they target specific keywords or search terms. Instead of designing a brand-specific ad and paying for it to run on a website, sponsored ads blend in with the retail media environment in which they appear. But don't be fooled. They're ads — bought and paid for. Learn more about sponsored ads at `https://advertising.amazon.com/library/guides/basics-of-success-sponsored-ads`.

Using alt tags

Use *alternative text* (ALT text) descriptions, which are a variety of ways to say the same thing. They allow search engines to locate your page. This is crucial, especially for those who use text-only browsers or screen readers. (There are alternate text generators you can find online.) The more descriptive you are, the better. Consider this example:

> **Before:** alt="Teacher pointing to a computer screen"

> **After:** alt="College professor using education software to instruct a business school student"

Understanding pay-per-click (PPC)

PPC is where search engines show ads. Each time someone clicks on the ad, the company that owns the ad pays a fee. If no one clicks, the company pays nothing. Essentially, it's a way of "buying" sites to the top of the listings. Today, more people are using the Internet to search for products and services relevant to their needs and interests, and this is a legal way to bring traffic to companies that are willing to pay.

Going organic (non-paid results)

This is achieved by obtaining a high-ranking placement based on substantive content rather than paying for advertising.

TIP

These tips help you rise up the rankings:

>> Make your headings and subheadings meaningful by using keywords people would use to find you.

>> Include bold, italics, and heading tags to highlight these keyword phrases — but don't overdo it.

>> Keep your site relevant and current.

>> Use metadata (described earlier in this chapter), especially title metadata. It's the most important metadata and is responsible for the page titles appearing at the top of the browser window.

>> Identify link-worthy sites. Check regularly to make sure the links work.

Standing Above Your Competitors

Competition is part of business. In addition to delivering what your customers want, you need to know what the competition is doing and how you're doing it better, how you're more cost effective, or how you perform differently. It's not enough to say that you have "excellent customer services" or "superior products." Everyone says that. Embrace unconventional thinking!

The number of competitors you face online grows daily. Ask yourself why your viewers should do business with you. You must be able to answer that, or it's only a matter of time before you go out of business. Also:

>> Understand what your customers want, and what your competitors don't offer.

>> Know the strengths and weaknesses of the competitors in your industry.

>> Become familiar with the product lines they offer.

>> Identify what makes each company competitive.

WARNING

Never post anything negative about your competition. However, you may say, *We're the only ones in this industry who . . .*

Competitive analysis software helps businesses gather and analyze data about their competitors' strategies, performance, and online presence. They offer valuable insights into various aspects, such as website traffic, SEO, content effectiveness, social media engagement, and email marketing strategies. By using competitive analysis software, businesses can gain a better understanding of their competitors' digital landscape and make informed decisions to improve their own strategies. Check out Semrush (https://www.semrush.com/), Similarweb (https://www.similarweb.com/), and Ahrefs (https://ahrefs.com/).

Crafting compelling and informational headlines

Make your headlines serve as ads for the copy that follows. Studies show that only one in five people read anything more than headlines. Here are some suggestions:

>> Include the single most important benefit you offer. For example, *Always on time and on budget.*

>> Mention your target in the headline. For example, if you target dentists, use *dentists* in your headline.

>> Include *you* and *your*.

>> Use power words such as *Discover, Now, Sale, Breakthrough* — words that grab attention.

Not overwhelming visitors with design or graphics

Contrary to popular belief, viewer's eyes aren't drawn to dazzling graphics in multitudes of colors. Viewers value substance over glitz. Here are some suggestions for using graphics appropriately:

>> Choose your text and background colors carefully. Dark text on a light background is easier to read than light text on a dark background.

>> Design your illustrations so they attract your visitor's attention, not distract from the content.

White space (also known as background space) is critical. It takes on an added importance on the web because more strain is placed on the eyes than with print material. Treat white space as more than just a background. Treat it as an integral part of your design. By doing so, you increase the power of your message.

Playing to the senses

Playing to a viewer's senses involves creating an immersive experience that engages multiple senses such as sight, sound, touch, taste, and smell. This can be achieved through various techniques such as using visually appealing designs, incorporating audio and video elements, providing interactive features, and using descriptive language to evoke sensory experiences. By appealing to multiple senses, you can enhance user engagement, create a memorable experience, and effectively convey information or promote products and services.

One easy way is to incorporate audio. Visitors respond to audio in a way they don't respond to words alone, no matter how great your copy is. Don't hit people with audio as soon as they arrive at your site, however. Provide a click so visitors can hear the following:

>> A message from you to remove some of the anonymity of the web experience.

>> Testimonials from clients/customers are social proof that make you very credible.

>> Playback of seminars or teleconferences so visitors can capture information they may have missed. (And they may promote you by passing this along to others.)

>> Tips that give short pieces of information quickly.

>> A how-to verbal guide.

Being Sensitive to International Visitors

Being sensitive to international viewers is crucial for creating inclusive and accessible content. This involves considering cultural differences, language preferences, and user experiences. By incorporating localization strategies, providing language options, and ensuring cultural sensitivity in visuals and messaging, you can effectively engage and connect with a global audience.

AI SPOTLIGHT

The following guidelines help you meet the needs of global visitors:

>> **Work with an AI and human translator.** If the site is to be translated, identify the languages. There are many translation tools out there that you can find with a quick search. In many cases, a chatbot will work just fine.

>> **Be aware of download time.** There are many parts of the world that have slow modems with Internet access that bills by the minute. Users in these regions will visit only sites that are quick to download.

>> **Create sites that are printable.** In parts of the world where Internet access is very expensive, viewers often share computers. They tend to print out websites and distribute hard-copy pages.

Writing for Comprehension

Comprehension is the ease with which your visitors read and understand your writing. When you improve the readability of your writing, you help visitors understand what you say quickly and clearly. (Check out Chapter 9 for readability tools.) Web visitors want information instantly, so it's critical to give them information at a glance. Here are some tips for writing for readability:

>> **Formatting**

- Always start with a compelling headline. Visitors read headlines if nothing else.
- Use lots of subheads.
- Include bold text sparingly. Bold works well for headlines. Don't, however, scatter boldface in the text because it can be distracting.
- Include bullets, numbers, graphs, and tables to convey critical information.
- List key information first, followed by supporting details.
- Sequence for emphasis. You capture visitors with the opening and closing.

>> **Text**

- Divide the text into manageable chunks of information.
- Use short, high-impact sentences.
- Use the active voice.
- Avoid internal jargon and language.
- Include quotes and testimonials, when appropriate.
- Cut anything that doesn't add value to the visitor.

》 Design

- Horizontal lines may be seen as a barrier and stop the visitor from scrolling. Vertical lines may indicate there's more to see.

- Keep headlines close to the text they describe.

- Write headlines in upper and lower case. That's much easier to read than all caps.

- When generating tables, remember that people typically scan down columns, not across.

- Use high contrast between background color and type. The best contrast is black type on white background.

TIP

Go modular. Think about the content and how the average person will access your pages. Keep the topic and content of each page focused and make each page one complete thought or idea. This means each page should stand alone, if possible. People have different browsing styles, so they view your website from different paths. Consider having the same information in several places. This isn't redundant; it's smart.

Keeping 'em Coming Back for More

Think of a store you keep returning to because of their high-quality goods, fair prices, logical arrangement of merchandise, wonderful customer service, and more. Those are the same attributes that keep people coming back to your website. Imagine what else you can offer to make your website one that people visit regularly and recommend to others. Perhaps some of these suggestions will serve you well:

- 》 Discounts

- 》 New product releases

- 》 Daily, weekly, monthly, or random specials

- 》 Newsletters

- 》 Contests

- 》 Online customer service

- >> Surveys

- >> Answers to commonly asked industry questions

- >> Weblogs

- >> Links to timely articles

- >> Weekly or monthly industry-related tip

AI SPOTLIGHT

CONVERSION TRACKING

Conversion tracking is a valuable technique that measures and monitors the actions of viewers following their interaction on your website. By observing whether visitors leave, explore other pages, or respond to your call to action, conversion tracking enables the assessment of ad effectiveness. Here are several conversion tracking options, some of which offer free features with the option to upgrade to paid plans, while others provide monthly or yearly subscription options:

- BuzzSumo (https://buzzsumo.com/)
- Clickervolt (https://clickervolt.com/)
- Crazy Egg (https://www.crazyegg.com/)
- Kissmetrics (https://www.kissmetrics.io/)
- Optimize Press (https://www.optimizepress.com/)

Without tracking conversions, it becomes impossible to accurately measure your return on investment (ROI) and gauge the effectiveness of your website. Tracking conversions is essential for obtaining meaningful data and insights into the impact of your online efforts.

When using tracking tools, especially for visitors from the European Union, it's important to consider General Data Protection Regulation (GDPR) compliance and user privacy. GDPR is a regulation that requires businesses to protect the personal data and privacy of EU citizens for transactions that occur within EU member states. Learn more at https://gdpr-info.eu/.

4

Crafting Noteworthy Professional Documents

Design informative instructions and procedures that capture readers' attention, rather than being skimmed through only in times of troubleshooting.

Explore the advantages of writing articles and grasp the processes of reading a masthead, submitting articles, and composing compelling query letters.

Master the art of writing formal and informal reports, strategically positioning them to have a significant impact and ultimately achieving the desired results.

Learn to write abstracts and executive summaries that effectively capture the essence of longer text.

Harness the potential of grant writing to attract potential funders and establish valuable partnerships.

Chapter **13**

Writing Instructions and Procedures: Step by Step

Get ready to embark on an exciting journey as this chapter equips you with the know-how to create instructions and procedures that are engaging, effective, and even enjoyable. It helps you master the art of writing instructions and procedures. So, whether you're a newbie or a seasoned professional, dive in and unlock your full potential with professionalism and a dash of fun!

Using AI as Your Assistant in Writing Instructions Procedures

AI SPOTLIGHT

If you're tired of your carefully written documents being ignored, let AI unleash its creativity. Here are some AI tools ready to assist:

>> Bit.ai (https://bit.ai/)

>> Scribe (https://scribehow.com/scribe-ai)

>> Paragraph AI (https://paragraphai.com/)

>> Tango (https://www.tango.us/)

You can use these tools to craft captivating introductions that establish the foundation for what follows. Additionally, the following are a few more touches these tools can provide:

>> Analyzing and understanding complex information.

>> Suggesting steps, descriptions, and clarifications for procedures.

>> Proposing titles to ensure clarity.

>> Processing vast amounts of data, extracting relevant information, and transforming it into concise and easy-to-understand instructions.

>> Assessing the target audience and adapting the instructions accordingly, using appropriate vocabulary and sentence structure.

>> Identifying potential ambiguities or inconsistencies in the instructions and suggesting revisions to make them more precise and unambiguous.

>> Generating a hierarchical structure that presents the instructions in a clear, sequential order.

>> Suggesting relevant reference materials, providing additional explanations, or offering alternative approaches.

REMEMBER

While technology can assist with writing, writer intelligence (WI) is still essential: Only human writers can customize instructions and procedures to suit diverse audiences; only human writers have the expertise to understand and accurately document tasks, including the intricate details and subtle nuances that may be overlooked by AI; and only human writers can identify and integrate modifications into documentation, thereby guaranteeing that instructions and procedures remain clear, precise, and current.

Generating Precise Prompts

Here are some suggestions for creating effective AI prompts, with a particular emphasis on instructions and procedures:

>> Identify the reader's level of knowledge.

>> Start with a clear objective that includes the intended outcome or goal.

>> Divide the instructions and procedures into small, manageable steps with ample detail.

>> Use simple language, free of jargon and acronyms.

>> Include necessary background information such as prerequisites.

>> Provide examples or visual aids that can be screenshots, photos, or more.

When writing instructions and procedures it's important to fill out the Kick-Start Brief in Chapter 4 to understand your reader, purpose, key issue, and the questions your readers will need answered. This Brief provides a foundation for you to customize your content.

Working Collaboratively

Writing instructions and procedures is often a collaborative effort. Collaboration is like a mouthwatering dessert recipe. It's not just about the ingredients, but how they can come together to create something amazing. Similarly, when it comes to collaboration, it's not just about the technology, but how the people can come together to create something amazing.

A collaborative team can consist of any combination of the following: leader, delegator, developer, writer, editor, and reviewer(s). It can even include people in marketing and sales, among others. Team members often assume more than one role. For example, you may be a lead writer and delegate sections to other writers. Your role may differ from project to project or within a project. You may write one section then be asked to edit someone else's section.

A strong team involves having strong leadership, putting the right people in place, knowing the role each person will play, creating a list of who does what, generating a production schedule, and setting up a comprehensive review process.

These collaboration tools can assist in creating a cohesive team by facilitating effective communication and seamless coordination:

>> Google Workspace (https://workspace.google.com)

>> Lucidspark (https://lucidspark.com/)

>> Miro (https://miro.com)

>> Monday.com (https://monday.com/)

>> Slack (https://slack.com/ai)

>> Trello (https://trello.com)

Transforming Documents from Sidekicks to Superstars

Imagine a world where instructions and procedures refuse to be mere sidekicks to products. A world where they stand out, captivate attention, and truly engage readers. No more dry, technical jargon. Instead they're sprinkled with humor, anecdotes, and relatable stories. Let your instructions make readers smile and chuckle, so they eagerly flip through pages to discover witty remarks and quirky illustrations. And don't overlook the power of visuals — captivating illustrations, infographics, and diagrams that can transform daunting instructions into an enjoyable visual journey. Embrace this imaginative approach and make instructions a memorable part of the product experience.

Here are some ways to create superstar instructions and procedures:

>> Begin with a relatable story. (You'll see a few later in this chapter).

>> Kick off each step using an action verb such as *press, proceed to, review,* and so forth.

>> Use metaphors and vivid imagery to transport readers into a world where documentation becomes an adventure.

>> Don't just write about the features and functions, bring them to life! Introduce the heroes of your documentation: tools, software, or processes. Give them personalities and quirks that make them memorable.

>> Inject some well-thought-out humor to lighten the mood and keep readers engaged.

- ≫ Break your content into bite-sized chunks of information, accompanied by eye-catching headings and subheadings.

- ≫ Alert readers to safety information and warnings with a whimsical icon or emoji.

- ≫ Use real-life examples, screenshots, or short videos to illustrate step-by-step processes. This hands-on approach will make your readers feel empowered and eager to try it out.

Inspiring Action with a Quick Tip Sheet

A *quick tip sheet* is a concise and easily accessible reference for a particular topic. It can be used to streamline the learning process and ensure that important information is readily available whenever needed. Additionally, it can serve as a quick refresher that saves time and avoids frustration. Whether you're writing tutorials that are self-study guides, do-it-yourself (DIY) guides, operator's manuals, service manuals, maintenance manuals, repair manuals, standard operating procedures (SOPs), or others, creating a quick tip sheet can help make the reader's task seem less daunting.

TIP

Consider the following section as your own quick tip sheet when writing instructions and procedures (whether you're writing on your own or using AI as your assistant):

- ≫ **Know your audience:** Understand who'll be using the product. Consider their level of expertise, familiarity with the subject matter, and any specific needs or challenges they may have. This will help you tailor the language and content to meet their needs.

- ≫ **Structure the contents:** Organize your instructions in a hierarchical structure, presenting them step by step. Begin with a broad overview, then delve into detailed topics and subtopics. If your document exceeds 15 pages, include a table of contents. Consider whether an index would be beneficial by asking yourself if you'd need one if you were the reader. The same holds true for a glossary.

- ≫ **Be descriptive:** Use clear and concise language to explain each step or process and start each step with an action word — a verb — what the reader is to do. Avoid jargon or technical terms that may be confusing. Provide enough detail to ensure that readers understand the instructions, but avoid unnecessary information that may overwhelm them.

>> **Write in the active voice:** This means referring to the doer of the action (either stated or implied) rather than the action being done. For example, write *Press the esc key*, rather than *The esc button should be pressed*. Chapter 8 offers more about active and passive voices.

>> **Include practical examples:** This can help readers understand how to apply the instructions in real-life situations and avoid any confusion.

>> **Use abundant visuals:** Visuals such as diagrams, illustrations, or screenshots can enhance and clarity of the instructions. See Chapter 7 for lots of information about visuals.

>> **Review and revise as needed:** After writing the initial draft of your instruction manual, review it for clarity, accuracy, and completeness. Make sure the instructions are easy to follow and there are no gaps or ambiguities. Check out Chapter 9 to learn more.

>> **Get feedback from a test group:** Once you have a well-documented draft, get feedback from a test group of representative users. Their input can help you identify any areas that may need further clarification or improvement.

REMEMBER

Developing instructions and procedures is an iterative process that often requires refinement even after the document is considered complete and the product has shipped. For example, if the help desk receives ongoing questions about certain instructions, it may be necessary to revise the instructions to improve their clarity and effectiveness.

AI SPOTLIGHT

AI tools such as UserGuiding (https://userguiding.com/) and others can help glean pertinent information that may work well for a tip sheet.

Identifying Questions Readers May Need Answered

In Chapter 4's Kick-Start Brief, you're encouraged to think about the questions readers may have and need answered. Table 13-1 shows some examples that specifically relate to instructions and procedures. Add additional questions that are relevant to your readers, and remove any that aren't.

TABLE 13-1   Questions Readers May Need Answered

Questions	What you may include
How do I _____?	Numbered list of steps
When do I _____?	List of conditions
What is _____?	Definitions and options
What's wrong with _____?	Explanation
Why did _____ happen?	Explanation (and perhaps a warning)
How does _____ work?	Explanation
Which is better?	Table comparing alternatives or list of criteria
Why do _____?	Explanation of purpose, goals, results, and list of benefits
Why not do?	List of costs, risks, and difficulties (even a warning)
How are _____ and _____ related?	Table of comparisons
Why is _____?	Conceptual explanation
Where is _____?	Explanation of where to find things
What does _____ contain?	List of parts
What can I do with _____?	List of uses
What must I do first?	List of prerequisites, if any
How do I recognize _____?	List of characteristics and/or visuals
What happens if _____?	List of results (and perhaps warning)
Is _____ true?	Confirmation or denial
How can I _____?	Measure success and meet goals

Understanding How People Process Information

We're all wired to process information differently. For example, intuitive learners prefer conceptual, abstract information. Sensory learners prefer concrete, factual information. That said, there are so many nuances and variables between each type and how they prefer to learn and that's what this section is about! You must understand how different professional and personality types process information. To learn more, visit the Myers-Briggs Type Indicator (https://www.themyersbriggs.com); although this is the most popular, you can find other options by checking out http://tinyurl.com/yrh4rkzk.

Here are some variables in a nutshell:

>> Academic, scientific, or technical people are *process-oriented* and relate to step-by-step instructions.

>> Business- and legal-minded people are *answer oriented* and want a quick way of accomplishing tasks.

>> Creative people are *visually oriented* and relate to drawings, charts, tables, flowcharts, illustrations, and photographs.

Knowing how the documentation will be used

Although online instructions and procedures have become the norm, they may be used in many different settings: indoors or outdoors, with good or poor lighting, in safe or dangerous settings, in areas with poor or no WiFi, and so on. Therefore, there's still a need for paper documentation in certain environments. Here are some guidelines to ensure that paper documentation can survive actual use:

>> Ensure they can lie flat on a work surface when opened. This helps to determine the binding.

>> Consider whether readers need to hold them and work at the same time. This helps to determine the size.

>> Provide durable covers and pages.

>> Take into account whether the document needs to resist water, oil, dirt, grease, and so on.

Sequencing for impact

The goal of sequencing a document for impact is to effectively communicate your message, engage the reader, and leave a lasting impression. By following the strategies shown in Table 13-2, you can create a document that's well structured, informative, and impactful.

TABLE 13-2　　**Structuring Documents for the Most Impact**

Method	Goal	Useful for . . .
Cause and effect	Show a plausible relationship between a situation and its causes or effects. *Tip:* Base your conclusions on the evidence you gather.	Experiments Accident reports
Chronological	Arrange events in sequential order to stress the relationship of what happened and when. Begin with the first event and continue to the last.	Trip reports Trouble reports Minutes of meetings Work schedules Manufacturing or scientific procedures Test protocols
Comparison	Point out similarities or differences, or advantages and disadvantages. *Tip:* Tables or graphs are great way to present these.	Feasibility studies Research results Trends and forecasts Proposals (some)
Decreasing order of importance	Start with the most important point and end with the least important point.	Reports for decision-makers who make decisions based on most important point.
Division and classification	Divide complex topics into small chunks of information.	Processes Instructions
General to specific	Begin with a general statement then provide facts to support it.	Reports Memos
Increasing order of importance	Start with the least important point and end with the most important point.	Personnel goals Oral presentations
Sequential	Explain something step by step.	Instructions User manuals
Spatial	Describe an item according to the grouping of its physical features. This relates to where things are from east to west, north to south, left to right, top to bottom, interior or exterior.	Activity reports Layout of equipment Building sites Research reports
Specific to general	Start with a specific statement and build to a conclusion. A good tool for persuasive writing.	Analogies Work orders Customer service responses Feasibility reports

Moving On to the Instructional Stuff

When it comes to learning, people have varying preferences (see the previous section), but there's a general inclination towards visuals. Visual instructions tend to be clearer and more memorable. An example of this can be seen in Figure 13-1 with visuals only. In certain cases, instructions can be effective by using a combination of both text and visuals, catering to different types of readers and their information-processing preferences.

TIP

If you're looking to enhance your materials with visuals, Chapter 7 provides valuable insights and guidance on this topic. It includes visual elements such as graphs, diagrams, images, drawings, charts, and other elements that can effectively inform and engage readers.

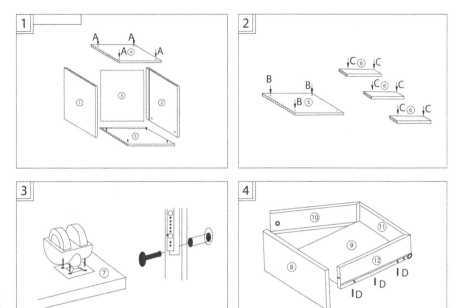

© New Africa/Adobe Stock Photos.

FIGURE 13-1:
Use pictures to show step-by-step assembly.

Identifying style and formatting

Written documentation should be brief, yet detailed enough to be easy to follow. Start each step with an action — a verb — which is what the reader should do. Look at the following figures and notice the difference in language and readability:

>> Figure 13-2, the "Before" document, has lots of unnecessary and confusing numbering. It doesn't say why this process is important, and it's loaded with gobbledygook that's unnecessary.

>> Figure 13-3, the "After" document, is clear and concise. It gets right to the point, gives information at a glance, and provides readers with a good reason to follow the instructions.

JOHNSON SPACE CENTER (MSC) HANDBOOK

101.1 Policy

It is the basic policy of JSC to take all practical steps to avoid loss of life, personal injury or illness, property damage or loss, or environmental loss or damage.

101.2 Goals and Objectives

101.2.1 Goals

a. To achieve a successful and unified occupational safety and health program while accomplishing JSC's objective for excellence in human space flight.

b. Of equal importance, to become a nationally recognized center for excellence for occupational safety and health. This excellence will also be a prominent feature of JSC's environmental protection and emergency preparedness program.

101.2.2 Objectives

JSC shall comply with all applicable regulations and standards, including those of the Occupational Safety and Health Administration (OSHA) and the Environmental Protection Agency (EPA). By exercising flexibility and creativity in striving for excellence, JCS will go beyond the minimum requirements of the regulations and standards to provide the best feasible protection for workers at JSC and the environment within the constraints of available resources.

....

FIGURE 13-2: "Before": Not effective and unclear.

NASA/Public Domain.

AI SPOTLIGHT

Instead of using the opening paragraph you see in Figure 13-3, you can enhance it even more with a storytelling approach, as detailed in Chapter 5. Here's a story-like opening created by AI, drawing readers right in:

> *Once upon a time, in the bustling space station of Nova Prima, there was a young and enthusiastic hypergol technician named Ethan who was known for his unwavering dedication to his craft. Ethan had always been diligent about strictly following all protocols and requirements.*
>
> *However, one fateful day an unexpected twist of events changed Ethan's life. Amidst the chaos of his busy work schedule, Ethan found himself overwhelmed and distracted. In a moment of carelessness, he neglected to follow safety protocols while handling a volatile fuel mixture. It resulted in a catastrophic fuel spill that haunts Ethan to this day.*
>
> *As the station's emergency response team fought to contain the danger, the spilled fuel came into contact with a fallen tool. It caused Juan and Alexi to suffer from caustic battery electrolyte burns on their hands. Both needed to be hospitalized and had residual scarring. Consumed by guilt, Ethan ultimately becoming a beacon of prevention within the department, inspiring others to prioritize safety above all else. Ethan is the driving force behind this document!*

WHY THIS IS IMPORTANT

This could be you. . . a hypergol technician didn't follow requirements and caused a major fuel spill. He was burned. He was using a tool that fell to the floor causing two employees spilled a caustic battery electrolyte on their hands. The batteries hadn't been through qualification testing. There were no requirements to prevent the technicians from working with unqualified batteries. That's why it's important to follow the guidelines in this handbook.

WHO MUST FOLLOW THIS HANDBOOK

This handbook applies to anyone at JCS headquarters or JCS field sites, unless exempted.

If you...	Then you must follow...
Are a federal employee	This handbook unless you work at a site that involves unique military equipment and operations.
Are a JSC contractor	This handbook as called out in your statement of work.
Work at a JSC remote site (such as the White Sands Test Facility) as a civil service employee or contract employee	All chapters that don't exempt you and local requirements that meet the intent of any chapter that exempts you.
Are a non-NASA or non-contract employee	This handbook while on JSC property.

FIGURE 13-3: "After": Clear and concise with key information appearing at a glance.

NASA/Public Domain.

Determining level of details needed

Write instructions with clarity and keen attention to detail. Never assume your reader will read between the lines or read your mind. Consider situations such as these:

>> **Be precise about locations such as top, bottom, left, or right.** Locations are subjective. If you write, *The switch is on the left,* that would depend on which way the reader faces. Instead write, *As you face the front of the room, the switch is on the left.*

>> **Use clockwise and counterclockwise to describe turns.** *Rotate the dial 45° to create a seal* doesn't tell the reader to rotate the dial clockwise or counterclockwise. When you say, *Rotate the dial 45° clockwise to create a seal*, the direction is clear. (It's a good idea to use symbols rather than words when writing technical documents.)

Describing the size of an object accurately

Remembering that accuracy and clarity take center stage, scale the size of an object being described. You can detail the dimensions of the object or scale it against something recognizable. In Figure 13-4, you see a hand scaling the size of a microcontroller chip. If additional context is needed, highlight specific features or any other relevant information that will aid readers in understanding the object's size and dimensions.

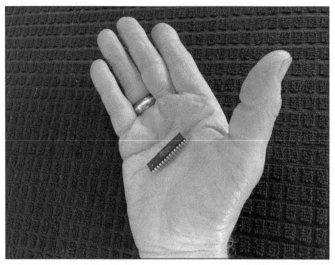

Courtesy of Sheryl Lindsell-Roberts.

FIGURE 13-4: Scaling the size of a microcontroller chip.

Writing equations

Even mathematical equations have a sense of style. When you write an equation as a sentence, give it the form of normal text or break it out on a line of its own:

In a sentence:　You may express $1/x + y$ as one line.

Broken out:　Or you may break it out on a line of its own.

$$\frac{1}{x+y}$$

Equation editors such as iMathEQ (`http://www.imatheq.com/corpsite/index.html`) and Wiris (`https://www.wiris.com/en/mathtype/`) create and format equations easily. They and others offer a wide range of mathematical symbols, functions, and formatting options.

DIFFERENTIATING BETWEEN BENEFITS AND FEATURES

It's important to differentiate benefits and features. Here's a breakdown of the two that include examples of AI's features and benefits.

Features are the specific attributes or characteristics of a product or service. They describe what the product or service does and what sets it apart from the competition. Features are often technical and provide factual information about the product or service. Here are a few of AI's features:

- Natural Language Processing (NLP)
- Artificial Neural Networks
- Machine learning
- Data ingestion

On the other hand, *benefits* describe why those features matter and how they can help the target audience. Benefits focus on the value and advantages that can be gained from using the product or service. They paint a picture of success and explain how the product or service can improve lives. A few of AI's benefits include:

- Increased efficiency
- Enhanced customer service
- Data analysis and insights
- 24/7 availability

To understand the features and benefits of something more tangible, let's look at an electric drill:

Benefits	Features
Makes clean, deep holes	Made of titanium
Drills holes in seconds	UL approved
Is lightweight	Cordless or corded
Wide range of sizes and prices	Variable speed control

Using the step-action table

SHERYL SAYS

I've been writing documentation for what feels like forever, and I've discovered that the step-action table is by far the easiest and most straightforward way to create clear instructions and procedures. Based on feedback from readers, it's the method that people find the most understandable and easiest to follow. Therefore, I present to you . . . the step-action table:

>> Create a title for each process or procedure.

>> Divide the table into two columns: Step and Action.

>> Start each step with a verb, something the user should do.

>> Use clear and understandable language.

>> Include in the Action column any notes, screenshots, results, graphics, if-then tables, or anything to further clarify the action.

>> Keep the language consistent. For example, don't call it a *manual,* then call it a *guide* or *handbook.*

What's wrong with the "Before" table you see in Figure 13-5? The steps don't start with verbs. Steps identified as 3 and 4 aren't steps; they're notes for Step 2. Step 5 combines the action with notes about the action.

Procedure Table (Before)

Step	Action
1	All official records must be signed in black or blue ink.
2	All mistakes must be corrected with a single line through the mistake, initialed, and dated with the correct date.
3	No whiteout or correction tape is allowed.
4	No back dating is allowed.
5	All incidents of lost documentation must be reported to the Documentation Supervisor. For a lost controlled document, the Documentation Supervisor will make a note in the controlled distribution record of the incident and will issue a replacement document. For a lost quality record, a memo will be placed into the appropriate file.

FIGURE 13-5: "Before": The steps don't start with action words and not all the actions listed are steps.

In the "After" table, as seen in Figure 13-6, each step starts with an action word. Also, helpful notes are included.

Procedure Table (After)

Step	Action
1	Sign all official records in black or blue ink.
2	Correct all mistakes with a single line through the mistake, initialed, and dated with the correct date. *Notes:* • You can't use white out or correction tape. • You can't backdate.
3	Report all incidents of lost documentation to the Documentation Supervisor. *Notes:* • For a lost controlled document, the Documentation Supervisor will make a note in the controlled distribution record of the incident and will issue a replacement document. • For a lost quality record, a memo will be placed into the appropriate file.

FIGURE 13-6:
"After": The steps start with action words and additional details are included in the frames.

Highlighting Dangers

Warnings of danger are particularly crucial when it comes to products that might be harmful or cause major consequences if misused. Your documentation should inform readers how to use the product safely and warn of potential dangers as a result of its misuse. This not only helps readers handle the product safely, but may discharge manufacturers from liability.

WARNING

In addition to telling readers what they should do, tell them what they shouldn't do. When performing a certain task may lead to something dangerous (electric shock, erasing a disk drive, toxic fumes, equipment damage, and the like) clearly highlight the danger with the word *Warning* or an icon representing danger. In addition to checking out the icon alongside this paragraph, here's another example:

 Airborne particles of respirable size of crystalline silica are known to cause cancer. They must be buried in approved land disposal facilities in accordance with federal, state, and local regulations.

Testing, Testing

REMEMBER

You won't know whether your documentation is easy to understand until you have it tested extensively. Are the instructions complete? Are they well organized and easy to follow? Are they technically correct? Are examples in sync with the text? Here are some suggestions for testing:

>> Ask a novice user to read the instructions to make sure they're accurate and easily understood. A novice often finds a need for explanations you take for granted. (This is absolutely critical if your users are novices rather than techies.)

>> Ask an expert in the technical area of the subject to review the instructions for accuracy. This is often referred to as a *technical edit*.

>> Test the instructions in typical user environments, if possible.

Determining FAQs

People often try to resolve their issues before reaching out to customer support. That's why online FAQs (frequently asked questions) are good business. They decrease the burden on customer support reps so the reps can focus on more pressing issues. Also, well-done FAQs are a unique opportunity to address the concerns of potential readers, removing obstacles on the path to purchase.

TIP

How do you know what questions to include? Scour your inbox and ticketing system, and quiz customer support reps to learn what callers typically struggle with. Social media channels can be a useful source of customer frustrations as well. Also, learn what doubts people have had before making a purchase. Here are some suggestions on writing FAQs:

>> Write questions from the reader's point of view, as if the reader is talking to a person. Example: *Can I use. . . ?*

>> Start with a *yes* or a *no* answer when you can. Then follow it briefly with the answer. Example: Q. *Do you test on animals?* A. *No. We do not test on animals.*

>> Categorize your topics. They may include Shipping, Updating Your Order, Sizing and Fit, Order Issued, Return Policy, Product FAQS, and more.

>> Make the FAQs searchable so users aren't forced to scroll through irrelevant questions to find what they're looking for.

>> Update your FAQ section whenever you roll out new features, products, or updates — or whenever you learn of the same questions that keep popping up.

>> Refer to other relevant text such as whitepapers or websites.

AI tools such as MonkeyLearn (`https://monkeylearn.com/`) and SentiSum (`https://www.sentisum.com/`) can analyze customer complaints for FAQ inclusion.

If customers are experiencing common problems because of faulty product design or programming snags, work with your company's development team to correct the problem rather than attempting to bury it in FAQs. With social media, these problems can escalate and damage a company's reputation.

Preparing an Instructional Video

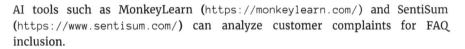

If you ever wanted to learn how to play an instrument, cook a gourmet meal, paint a masterpiece, or even fix a broken appliance, chances are you've turned to a "how-to" video on YouTube (`www.youtube.com`). Yes, YouTube has revolutionized the way we learn. In addition to YouTube, options include Vimeo (`https://vimeo.com/`), Wistia (`https://wistia.com/`), and SpoutVideo (`https://sproutvideo.com/`).

To prepare an instructional video, consider using a *storyboard,* a visual representation that breaks the action into individual frames as you see in Figure 13-7. Limit your video to about five minutes because people have short attention spans. For a complicated or lengthy topic, consider a series of short, chapter-like segments. Chapter 20 includes lots of information about storyboarding options.

Here are things to consider:

>> Determine if your video will be animated or live action.

>> Decide on the length and number of segments.

>> Think in terms of images and tell a story. (Yes, even instructions can be in story form.)

>> Use humor cautiously and only when appropriate.

>> Engage an experienced narrator if the budget allows.

>> If you're including music, make it appropriate for the industry. (Use license-free music or pay for the rights. Otherwise your video will be removed from social media or major streaming services.)

Sample Video Script: How to Fly an XXX Aircraft

Tell	Visuals	Duration
	Aerial view flying over New York City Accompanying music: TBD	10 seconds
Welcome to the XXX Aircraft. This exciting journey will take you. . . (Objectives and outcomes)	TBD	2 minutes
Before we begin with your journey, let's examine some of what. . . . (Describe in detail what learners will see.)	Show the cockpit	10 minutes
Now sit back and enjoy the ride.	TBD	12 minutes

FIGURE 13-7: Sample video script storyboard.

AI SPOTLIGHT

AI tools offer a range of features to enhance the entire process of producing videos. Here are some popular AI tools to assist with streaming productions:

- **DeepBrai** for general-purpose video productions: `https://www.deepbrain.io/features/training-video`

- **Descript** for video editing: `https://www.descript.com`

- **HourOne** for general-purpose video productions: `https://hourone.ai/lnd/ai-training-video-generator-v2`

- **Jasper** for script writing: `https://www.jasper.ai`

- **Synthesia** for generating avatars: `https://www.synthesia.io`

- **Visla** for turning a script into a video: `https://www.visla.us/`

- **Wave** for general-purpose video productions: `https://wave.video/`

Chapter **14**

Articles: From Headline to Byline

When you see your name in a published article, it's a little boost of awesomeness! Not only does it make you look credible, but it also helps you build your own personal brand. Plus, it's like having a VIP pass to all kinds of opportunities. And guess what? Your article becomes a magnet for readers, driving traffic and engagement to your website and social media sites.

Using AI as Your Assistant for Writing Articles

AI SPOTLIGHT

ChatGPT (https://chat.openai.com), Copy AI (https://www.copy.ai/), Grammarly (https://grammarly.com), Rytr (https://rytr.me/), Jasper (https://www.jasper.ai/), You.com (https://you.com/), and others can aid in writing articles for a plethora of topics. Here's what many of these tools offer:

>> **Time-saving:** Generate an article in minutes. This is especially useful if you need to produce a large amount of content in a short timeframe.

>> **Efficiency:** Create content quickly. If you're experiencing writer's block, AI gets you started.

>> **Variety:** Produce different types of articles. This versatility allows you to tailor the generated content to your specific needs and target audience.

>> **Titles and headlines:** Come up with jazzy titles and headlines that grab attention.

>> **Consistency:** Maintain consistency in writing style, tone, and formatting across multiple articles. This can be particularly useful if you have a specific brand, voice, or style that you want to maintain throughout your content.

>> **Support for research:** Gather information and create well-researched articles on a wide range of topics. Get relevant links, results, solid conclusions, references, and bibliographies.

>> **SEO assistance:** Improve your content marketing strategies, such as SEO analysis and performance tracking.

REMEMBER

When writing articles, it's important to fill out the Kick-Start Brief in Chapter 4 to understand your reader, purpose, key issue, and the questions your reader will need answered. This Brief provides a foundation for you to customize your content to precisely meet the needs of your reader.

Generating Precise Prompts

AI SPOTLIGHT

Here are some suggestions for creating effective AI prompts, with a particular emphasis on articles:

>> Define the target audience and level of complexity.

>> Outline the structure to include introduction, main points, arguments, and conclusions.

>> Specify the tone and style such as formal, informal, conversational, academic, and so forth.

>> Include key points or information.

>> Provide specific sources or research materials, if you have any.

>> Request reference material, if needed.

>> Encourage creativity and uniqueness for engaging content.

Writing Academic or Non-Academic Articles

Whether your writing is academic or non-academic, there's a whole array of article types out there waiting for you to try. Each one has its own unique charm and purpose:

>> **Perspective/Opinion articles:** They express the author's viewpoint and are often based on the author's expertise and experience in the field. They may provide critical analysis, propose new ideas, or offer insights into current issues or debates.

>> **Research articles:** They present the findings of original research studies and follow a specific format, including sections such as introduction, methods, results, and discussion. This type of article may undergo rigorous *peer review* (where experts in the field review the article for quality and originality).

>> **Review articles:** This may be a comprehensive summary or discussion of research on a specific topic. The article may be analyzed and synthesized, often providing a new perspective or conclusion. They're valuable for researchers to identify gaps in knowledge and provide a broader understanding of a subject area.

>> **Case studies:** These are commonly used in business, medicine, psychology, and such to explore real-life situations. They often involve in-depth examination and interpretation of data or evidence.

>> **News articles:** They're often written by journalists who report on current events, developments, or issues. They should provide factual information.

>> **Editorials:** There are two types of editorials: Opinion pieces submitted by readers of a publication, and those written by the editorial board or invited experts of a publication. They express the publication's stance on a particular issue, provide commentary, or highlight important topics or events.

So go ahead, write that killer article and shine. And remember to use your writer intelligence (WI) to check for anything that doesn't belong. After all, this has your byline on it!

Unraveling Hypothetical Threads

AI SPOTLIGHT

Here's an example of using AI to help with an article. Gerhard works for a land management improvement company and was asked to write an article to appear in a journal on the role trees play in the environment. He didn't know where to start because it's such a broad topic. So he turned to You.com. Figure 14-1 shows the results of Gerhard's request for the chatbot to list six topics about trees. Figure 14-2 shows what the chatbot spewed out when Gerhard clicked the button on the bottom left to learn of the benefits of trees. Needing some visuals, Gerhard clicked on the button marked images across the top. See what popped up in Figure 14-3.

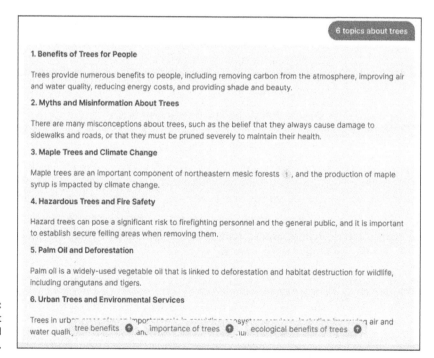

FIGURE 14-1: Topics about trees generated from a chatbot.

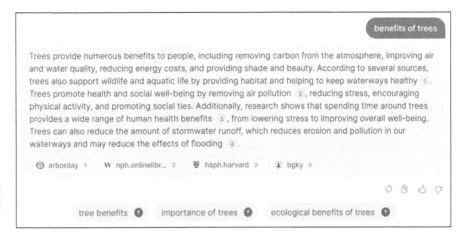

FIGURE 14-2:
Then the chatbot spewed out the benefits of trees.

FIGURE 14-3:
Now for some visuals.

You.com

Delving Into the Perks of Writing an Article

There are several thousand technical, business, and academic, scientific, and trade publications that professionals use to tell peers and institutions about their work. Technical people write technical articles for other technical professionals. Here are several benefits of getting a technical article published:

>> Personal satisfaction.

>> Professional prestige.

>> Increase in your status as a technical expert.

>> Good publicity for you and your organization.

>> Contribute to a pool or technical knowledge to help others.

You don't need to write like Shakespeare. Publications have editors who polish manuscripts to make them more readable and more interesting. However, your article should be well thought out, well organized, and neatly presented.

WARNING

If your topic is revolutionary or very controversial, you may face some obstacles in getting your article published. Editors aren't necessarily crusaders. Crusaders in the publishing world either receive journalism awards or find their golden futures behind them. But don't be discouraged. This just adds an extra challenge.

The value of a byline

A *byline* is where the name of the writer appears. Writing an article under your byline is one of the most effective ways to promote yourself or your business. Don't be intimidated by the prospect of getting published. Editors are always on the lookout for good material and competent writers. Not all publications pay for articles or offer honoraria. The payoff is gaining new customers/clients or driving traffic to your website or blog, gaining prominence, and adding a credible item to your resume. Here's some of the mileage you can get from your article:

>> **Increased visibility and credibility:** You and your article become visible to a wider audience, which can enhance your credibility and increase your visibility within your field. This can be particularly beneficial for academics, researchers, and professionals.

>> **Professional development:** This can be a significant milestone in your professional development. It can provide a sense of accomplishment and contribute to your overall growth as a researcher or professional.

>> **Speaking and networking opportunities:** You may receive invitations to speak at conferences or be asked to collaborate on future projects where you can network with others in your field.

>> **Career advancement:** You're demonstrating your knowledge and expertise in your field, which can contribute to career advancement opportunities. It can also signal to potential employers that you're committed to your profession and are actively engaged in research and development.

Where your article may appear

When you write an article, it should appear in a publication or platform relevant to your target audience. Here are some common places where articles appear:

>> **Scientific journals:** If you are writing a research article in a scientific field, it should ideally be submitted to a reputable peer-reviewed scientific journal.

These journals specialize in publishing original research and provide a platform for researchers to communicate their findings to the scientific community.

>> **Professional publications:** Depending on your field or industry, there may be professional publications or trade magazines that cater to professionals in that sector. These publications often accept articles that provide insights, analysis, or best practices relevant to their audience.

>> **News outlets:** If you are writing a news article or an opinion piece on a current event or topic, you can submit it to newspapers, magazines, or online news outlets. These platforms reach a wider audience and can help you share your perspective or analysis on a particular issue.

>> **Blogs and websites:** Many websites and blogs accept guest posts or feature articles on specific topics. If you have expertise in a particular area or want to share your knowledge or experiences, you can reach out to relevant blogs or websites and inquire about guest posting opportunities.

>> **Academic conferences:** In academic settings, you can present your research findings or ideas at conferences and submit your article as part of the conference proceedings. This allows you to share your work with peers and receive feedback from experts in your field. Check Chapter 16 to get information on preparing an abstract, which should accompany your article.

>> **Online platforms and forums:** Online platforms such as Medium (`https://medium.com/`), LinkedIn (`https://www.linkedin.com`), or specialized forums provide opportunities to publish articles on a wide range of topics. These platforms are accessible to a large audience and allow you to engage with readers through comments and discussions.

Note that open-access publications have the potential to shake things up in academia by making research freely available to everyone. This means that more people can access and benefit from the latest findings, which can lead to increased collaboration and knowledge sharing among researchers worldwide. It's like opening the doors to a whole new level of academic exploration and discovery!

Reading the Masthead

One of the first questions writers ask about submitting to a publication is "Where do I send my submission?" The *masthead* — the who's who of the publication — is essentially a one-page informational overview of a publication and everyone involved in its creation. You can typically find it in the front pages, often on one of the initial pages or on the table of contents page. It's useful for writers because it has information about the magazine, such as the names of the editorial team, the publisher, and other contributors, along with email addresses.

Deciphering the masthead can be a challenge. With all those names and titles to choose from, who is the right person to contact? What do all those people do? Pay attention to the specific sections or topics each editor is responsible for, as this will help you determine who to contact for your article submission. If you can't figure out the person you need to connect with, contact the publication.

Following the Publisher's Guidelines

Publishers are bombarded with article submissions but only select a few. You know what publications people in your profession read, so contact these publications and ask for guidelines. Here are some basic guidelines to help tip the scales in your favor:

>> Read several issues of your target publications to become familiar with the style and types of articles they publish.

>> Write powerful headlines that call out key information throughout the article (Remember that AI can be a great help with generating headlines.).

>> Use callout boxes to bring attention to a critical piece of information.

>> Ensure you have permission to use any copyrighted material and that you've cited all sources used in your research.

>> Use proper grammar, punctuation, and spelling.

>> Limit your biographical information to six lines or less.

If you're submitting to a professional journal there may be a peer review process. Be prepared to make revisions based on the feedback received during the peer review process.

TIP

Unless you get paid a substantial fee, retain the rights to your article. If you submit the same article to several journals, consider making some changes — modify the title and 25 percent of the text.

Composing a Meaningful and Compelling Title

AI SPOTLIGHT

Think about who your audience is and what might interest them. Get to know them by using the Kick-Start Brief in Chapter 4. Use language and phrasing that would appeal to them and address their needs. There are loads of AI title generators. Search for "AI title generators" and take your pick. Here are a few things to consider:

>> Use relevant keywords so readers can find your article through search engines.

>> Create attention-grabbing headlines with catchy phrases, intriguing questions, or interesting statistics. (However, avoid clickbait, which is a title that's misleading.)

>> Make your title reflect the content of your article so readers have an idea of what to expect.

>> Try out different titles and run them by people whose opinions you trust.

TIP

Here are some ideas for effective titles:

>> **Use numbers:** A Dozen Ways to . . .

>> **Include the word "guide":** Expert's Guide to . . .

>> **Include a *Who? What? When? Where? Why? How?* question:** Why It's Wise to . . .

>> **Tug at emotions:** Jaw-Dropping . . .

>> **Promise a major change:** Forget . . . and Try . . .

>> **Include savvy:** Go-Getter's Guide to . . .

>> **Add shock value:** The Alarming Truth Behind . . .

>> **Arouse curiosity:** Little-Known Facts About . . .

>> **Use negatives:** Don't Even Think About . . .

AI SPOTLIGHT

With the right prompts (more about that in Chapter 23), AI can use its magic to understand the content and generate relevant and captivating titles. Try it — not only for articles but for any document where you need to generate titles and headlines. I used AI to generate several titles and headlines in this book.

Composing a Persuasive Query Letter

A query (cover) letter is the first impression an editor gets of your writing style and thought process. It's not necessary to send the article itself, unless you choose to or it's required. However, you want to pique the editor's interest enough to make them request it. Here are some tips for crafting a successful query letter, as illustrated in Figure 14-4 (which resulted in a positive response from the editor and publication of a three-page article):

>> **Be concise:** Ideally, limit it to one page. Editors receive numerous submissions, so respect their time.

>> **Showcase your writing style:** It should be engaging, well-crafted, and reflective of your expertise in the subject matter.

>> **Capture the editor's interest:** Start with a hook to entice the editor to continue reading and consider your submission. Be sure to address the editor by name to demonstrate your professionalism (you'll find their name listed in the masthead).

>> **Generate a working title:** This gives the editor an idea of what to expect and helps them envision how it would fit within their publication.

>> **Highlight your expertise:** Briefly mention your qualifications, experience, or any relevant credentials that establish you as a writer on the topic. This will assure the editor of your expertise and increase the chances of them considering your article.

>> **Provide a concise summary:** Outline the key points, unique angles, or fresh insights it will offer. This will give the editor a clear understanding of what the article entails.

>> **Mention available resources:** If applicable, mention any resources, research, or photographs you have that can enhance the article. This demonstrates your preparedness and can help convince the editor to request the article.

>> **Express your enthusiasm:** Convey your passion and enthusiasm for the subject matter and the opportunity to contribute to their publication. Editors appreciate writers who are genuinely excited about their work.

>> **Proofread and polish:** Meticulously proofread it for any errors or typos. Ensure that the letter is well structured and professional in tone.

> Dear [Editor's Name]:
>
> A favorite conversation among boaters is always boat names. Boat owners like to share how or why they named their boats. I thought [publication] would be an ideal place for a boat owner to do just that.
>
> **Working Title: "What's in a Name: It's Absolutely Lunar Sea"**
>
> As an enthusiastic sailor for more than 20 years, I sent out questionnaires to boat owners and have accumulated dozens of funny and heartwarming stories. In addition, many boat owners sent high-quality photographs of their boats showing the names. This article would make wonderful reading for boaters in your audience. I also have pictures of several of the boats with permission of the captains (owners).
>
> <u>Next step</u>
>
> Please let me know if you're interested in reading my 1500-word manuscript with a view toward publishing it. I look forward to hearing from you and sharing these wonderful stories with your readers.
>
> Sincerely,

FIGURE 14-4: Query letter example.

TIP

If your query letter doesn't get a response within a month, give the editor a call or send an email. They're probably swamped with submissions and may not have read yours. By calling, you may help your query rise to the top. If one publisher rejects you, send your submission to others. A rejection isn't necessarily a rejection of your topic or your writing. It may merely mean that the topic isn't appropriate for that particular publication or the publication doesn't have that topic scheduled on its calendar.

KNOWING THE DIFFERENCE BETWEEN AN ARTICLE AND A RESEARCH PAPER

Research articles are typically published scholarly, peer-reviewed journals. The articles often contain headings such as Literature Review, Method, Results, Discussion, and Conclusion. Research papers are different because they:

- Are based on original research and present the findings of a study.
- Represent the findings of a study, while articles can reflect opinion, news, research, reviews, instruction, or any other focus.

(continued)

(continued)

- Involve collecting and analyzing raw data and conducting an original investigation.

- Are based on the analysis and interpretation of this data.

- Are longer than articles (usually between 5 and 20 pages).

When you publish in a research journal you gain visibility among other researchers in your field and those outside of your immediate circle of contacts and colleagues. You add information to the public discussion of contemporary topics beyond academic circles. And you preserve your work in the permanent records of research in the field.

The following AI tools can assist with research papers: Scholarcy (https://www.scholarcy.com/), Jenni AI (https://jenni.ai/), Paperpal (https://paperpal.com/), Grammarly (https://app.grammarly.com/), and QuillBot (https://quillbot.com/).

Use caution when using AI tools to conduct critical research tasks such as data analysis or hypothesis formation, While AI can aid in these processes, it can't replace the creativity, intuition, and critical-thinking skills essential in scientific research. Over-reliance on AI may limit diverse perspectives and hinder scientific discoveries, as well as overlook important biological factors. Therefore, it's important to view AI as a tool to complement, rather than replace, critical thinking in research endeavors.

Understanding the Blogosphere

Blogs are a great way to build a following, share your expertise, and establish an online presence that can help increase your bottom line. In social networks, influencers are people who've established credibility, authority, and have a dedicated following in a specific industry or niche. They have the power to influence the opinions, behaviors, and purchasing decisions of their readers. The terms blogger and influencer (although they're slightly different) are often used interchangeably. Although having a blog doesn't necessarily qualify you as an influencer, you increase your chances of becoming one through your writing by developing a niche and creating high-quality content.

REMEMBER

The lines between blogs and articles have become increasingly blurred in recent years, but there are nuanced differences between the two. Here's some of what sets a blog apart from an article:

>> **Point view:** A blog post is often written in the first person using *I* or *we*, as if the blogger is having a conversation with readers.

- **Where it's published:** Blogs are published on individual blog sites. Articles may be published on websites as well, but they often appear in external publications such as newspapers, magazines, and periodicals.

- **Tone:** Blogs are written in a more casual tone, allowing bloggers to connect with readers on a more personal level.

- **Personal opinion:** Blogs often describe things from a personal perspective, rather than on information and statistics.

- **Length:** The correct blog length is a hotly debated SEO topic. In general, they range from 300 to 1,000 words. Blogs are meant to provide quick information and engage readers with easily digestible content.

- **SEO keyword optimization:** Blogs are built around SEO keywords and the writing is often changed to incorporate keywords (find out more in Chapter 12).

- **Updates:** Bloggers often publish new content regularly (daily, weekly, monthly, or as needed) to keep readers engaged and encourage return visits.

The big advantage of a blog is that it helps readers connect with a person and/or business without drowning them in technical details. Here are some tips for writing a successful blog:

- Use catchy titles and headlines for each blog entry.

- Include lots of bullets for readers who skim.

- Shake things up now and then by changing your format, using a different font, and so on.

AI SPOTLIGHT

AI writing tools, such as GrowthBar's AI Blog Idea Generator (`https://www.growthbarseo.com/ai-blog-idea-generator/`) and Ahrefs Content Idea Generator (`https://ahrefs.com/writing-tools/content-idea-generator`) can help you to generate blog ideas. These tools can help overcome writer's block and generate content ideas quickly and efficiently so your blog can shine like a beacon.

» Generating precise prompts

» Placing important details
strategically

» Presenting reports in a systematic
order

» Reporting in an informal manner

Chapter **15**

Reports: "Elementary, My Dear Writer"

I n the realm of business communication, the iconic phrase "Elementary, my dear Watson" (Figure 15-1) takes on a new meaning as it pertains to writing business reports. Just as Sherlock Holmes — the famous fictional detective — deduces complex mysteries through keen observation and logical reasoning, crafting effective business reports requires a similar approach. By gathering and analyzing data, identifying key patterns and insights, and presenting them in a clear and concise manner, you can unveil the hidden truths within a business context. However, in the case of a business report, the drama might come from the quarterly budget rather than a smoking gun.

And like Sherlock guiding his assistant Dr. Watson through the intricate web of clues, you can shepherd your reader through the report, providing them with a comprehensive understanding of the subject matter and strategically guiding them to the findings or conclusions. Therefore, in the realm of business reports, the mantra becomes "Elementary, my dear writer." The art of deducing and presenting information becomes a crucial skill in effectively communicating business insights.

FIGURE 15-1:
In the case of business reports, it's "Elementary, my dear writer."

Using AI as Your Assistant for Writing Reports

AI SPOTLIGHT

Much like Sherlock's ability to unravel mysteries through astute observation and logical reasoning, AI has the capability to analyze vast amounts of data and extract meaningful insights. With the assistance of AI, you can generate reports at all levels of understanding, improve readability and clarity, perform data analyses, and assist in project management. Check out `https://www.capterra.com/` to learn of several applicable report-writing tools.

In Figures 15-2 and 15-3, I asked You.com to write two paragraphs for a report about soccer — one with advanced vocabulary words and the other with elementary vocabulary words. Notice the difference. (Find out more about different levels of reading comprehension in Chapter 9.)

REMEMBER

When writing reports, it's important to fill out the Kick-Start Brief in Chapter 4 to understand your reader, purpose, key issue, and the questions your reader will need answered. This Brief provides a foundation for you to customize your content to precisely meet the needs of your reader.

FIGURE 15-2:
AI-generated
paragraph using
advanced
vocabulary
words.

paragraph on soccer using advanced vocabulary words

Soccer, a sport revered for its captivating display of skill, agility, and strategic finesse, stands as a testament to the epitome of athletic prowess. The resplendent dance of the spherical orb, deftly maneuvered by the players, evokes a symphony of rhythmic precision on the undulating pitch. The players, adorned in their vibrant kits, exude an aura of determination as they engage in a symposium of tactical brilliance, employing astute passes and calculated runs to confound their adversaries. The fluidity of their movements, akin to a ballet performance, showcases their dexterity and acumen, leaving spectators in awe of their artistry. The cacophony of cheers reverberates through the stadium, as the players, undeterred by the cacophony, remain steadfast in their pursuit of victory, their indomitable spirit manifesting in every flick, feint, and thunderous strike. Indeed, in the realm of sports, soccer reigns supreme, an exquisite amalgamation of athleticism, strategy, and unyielding passion.

FIGURE 15-2:
AI-generated
paragraph using
advanced
vocabulary
words.

paragraph on soccer using elementary vocabulary words

Soccer is a fun and exciting game that people all around the world love to play. It's played with a round ball on a big field, and the aim is to kick the ball into the opponent's net to score a goal. The players run, pass, and kick the ball to try and outsmart the other team. They wear special jerseys and have teammates who help them during the game. Soccer matches can get really loud, with fans cheering and clapping for their favorite players. It's a great way to stay active, make friends, and have a good time!

FIGURE 15-3:
AI-generated
paragraph using
simplified
vocabulary
words.

Generating Precise Prompts

AI SPOTLIGHT

Here are some suggestions for creating effective AI prompts, with a particular emphasis on reports:

>> Define the purpose and call to action.

>> Specify the audience.

>> Identify the key elements such as abstract, executive summary, methodology, findings, analysis, recommendations, and conclusion.

>> Provide relevant data or information that may include data points, statistics, or research findings.

>> Specify the format and style such as formal, informal, and citation style.

>> Set the structure to include headings and subheadings.

>> Encourage analysis and insights beyond mere facts.

>> Pinpoint any visual elements.

Positioning for Maximum Impact

In the story "The Adventure of Silver Blaze," Sherlock asks, "Is there something specific you want to emphasize and bring to my attention?" This is a question you should ask yourself. By placing important details strategically, you can engage your reader and guide their attention towards what will have the biggest impact. Where you position these details depends on the kind of reaction you expect from your reader. Your Kick-Start Brief (see Chapter 4) should ask if your reader's reaction will be positive, neutral, or negative. This will determine how to position the information.

Delivering positive or neutral news

When your report is delivering good or neutral news, use the BLUF method — Bottom Line Up Front. Don't make your reader wade through page after to page to find the key piece of information they're looking for . . . the bottom line. After all, this isn't a joke where you have to put the punch line at the end.

Bluffing is a tactic Holmes occasionally uses to deceive his opponents, gather information, and manipulate a situation to gain an advantage. Although you're not trying to deceive, you can use bluffing to gain an advantage. Here's how: For a report that delivers positive or neutral news, put the key issue at the beginning of the report. This expedites clarity and efficiency, increases engagement and interest, reduces anxiety, and aids in useful decision making. (You'll learn about bluffing for negative news in the next section.)

TIP

Use headlines to your advantage to call out the good or neutral news. Here are some examples:

Conclusion: *Record-breaking quarter — Exceeding expectations*

Findings: *Survey reports 25% increase in customer satisfaction*

Recommendations: *We will need to reassess in six months*

Articulating negative news

All leaders — whether they lead nations, corporations, departments, or projects — must at some time deliver less-than-rosy news. Yes, it's uncomfortable. Yes, you may get pushback. What matters most is the way you handle yourself and the situation. You must own it. Provide your reader with insight, understanding, transparency, responsibility, accountability, and empathy. Let them know you're in control of the situation.

Here are some things to consider:

>> **Don't lead with the bad news.** Soften the impact by opening with a buffer such as background information. This can help prepare the reader for the upcoming news with an understanding of "why."

>> **Be clear and concise.** Use simple and direct language without ambiguity or unnecessary harshness.

>> **Offer a clear and logical explanation.** This can help the reader understand the reasons that resulted in the bad news.

>> **Show empathy.** Let them know that you understand the impact and that you're sensitive to what they're feeling.

>> **Offer solutions or alternatives.** Whenever possible, give potential solutions or alternatives to mitigate the negative impact. This shows that you're proactive and committed to finding a way forward.

>> **Maintain professionalism and empathy.** Avoid personal attacks or derogatory language. Focus on issues, not on people.

To articulate negative news, cushion the key issue between a positive opening and closing. You don't want to hit them between the eyes with bad news until you've had a chance to build up to it and explain why. Depending on the situation, you can either use the bad-news sandwich approach or a direct approach.

Bad-news sandwich

If you're not familiar with the sandwich approach, it goes like this:

1. **Start with something soft (like a slice of bread).** This means starting with genuine empathy, a compliment, or positive statement about the issue.

2. **Then pack it with meat.** You can use transitional words such as *regrettably*, *unfortunately*, or *however*. . . to address the meat of the matter.

3. **Close with the soft slice of bread.** This offers something positive or encouraging.

AI SPOTLIGHT

AI can be a valuable tool in shaping the tone of a message, especially when delivering bad news. It can assist in creating content in the desired tone of voice, ensuring consistency, and providing guidance on preparing for the conversation, choosing the right setting and time, reducing misunderstandings, and expressing empathy. By leveraging AI you can enhance the effectiveness and impact of your message with a tone appropriate for the reader.

CASE STUDY OF A BAD-NEWS SANDWICH

Sofia was the president of a privately owned manufacturing company. The company was experiencing an ongoing drop in revenue and was seeking ways to cut expenses. After throwing around a number of ideas, the management team decided they could save money by delivering paychecks twice a month rather than every week.

They knew this message wouldn't be well received because there would be times employees would need to wait nearly three weeks for a paycheck. Many of them are factory workers, and are living from paycheck to paycheck. To help with budget planning, the company was going to offer an Employee Assistance Program (EAP). Employees are geographically disbursed, so Sofia had to no choice but to deliver the report via email.

Sofia contacted me for help in drafting this difficult message. I asked her what other options had been on the table. She said: *Cutting the 401K match . . . asking employees to contribute more to their healthcare premiums . . . eliminating year-end bonuses . . . cutting jobs.* The fact that these options were taken off the table was good news, so we started with them.

Here's the finished email that Sofia sent:

Subject: Positive resolution to rumors about financial difficulties

Opening paragraph (first slice of bread):

Many of you have heard about the financial uncertainties of this company. Well, the management team has come up with a solution you should all be happy to hear. Rather than cutting your 401K match . . . Rather than asking you to contribute more to your healthcare costs . . . Rather than eliminating year-end bonuses . . . Rather than cutting jobs . . . we've found a way to keep all your jobs and benefits intact.

Sofia could almost hear each employee breathing a sigh of relief. Whatever followed couldn't be as bad as what they had anticipated.

Middle paragraph (meat):

Fortunately, we found a better option for everyone that can solve many of our financial difficulties. We'll be delivering paychecks twice a month instead of every week. And we have a solution for those of you who may need assistance with budgeting.

Compared to what might have been, that was palatable news.

Direct approach

Once the rumor mill has started, deliver your message ASAP. Define what happened without blaming anyone or anything. You'll earn points by showing you're in charge and are being forthright. Here are some tips:

» **Be honest and authentic.** Don't skirt the topic, don't give false hope, don't sugarcoat, and don't overly explain. Be brief, straightforward, and to the point. Keep strategies for moving forward in the forefront.

» **Get to the point.** Don't drown your audience in a sea of endless numbers and data points. Present the news in terms of critical takeaways, not data dumps.

» **Give a point of contact.** If appropriate, give readers someone they can contact for more information.

REMEMBER

Regardless of which approach you use, focus on the future. Describe your plans, what measures will be taken to resolve the situation, or how this may be avoided in the future. End on a positive note giving your audience some hope and reassurance.

Considering how the report will be routed

When you write a report, even if the report is delivered via email, take into consideration how the report will be routed. The routing should impact your tone, visual design, and what to include. The different routes might be:

» **Downward from managers to support staff.** This can be managers informing the team of an impending decision.

- >> **Peer to peer.** May be used for a team to coordinate activities.

- >> **One person or committee to management.** Managers can't participate in all department activities, so this gives them insight into what was discussed, decisions that were reached, and so forth.

- >> **Inside the organization to outside the organization.** This is a report that may be distributed to customers, stockholders, or other people who are not part of the organization.

Sequencing Formal Reports from Top to Bottom

Sherlock meticulously unravels cases from top to bottom, employing his keen observation skills and deductive reasoning to connect the smallest details and reveal the truth. You too should approach business reports with top to bottom precision, logical reasoning, and a systematic presentation of information in a clear and concise manner. A formal report serves as the culmination of a project, often involving a team who've dedicated weeks, months, or even longer to its completion.

Formal reports can cover a wide range of topics, such as developments in a field, feasibility studies for new products, service expansions, periodic reviews, and more. Despite the term "formal," these reports aren't inherently stuffy, but they are typically divided into three main parts: front matter, body, and back matter. Many reports start with a transmittal letter, which isn't considered one of the three parts.

Transmittal Letter

The letter of transmittal, as the one shown in Figure 15-4, sits on top of the report giving it a more professional look. It should identify what and why you're sending the report. If you send the report via email, the letter of transmittal can work as the body of the email with the report attached. If you're sending hard copy, place the letter on top of the cover page. (Check out Chapter 19 for more on writing letters.)

FIGURE 15-4:
Letter of
transmittal
for email or
hard-copy
reports.

Subject: Surpassing your goal of 25% growth

We're very excited about the prospect of helping A&D Engineering surpass its aggressive business goal of 25% growth in revenue over the next two years. We're convinced that the implementation of our open architecture data system will be a major factor in yielding that growth.

Here's our solution

The attached proposal addresses in detail the specific technical, implementation, and investment requirements you provided at our last meeting.

Let's move forward

We've successfully helped companies such as yours meet ambitious goals, and we're anxious to help you meet yours. We thank you for this opportunity and will call you next Tuesday to discuss our next step.

Sincerely,

Part 1: Front Matter

Number the pages in the front matter with lower case Roman numerals. Front matter may include:

- **Title page:** This is a non-numbered page that identifies the name of the report, the completion date, name of the preparer, and to whom it's presented.

- **Abstract:** A condensed version of the report. (See Chapter 16 for details.)

- **Table of contents (TOC):** This can either be a list of section titles or titles broken into subheads. See the beginning of this book for the difference between the two.

- **List of figures and tables:** Next comes the lists of figures and tables. Take a look at Figure 15-5 to see a sample.

- **Preface:** This is optional and the decision is generated by the corporate style. You may include a preface to announce the purpose, background, scope, and acknowledge people who participated in the project or helped with the report.

- **List of abbreviations and symbols:** This is the final entry in the front matter and lists all the abbreviations and symbols (what else were you expecting?) that readers may not be familiar with.

FIGURE 15-5:
Lists of figures and tables.

AI SPOTLIGHT

Here are some AI tools to generate specific portions of the front matter:

- TOC generator: https://nichesss.com/tools/table-of-contents-generator-J3bvn72gU

- Abstract generators: https://x.writefull.com/abstract-generator or https://www.editpad.org/tool/abstract-generator

- List of abbreviations: https://www.scribbr.com/dissertation/list-of-abbreviations/

Part 2: Body

This is the meat and potatoes of the report. Number these pages with Arabic numerals. The body may include:

- **Executive summary:** This serves the important purpose of giving key information at a glance for people who don't read the entire report. Just as you can't write a book report before you read the book, you can't write the executive summary until you've written the report. (Check out Chapter 16 for a full discussion of executive summaries.)

- **Introduction:** This is a thesis statement that tells the reader the importance or significance of the research or problem to be reported, the purpose of the report, issues to be discussed, limitations of the report, and assumptions made. This too should be written after the report has been completed so you include all relevant material.

REMEMBER

If you're delivering good or neutral news, start the introduction with a relevant story.

- **Text:** This is where you elaborate and include methodology. The text should be clear, concise, and written at the level of your readers. Be sure to include strong headlines that give information at a glance in addition to charts and tables, where needed. Use real-world examples, anecdotes, and storytelling to bring your report to life, as you can discover in Chapter 5.

- **Conclusions or recommendations:** This section gives you the opportunity to summarize or review your report's main ideas and recommendations, and suggest actions to be taken in response to the findings. If this is good or neutral news, put it right up front rather than waiting until the end.

- **References:** This is where you give details about sources so readers have a good understanding of what you've used and how to find the source themselves. This differs from a bibliography that lists all the sources you used to generate your ideas (see the next section).

AI SPOTLIGHT

Here are some AI tools to generate specific portions of the body:

- **Executive summary:** https://quillbot.com/summarize or https://www.longshot.ai/templates/executive-summary-generator

- **Introduction generator:** https://koala.sh/tools/free-ai-blog-post-introduction-generator

- **Text:** https://www.grammarly.com/ or https://www.jasper.ai/

Part 3: Back Matter

This is the final section that included additional information. It can provide details that can't easily fit in the body of the report such as resumes, charts and tables, and analytical reports. Number these pages with Arabic numerals. The back matter may include:

- **Bibliography:** This is an alphabetic listing of all sources you consulted.

- **Appendixes:** Use these judiciously to avoid overloading reports. When one is necessary, this may consist of figures, tables, maps, photographs, raw data, computer programs, resumes, interview questions, sample questionnaires, and anything else that's necessary to supplement the body of the report.

- **Glossary:** This is appropriate when the words, phrases, and abbreviations used within the content relate to a specific discipline or technology area. Keep in mind the route this report will travel, as mentioned earlier in this chapter.

- **Index:** When you bookend your report with a table of contents and an index, readers will have no excuse for not finding the information they're after.

Here are some AI tools to generate specific portions of the back matter:

- **Bibliography:** https://www.taskade.com/generate/research/bibliography or https://zbib.org/

- **Appendixes:** https://perrla.zendesk.com

- **Glossary:** https://nichesss.com/tools/glossary-generator-9qBrcEYWc or https://www.jamesmurdo.com/glossary_generator.html

- **Index:** https://thedocumentindexgeneratorweb.azurewebsites.net/, https://ai-solutions.com/_help_Files/terrain_index_generator.htm, or https://www.scribendi.ai/cindex/

REMEMBER

Proofread and edit fiercely. Use the tools mentioned in Chapter 9 but always remember that writer intelligence (WI) is mandatory. For example, the transposition of a single digit or an incorrect date can have catastrophic results.

Writing Informal Reports

Sherlock, the master of deduction, writes reports with the precision of a surgeon and the flair of a Shakespearean actor. Armed with a pen as sharp as his wit, he weaves words into intricate tapestries of logic, leaving no detail unexplored and no pun un-punned. As a writer, you require meticulous attention to detail and a keen eye for uncovering hidden insights, but instead of a magnifying glass, you're armed with a computer and a strong cup of coffee.

Informal reports are short written communications typically shared within an organization. They can be in the form of emails, letters, memos, or even presentations. Each company may have a different style for informal reports, so it's important to be familiar with your organization's specific style before you start writing.

REMEMBER

Sequence for maximum impact. Figure 15-6 is sequenced for an unresponsive (negative) reader, giving the background first.

Subject: Bringing the Successful Money Management Seminar In-House

Background

I was asked to attend the Successful Money Management seminar on April 18, 20XX at the Gateway Hotel in order to evaluate whether this is a suitable seminar to bring in house.

The Seminar's Structure

This is how the seminar was structured:

Section 1

- Foundation for Financial Independence
- Making Your Dollars Work for You
- Money Markets, Stock & Bonds, Balanced Funds and Limited Partnerships

Section 2

- Tangible Assets
- Retirement Planning
- Risk Management

This is Just What We've Been Looking For

I found the content to be extremely valuable. The facilitator provided real-world examples that even a novice investor could understand. The atmosphere was relaxed with lots of interaction, and each participant was given opportunities to discuss individual situations. This is well worth the investment of time and expense.

Next Step

Brooklyn Zell, the company president, would be happy to tailor the seminar for our needs, and she looks forward to hearing from you. Her number is 408.456.2356. Please give her a call.

FIGURE 15-6: Informal report using strong headlines and strategic sequencing.

Chapter **16**

Being Concise: Abstracts and Executive Summaries

bstracts and executive summaries are nuggets of wisdom that distill complex ideas into bite-sized brilliance. They're the antithesis of information overload, swooping in to save readers from drowning in a tsunami of "infoglut." They're like the little black dresses of the literary world — elegant, versatile, and oh-so-stylish. In a world that moves at the speed of a million tweets per minute, we could all use a little brevity.

REMEMBER

Abstracts and executive summaries are like movie trailers. Just as you can't make the trailer without first making the full-length film, you can't create an abstract or executive summary before writing the entire document.

Using AI as Your Assistant in Writing Abstracts and Executive Summaries

AI SPOTLIGHT

AI tools can abridge your text and cull the most significant parts. Search the Internet for "summary generators" and you'll find many listed. Here are some of the popular ones. Most of them have free versions with word limitations in addition to more robust versions for a fee:

>> EditPad (`https://www.editpad.org/tool/abstract-generator`)

>> Grammarly (`https://app.grammarly.com/`)

>> Notion AI (`https://www.notion.so`)

>> Quillbot (`https://quillbot.com/summarize`)

>> Summarizer (`https://www.summarizer.org/`)

Despite the aid of AI, remember that human input is critical. AI models are trained on existing data, but they lack the understanding and contextual knowledge that only humans can supply. Only you know what's truly important for your audience.

REMEMBER

When writing abstracts or executive summaries it's important to fill out the Kick-Start Brief in Chapter 4 to understand your reader, purpose, key issue, and the questions your reader will need answered. This Brief provides a foundation for you to customize your content to precisely meet the needs of your reader.

Generating Precise Prompts

AI SPOTLIGHT

Here are some suggestions for creating effective AI prompts, with a particular emphasis on abstracts and executive summaries:

>> Specify whether this is for a research paper, business proposal, book, or whatever else.

>> Highlight the key points, main arguments, findings, or essential information.

>> Specify the target audience such as newbies, experts, stakeholders, investors, or a general audience.

>> Mention the number of paragraphs or word count limit.

>> Provide any necessary contextual information such as background methodology, main sources, or any relevant data or statistics.

Writing an Abstract

The purpose of an *abstract* is to provide an overview of the objectives, methods, and results, enabling readers (usually technical readers) to grasp the main points of the paper without having to read the entire document. An abstract has two main purposes:

>> Giving readers a peek of what the document is about so they can determine if they want to read the entire text.

>> Helping readers to identify, locate, and retrieve work via search engines, databases, and other informational repositories that rely heavily on abstracts for such retrievals.

Abstracts are often used when submitting an article to a journal, applying for a research grant, writing a proposal for a conference paper, completing a college-level degree (from bachelors to doctorates), writing a proposal for a book, or applying for a patent.

Unlocking the influence of abstracts

Abstracts can stand alone or be part of the longer text. When they stand alone, always let readers know where they can find the full document — in print and/or electronic form. The following are examples of how abstracts may be used:

>> **Research papers:** In academic and scientific research papers, abstracts are typically included at the beginning of the paper. They serve as a preview of the study, summarizing the purpose, methodology, results, and conclusions. Readers can quickly assess whether the paper is relevant to their interests and decide whether to read the full paper.

>> **Conferences and trade shows:** Abstracts are often required when submitting proposals for conference presentations and trade shows. They provide a concise summary of the proposed research or presentation, allowing conference organizers to evaluate the relevance and quality of the submission.

>> **Journal articles:** Many scholarly journals require authors to include an abstract with their articles. The abstract provides a summary of the article's main points, helping readers determine whether the article is worth reading. Abstracts also appear in databases and search results, making it easier for researchers to find relevant articles.

>> **Literature reviews:** In literature reviews, abstracts are used to summarize the main findings and conclusions of multiple studies. Researchers can quickly assess the relevance and quality of each study by reading the abstracts, helping them determine which studies to include in their review.

>> **Indexing and cataloging:** Abstracts are often used for indexing and cataloging purposes. They provide a brief description of the document's content, making it easier for researchers to locate relevant materials in databases, libraries, and archives.

>> **Decision making:** Abstracts are useful for decision-making purposes. For example, policymakers may rely on abstracts to quickly understand the key findings and implications of research studies, helping them make informed decisions.

>> **Information retrieval:** Abstracts play a crucial role in information retrieval. When conducting literature searches, researchers often rely on abstracts to determine the relevance and quality of articles before reading the full text.

When an abstract is part of the longer text that appears in a professional journal or bound publication for a conference, it precedes the article as you see in Figure 16-1. This is the first page of a paper that appeared in a technical publication prepared for the IMAPS (International Symposium on Microelectronics) Proceedings. The author presented the paper at the IMAPS conference. The entire article was bound in a publication that was distributed at the conference. Here are a few things to notice in this abstract:

>> **The title states the bottom line:** For anyone who doesn't have time to read the abstract, they can determine that "Stencil Printing Holds High Promise for Wafer Bumping."

>> **Keywords were extracted from the longer document:** Solder bumping, semiconductor wafer application, stencil printing process were mentioned throughout the longer document. (*Keywords* are often used by search engines and bibliographic databases to index and categorize research papers.)

>> **Conclusion:** The wrap-up is drawn from the research and gives readers important information at a glance: "This work helps to determine the direction to further refinement."

Stencil Printing Holds High Promise for Wafer Bumping

Jon Roberts
Cookson Performance Solutions
Foxborough, MA 02035
Phone: 508-698-7225
E-mail: jroberts@cps.cookson.com

Abstract

Solder bumping for semiconductor wafer applications requires scaling a stencil printing process from the current 50-mil geometries downwards by an order of magnitude, while driving defect densities even lower to maintain high yield. In particular, wafer bumping moves the process to smaller area ratios, where the print covers a smaller area on the wafer, but using a thicker stencil to achieve a high print volume. The effects of aperture periphery begin to dominate the printing quality, and the paste particle size approaches the of the stencil thickness. A successful process calls for an integration of printing equipment technology, solder paste development, stencil manufacture improvements and reflow furnace advances. In this paper, we describe some of the metrics used to evaluate these components and give early results of some of the tests. This work helps to determine directions for further refinement.

As a packaging choice for IC's that's been around for decades, flip-chip with solder bumps has witnessed improvements in many of the alternative die assembly processes. Although solder bump users have made their own advances, the benefits just haven't yet outweighed the problems and costs involved with its implementation. Electroplating (Solders or gold) and evaporation/sputtering as methods of making bumps haven't kept up with the advances in automated wire bonding.

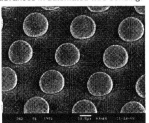

Figure 1 Typical printed solder bumps after reflow and cleaning

Stencil printing, however, brings promise of high yield and throughput, low tooling costs, and full automation to the competition. Including wafer handling and printing, a production rate in excess of 40 wafers per hour is easily achieved. Adaptable for a variety of solder paste compositions, there is no penalty for wafer size evolution and

printing speed is independent of pattern density and bump size. Figure 1 shows eutectic solder bumps printed with Alpha Metals's WS 3060 paste to a pattern at 10-mil pitch, reflowed, and cleaned, ready for flip-chip or direct chip attachment.

Process integration for wafer printing calls for more than just scaling down the stencil dimensions. The typical aperture size, about 125 microns, violates the aspect ratio rule for stencils thicker than 85 microns. But high-density patterns to make large bumps require large, closely spaced apertures in thick foils. Getting past the aspect ratio rule puts increased demands on the paste release and stencil wipe processes and frequency. Reflowing the paste into uniform bumps requires the collection of all printed paste beads into the melt – flux chemistry and reflow atmosphere control are critical to successful reflow. And reflow must leave flux residues which can be cleaned with chemistries friendly to semiconductor wafers as well as to the environment.

Stencil Development is the Key to High Yields

The stencil represents a critical limiting factor in the quality of the printed wafer. The reflowed bump's size variation can be no better than the variation of the aperture size. Although the reflow process will re-locate a paste brick to perfect position on the UBM pad, the alignment of the aperture to the pad

33rd International Symposium of Microelectronics IMAPS 2000 Proceedings September 20–22, Adapted from 2000 Boston, Massachusetts.

FIGURE 16-1: Highlights in abstract form.

Knowing what to include

The abstract is often considered the most important part of any longer work such as a thesis, dissertation, or research paper. It's been estimated that 90 percent of journal readers will read abstracts, but very few read the full papers. Abstracts can become critical segments of journal articles, theses, book proposals, grant applications, and more. Keywords are important because online databases use abstracts to make it easier for people to research a particular subject or find a full body of work. Because abstracts contain the gist of a longer document, they've proven to be very helpful in providing essential information to a wide range of users.

The specific requirements for an abstract may vary depending on the guidelines of the publication or discipline. Pay close attention to specific formatting requirements or word limitations. Key parts should include the following:

>> **Purpose:** Start with a brief, precise statement of the problem or issue you're addressing.

>> **Methods/Procedure/Approach:** This would include a brief description of the research method and design including the data collection process, sample size, and specific techniques used.

>> **Results/Findings:** Concisely highlight the key results or outcomes that are most relevant to your thesis.

>> **Summary/Conclusions/Implications:** End by summarizing the conclusions you've drawn from your research and the implications. Include any recommendations for further research or action.

REMEMBER

Avoid wishy-washy words such as *seem* and *appear* and needless adverbs. Write in the third person, use active verbs, and write in the past tense. Because of the brevity of an abstract, be sure every word has a clear function, and pay attention to key phrases and keywords.

Looking at different types of abstract

There are four basic types of abstract: The most commonly written is the informative abstract; therefore, it's explained in greater detail. Also used (as appropriate) are descriptive, critical, or highlight abstracts, which are discussed here in less detail.

AI SPOTLIGHT

AI can be used for culling key information for all four types of abstracts. They provide multiple benefits, including time-saving capabilities, accuracy and objectivity, the ability to generate multiple versions of abstracts for different purposes, and the opportunity for learning and improvement in academic writing skills.

Additionally, the major AI chatbots can determine if an abstract is clear by either selecting salient sentences that represent the main idea of the text or by understanding the text and generating new sentences that capture the essence of the content. While these tools serve as a starting point, always remember the importance of writer intelligence (WI) to review and revise.

Informative abstracts

An informative abstract is a detailed summary of the paper, including the purpose, methods, results, and conclusions. It gives readers a clear understanding of the research and its findings. You write informative abstracts to stand alone or to be part of a lengthy paper. Limit informative abstracts to no more than 300 words. It's important to note that an informational abstract should not include personal opinions, judgments, or interpretations. Instead, it should focus on presenting the objective facts and key points of the work. Here's what to include in an informative abstract:

>> Subject, scope, and purpose of the study

>> Methods used

>> Results

>> Recommendations, if any

REMEMBER

Touch upon all parts of your project. This includes a summary of the discussion or conclusion of your study. Some authors omit interpreting their results, expecting the reader to wait until they've read the entire document. While this approach may have its merits, it can also result in readers skipping the abstract if they're seeking specific details. Here's what you should consider removing from the abstract:

>> A detailed discussion of routine methods

>> Illustrations, charts, tables,

>> Any information that doesn't appear in the full text

>> Undefined abbreviations or acronyms

>> Citations or references

Descriptive abstracts

A descriptive abstract is often used for humanities and social science papers or psychology essays. In about 100 words a descriptive abstract provides an overview of the content dealing with the intended purpose, scope, and method to be used.

This is often written as a preview of research that hasn't been carried out; therefore, it doesn't include findings, conclusions, or recommendations. Include keywords found in the overall text. Here are some tips for writing a descriptive abstract:

>> **Don't include what you hope to find.** The purpose of a descriptive abstract is to provide a quick overview of your work and its key points, not your expectations or aspirations.

>> **Give general background information about your topic.** This is often restricted to one or two sentences, mentioning the study topic and/or general problem to be addressed.

Example: *Discontent of one's body has negative effects on people's psyche, especially on women of all ages.*

>> **Describe the general problem your research will explore.** In one sentence, describe the specific concepts that the study will investigate.

Example: *This paper aims to explore how applying self-compassion can create a positive body image and a sense of self-worth.*

Critical abstracts

A critical abstract provides a summary of a research paper or article, along with a judgment or comment about the validity, reliability, or completeness of the study. In addition to describing the main findings and information, a critical abstract evaluates the paper and often compares it with other works on the same subject. Critical abstracts are typically approximately 500 words in length. When writing a critical abstract, there are some general guidelines to follow:

>> State the problem in the form of a question or series of questions.

>> Provide a summary of the main findings and information from the paper.

>> Evaluate the paper by discussing its validity, reliability, or completeness.

>> Compare the paper with other works on the same subject.

Highlight abstracts

Highlight abstracts in scientific papers provide a concise summary of the purpose, procedure, results, and implications of a study. They go beyond simple descriptions, including main arguments, important results, evidence, and recommendations. They serve as surrogates for full papers, helping readers quickly grasp key points without reading the entire document. Different disciplines and journals may have variations, but the goal of providing a concise and informative summary remains consistent.

Highlight abstracts gained popularity in the art world during the modern era, influenced by movements such as Cubism and Fauvism. In academic research, abstracts have long been used to summarize scholarly texts, but their use in navigating scientific literature became more prominent after World War II.

Writing an Executive Summary

An *executive summary*, which is longer than an abstract, covers the information in greater detail. It's a concise overview of the main points of a larger document and is typically written to provide key information to executives who may not have the time to review the entire text. This document should be tailored to the audience's expertise and level of interest.

The purpose of an executive summary is to allow readers to make informed decisions based solely on the summary itself. An executive summary may include charts, graphs, or other visual aids that summarize the full text into a few pages. In general, it should include the following elements:

>> **Purpose:** Clearly state the purpose of the document.

>> **Key points:** Summarize the main points and findings of the document.

>> **Results, conclusions, and recommendations:** Describe any results, conclusions, or recommendations presented in the full document.

>> **Sufficient information:** Provide enough information for readers to understand the content of the full document without having to read it in its entirety.

Recognizing the bare necessities of executive summaries

WARNING

When an executive summary is not well-written or the key information hasn't been extracted, it can lead to faux pas or mistakes that can negatively impact the overall effectiveness of the original document and lead to flawed decision making. It's worth noting that politicians admit to voting on bills of several hundred pages, having read only the executive summary.

I wrote a book titled *Loony Laws & Silly Statutes* (Sterling Publishing Co., 1994), that lists weird laws that are or have been on the books because lawmakers relied on executive summaries and didn't read the bills. Perhaps it's why we have (or have had) laws on the books such as these:

>> A law in Kansas reads: "When two trains approach each other at a railroad crossing, both shall come to a full stop and neither shall start up again until the other has gone."

>> A law in Belvedere, California says, "No dog shall appear in public without its owner on a leash."

>> In Bayonne, New Jersey, "It's against the law for a pigeon to fly overhead without a license."

Although these laws are on the lighter side, they earmark the dangers of not including — or deliberately excluding — key information. You've probably heard of *pork barrel projects*. They refer to government spending initiatives that are included in bills to benefit specific constituencies or lawmakers' districts, often without proper scrutiny or evaluation. When these projects are buried within bills and not highlighted in the summary they result in lack of transparency, misallocated resources, wasteful spending, distraction from key issues, and undermining public trust.

This all speaks to how a flawed executive summary can have ambiguities and negative consequences that impact the understanding, perception, and effectiveness of the document it represents — and another reason why WI is absolutely necessary.

Understanding what executives want and need to know

Busy executives don't have the time or inclination to read exhaustive details. They make decisions about personnel, funding, policies, and other key issues based on information they digest in a few pages of executive summary. Make those pages action packed. Use the Kick-Start Brief Sheet in Chapter 4 to gather as much information as you can about your reading audience.

A study by Westinghouse Electric Corporation entitled "How Managers Read Reports" confirms that managers read executive summaries even though they may read little else. Here's a breakdown of what managers read in a report:

>> Executive summary: 100 percent

>> Introduction: 65 percent

>> Body: 22 percent

>> Conclusions: 55 percent

>> Appendix: 15 percent

Writing the executive summary after you finish the longer document

Keep in mind that high-level executives need high-level information. That's the reason a very small percentage of executives read the body or the appendix of a report. Here's how to begin to write an executive summary that's meaningful:

>> Scan the overall document to determine the content, structure, and length.

>> Review your research to determine the key ideas and concepts.

>> Group ideas logically.

>> Outline the key elements and minor points that support the key element.

>> Include findings or conclusions.

>> Include graphics that make a strong statement.

TIP

Although executive summaries can vary in length, here are some guidelines: If the document is about 50 pages, the summary should be one or two pages. If it's between 50 and 100 pages, consider an executive summary of two or three pages. If it's longer than 100 pages, a three- or four-page summary is appropriate.

Using technical terms cautiously

Use technical terms only when you're sure the executives reading the report are familiar with them. Not all executives have technical backgrounds, so err on the side of being conservative or offering explanations. For example, if you're using initialisms or acronyms, spell them out and follow with the abbreviated form. Here's an example:

Modern Language Association (MLA)

Showing a positive attitude

SHERYL SAYS

This makes me think of a story in *The Art of Possibility* (Harvard Business School Press, 2000), written by Rosamond Stone Zander and Ben Zander. It tells of two shoe factory scouts sent to Africa to prospect business. One scout sends a telegram saying, SITUATION HOPELESS [STOP] NO ONE WEARS SHOES. The other sends a telegram saying, GLORIOUS BUSINESS OPPORTUNITY [STOP] THEY HAVE NO SHOES. If these headlines were presented in an executive summary as "Findings," which would please the executive more?

Taking charge with the active voice

The active voice is stronger and more alive than the passive voice. When you use the active voice, you place the focus on the doer of the action. When you use the passive voice, you place your focus on the action, not the doer. The passive voice is dull and weak, as you see in the following sentence:

> **Active:** *Jose will present the findings next Friday.*
>
> **Passive:** *The findings will be presented by Jose next Friday.*

Check out Chapter 8 for more information about the active voice and lots of other good "tone" stuff.

WARNING

Think seriously about being funny. Incorporating humor into an executive summary (or into any part of your report for that matter) isn't appropriate. Your company isn't paying you to be a humorist, and humor is very subjective. What you think is funny may be offensive to others, especially in a business setting.

Sequencing information to have the most impact

Executives may use an executive summary as the basis for major decisions. Therefore, sequencing is critical. For executives who'll be positive or neutral, put the key issue at the beginning. There's no need to hide it. For executives who'll be negative, put the key issue at the end — giving you a chance to build up to the reasoning.

SHERYL SAYS

I was asked by a commander in the U.S. Coast Guard to edit a 296-page report because he thought it was slightly too long. (That was a gross understatement.) The document was filled with repetitive, redundant, and repetitious information about Coast Guard ports and more. Notice the difference between the two documents in Figures 16-2 and 16-3, which are for a neutral reader.

In Figure 16-2 you see a very lackluster executive summary presented in the typical order: Background. Approach. Findings. Nothing jumps out. It's rather mundane and gives the reader no information at a glance.

In Figure 16-3 you see a very different document that shares the same information. It leads with the Findings (key information readers need to know) with additional information called out. The three ports are detailed in a table. The Approach was numbered (rather than bulleted) because these were steps in a process. The Background appears at the end. Those reading the executive summary know the Background but it needs to be included for historical purposes. It's the least important piece of information; therefore, it's at the end.

AI can swiftly identify the most relevant sections, highlight important insights, and condense lengthy texts into a coherent and digestible format. This means that executives can swiftly grasp the essence of extensive reports, enabling them to make informed decisions quickly and efficiently.

EXECUTIVE SUMMARY

BACKGROUND

This study documents the costs and benefits of potential U.S. Coast Guard Vessel Traffic Services (VTS) in selecting U.S. deep draft ports in the Atlantic, Gulf, and Pacific coasts. The concept of VTS has gained international acceptance by governments and maritime industries as a means of advancing safety in rapidly expanding ports and waterways. VTS communications are advisory in nature, providing timely and accurate information to mariners, thereby enhancing the potential for avoiding vessel casualties. This study builds on the experience of earlier efforts and provides the most comprehensive and quantitative analyses of VTS costs and benefits.

APPROACH

The following summarizes the steps used to gather the data:
- Defining study zones and subzones.
- Analyzing historical vessel casualties.
- Forecasting avoidable future vessel casualties in each study zone.
- Estimating the avoidable consequences in each study zone, the associated physical losses, and the dollar values of these avoidable losses.
- Estimating the costs of a state-of-the-art VTS Design for each study zone.
- Comparing the benefits and costs among the 23 zones.
- Analyzing the sensitivity of relative net benefits among study zones to a range of uncertainty in key input variables.

FINDINGS

The study was done over the period of one year. The findings show that the 23 zones can be divided into three groups in terms of their relative lifecycle net benefits. The following groupings are divided into areas of sensitivity. The net benefit is positive in New Orleans, Port Arthur, Houston/Galveston, Mobile, Los Angeles/Long Beach, and Corpus Christi. It is sensitive in New York, Tampa, Portland (Oregon), Philadelphia/Delaware Bay, Chesapeake North/Baltimore, Providence, Long Island Sound, and Puget Sound. And it's negative in Jacksonville, Wilmington, Santa Barbara, Portsmouth, Portland (Maine), San Francisco, Anchorage/Cook Inlet, and Chesapeake/South Hampton Roads.

FIGURE 16-2:
The "Before" executive summary where nothing pops out.

Executive Summary

This study documents the costs and benefits of potential U.S. Coast Guard Vessel Traffic Services (VTS) in selecting U.S. deep draft ports on the Atlantic, Gulf, and Pacific coasts.

Findings

The study indicates that the 23 study zones can be divided into three groups in terms of their relative life cycle net benefits. The following groupings are divided into areas of sensitivity:

Net benefit	Port
Positive	New Orleans, Port Arthur, Houston/Galveston, Mobile, Los Angeles/ Long Beach, Corpus Christi
Sensitive	New York, Tampa, Portland (Oregon), Philadelphia/Delaware Bay, Chesapeake North/Baltimore, Providence, Long Island Sound, Puget Sound
Negative	Jacksonville, Wilmington, Santa Barbara, Portsmouth, Portland (Maine), San Francisco, Anchorage/Cook Inlet, Chesapeake South/Hampton Roads

Approach

The following summarizes the seven steps used to gather the data:

1. Defining study zones and subzones.
2. Analyzing historical vessel casualties.
3. Forecasting avoidable future vessel casualties in each study zone.
4. Estimating the avoidable consequences in each study zone, the associated physical losses, and the dollar values of these avoidable losses.
5. Estimating the costs of a state-of-the-art Candidate VTS Design for each study zone.
6. Comparing the benefits and costs among the 23 zones.
7. Analyzing the sensitivity of relative net benefits among study zones to a range of uncertainty in key input variables.

Background

The concept of VTS has gained international acceptance by governments and maritime industries as a means of advancing safety in rapidly expanding ports and waterways. VTS communications are advisory in nature, providing timely and accurate information to mariners, thereby enhancing the potential for avoiding vessel casualties. This study builds on the experience of earlier efforts and provides the most comprehensive and quantitative analyses of VTS costs and benefits.

FIGURE 16-3: The "After" executive summary where key information pops at a glance.

IN THIS CHAPTER

» Using AI as your grant-writing
assistant

» Generating precise prompts

» Adding the human touch

» Doing your homework

» Taking your readers on a journey

» Including the right information

» Understanding the review process
and becoming a finalist

» Following up if your grant is denied

Chapter **17**

Grant Proposals: The Funding Frenzy

airing grantors and grantees is somewhat like speed dating, where both sides have a limited time to make a connection and determine compatibility. Just like in speed dating, grantors and grantees come together with specific intentions and expectations. Grantors have certain criteria they're looking for, such as alignment with their funding priorities and a track record of success. Similarly, grantees present their projects and qualifications, hoping to catch the grantor's attention.

In this fast-paced and time-constrained environment, both parties must quickly assess if there's a potential match, considering factors such as shared values, goals, and the potential impact of the partnership. Ultimately, the pairing process requires effective communication and a dash of intuition to find the perfect match that can ignite transformative change. So, if you're ready to unleash your grant proposal prowess, jump into this chapter and make some magic happen!

Using AI as Your Assistant for Writing Grant Applications

AI SPOTLIGHT

Here are ways in which AI tools can assist writer intelligence (WI) to streamline the grant-application process:

» Identifying relevant funding opportunities.

» Evaluating the competitiveness of grant applications.

» Providing recommendations based on historical data and predictive analytics.

» Uploading the request for a proposal (RFP) from which to pull requested information.

» Analyzing the requirements and matching them with potential reviewers who have relevant expertise.

» Gathering and analyzing large amounts of data.

» Analyzing past grant applications and funding outcomes to identify patterns and trends.

» Creating accurate and comprehensive budgets for the projects by analyzing historical data and providing recommendations on budget allocation.

» Providing iterative learning from past funding outcomes.

» Generating drafts based on predefined templates and guidelines.

Although there are subtle differences among the following AI tools, here are a few top-rated ones to help facilitate the grant-application process:

» AmpliFund (https://www.amplifund.com)

» Grantboost (https://topai.tools/t/grantboost)

» Optimy (https://www.optimy.com/)

» ProposalGenie (https://www.proposalgenie.ai/)

» Wizehive (https://www.wizehive.com)

REMEMBER

When writing grant proposals, it's important to fill out the Kick-Start Brief in Chapter 4 to understand your reader, purpose, key issue, and the questions your reader will need answered. This Brief provides a foundation for you to customize your content to precisely meet the needs of your reader.

Generating Precise Prompts

AI SPOTLIGHT

Here are some suggestions for creating effective AI prompts, with a particular emphasis on grant proposals:

» Prompt AI to create a tone of empathy and compassion to resonate with potential funders.

» Specify the section, topic, and objective.

» Request assistance in presenting the problem statement in a clear and compelling way.

» Develop a comprehensive methodology for a robust approach, including steps, strategies, and techniques.

» Present supporting evidence and data that showcases evidence or data to validate the feasibility and effectiveness of your proposed solution.

» Address past successes.

Realizing the Human Touch is Crucial

WI is critical in grant writing because it brings a unique perspective and personal connection to the process. AI has the expertise to craft compelling applications, but it's the human touch that adds the emotional appeal and storytelling elements that resonate with funders. By infusing passion, creativity, and a personal touch into the application, you can effectively convey the impact and importance of the project, increasing the chances of securing funding. It's about connecting with the reader on a deeper level and making them understand why the project matters. The human touch sets your application apart and makes it more compelling, increasing the likelihood of success.

Grantors don't hand out funding to robotic-sounding text. Here's why the human element is crucial:

>> **Crafting persuasive narratives/stories:** The text needs to tell a compelling story that resonates with the grantor. Humans are skilled at crafting narratives that engage and persuade. They can use their creativity and emotional intelligence to present ideas in a way that captures the grantor's attention and convinces them of the value proposition. (Check out Chapter 5 to learn more about storytelling, and see examples later in this chapter.)

>> **Understanding the grantor's needs and building relationships:** This requires strong and effective communication, active listening, and empathy. Humans are able to connect with clients on a personal level, understand their pain points, and tailor grant proposals to meet their specific requirements.

>> **Collaborating and teamwork:** Humans can work together, leverage their diverse skills and perspectives to create comprehensive and well-rounded grant proposals. Collaboration fosters innovation, ensures all aspects are addressed, and increases the overall quality of the proposal.

>> **Bringing flexibility and adaptability:** Sometimes adjustments are needed based on the grantor's feedback or changing circumstances. Humans can quickly respond to changes, brainstorm alternative approaches, and modify proposals accordingly.

>> **Customizing solutions:** Only humans can assess the situation, ask relevant questions, and tailor solutions that address the specific needs of the grantor.

>> **Building trust and credibility:** These are vital components in any business relationship.

Base your request on the idea that you have the capacity to solve a specific problem or need but don't have the dollars to implement the program. In addition to the Kick-Start Brief mentioned in Chapter 4, Figure 17-1 is a Start-Up Sheet to help you fine-tune your grant proposal.

Start-Up Sheet: Fine Tuning Your Grant Proposal

1. Does this overlap another grant (internal perhaps)? If so, what makes your request different?

2. What are your specific needs? (Remember you should follow the needs, not the money)

3. What is your goal? (State in one sentence.)

4. What are your objectives?

   - Short- and long-term?

   - How will you measure success?

5. What are your budgetary needs?

6. What's the timeline?

7. What's the sustainability?

8. What are your plans for promoting the program?

9. Who is your target population?

10. What are the best practices?

11. Who is your reader?

12. Is anyone else working on another aspect of this proposal?

13. Why is your organization more qualified than others to do_____?

14. What's the one *key point* you want your readers to remember?

FIGURE 17-1:
Start-Up Sheet for
grant proposals.

Doing the Preliminaries

Before applying for a grant do your homework. Research grant providers, understand the requirements, identify how your project fits, and prepare supporting documents. The following sections describe some key preliminary steps.

Finding grantors

If you're new to the realm of writing grant applications, it can feel overwhelming trying to find the right grantor(s) for you or your organization or project. Here are some websites to get you started:

>> https://usafundingapplications.org/v9/

>> https://www.grants.gov/

>> https://www.thegrantportal.com/

>> https://www.instrument1.com/blog/best-places-to-find-grants

>> https://www.nerdwallet.com/article/small-business/small-business-grants

Acquiring guidelines

Request guidelines from the potential grantor and read them very carefully. Guidelines tell you about deadlines, eligibility, format, timetable, budgets, funding goals and priorities, award levels, evaluation process and criteria, contact information, and other submission requirements.

Starting with the planning

TIP

Successful grant writing involves the coordination of several activities: planning, searching for data and resources, writing and packaging the grant, submitting the grant, and following up. It's critical to put the time into planning in order to reap the rewards. Here are some planning tips:

>> Define your project.

>> Clarify its purpose with a mission statement.

>> Define the scope of work.

>> Determine the goals and objectives.

>> Understand what sets you apart from your competitors.

Building partners, not grantors

Envision the intended grantor as your spirited partner in a grant quest, rather than as a mere benefactor. This will open up the realm of possibilities. I'll get to storytelling in the next section, but for now picture this: You (the valiant grant seeker) and the grantor (a fellow adventurer) are standing shoulder to shoulder, fueled by shared purpose and determination. Together, you forge a path toward your noble goal, weaving dreams into reality, and leaving bureaucratic hurdles in your wake.

Paint a vivid picture of how your organization and the grantor will waltz through challenges, hand in hand. The grant application becomes more than words; it becomes a symphony of collaboration, a crescendo of impact. Focus on these issues:

>> **What's the need or problem?** Cast the question in terms of the need for the greater good, not your need.

>> **Who else is addressing this need or problem?** Identify any gaps that can be problematic.

>> **How do you propose addressing the need or problem?** "Paint a picture" so your prospect sees your plan in action.

>> **How will the grant funding solve the need or problem?** State what will be different or improved when the project is completed.

>> **How will you know that you're successful?** Include the measurements you'll use to determine success.

>> **What resources do you already have?** Give information about your resources — both paid and volunteer.

>> **What are your qualifications?** List your history, key accomplishments, past successes, and anything else showing you're the one who can solve this need or problem.

>> **What problems or barriers do you foresee?** Demonstrate that this project is well thought through by discussing any roadblocks you anticipate and how you plan to overcome them.

Taking Your Readers on a Journey

Both stories and testimonials have the power to bring a human touch to issues and people that are often overlooked or forgotten. When you incorporate stories and testimonials into your grant proposal, you not only provide a compelling narrative, but demonstrate the urgent need for collaboration between you and your grantors to address these challenges. While facts and statistics are important, it's crucial to highlight the impact of personal experiences. Unfortunately, stories and testimonials are often overlooked in grant proposals, but they have the potential to create a lasting impression and help you to be the one granted the funding.

Creating stories that appeal to emotions

SHERYL SAYS

In the course of my writing career, I've helped dozens of companies write winning grant proposals. I did this by embracing Steve Job's philosophy of storytelling: "The most powerful person in the world is the storyteller. The storyteller sets the vision, values, and agenda."

If you look around modern marketing, the most successful ads and commercials are based on storytelling. That's how humans relate. Stories are concrete. Stories appeal to our senses and our emotions. Stories persuade. Stories leave a lasting impression.

TIP

Check out Chapter 5 to learn how you can convey stories and incorporate them into your grant proposals.

Using stories that appeal to emotions when applying for a grant allows you to establish a personal connection with the reader. By weaving narratives that highlight the real-world impact of the proposed project, you can evoke empathy, compassion, and a sense of urgency, making your case more compelling and memorable. Stories have the power to engage the emotions of the grant reviewers (also known as *evaluators*), helping them understand the significance of the project on a deeper level and increasing the likelihood of their support.

AI SPOTLIGHT

Write a prompt that includes basic details from your story. Then ask AI to enhance it with a tone of empathy. Here are two examples of stories amplified with the help of AI:

Example 1: Grant for community development

In [city], a group of teenagers found hope and opportunity when a generous grant transformed an abandoned building into a vibrant community center. Walls that were once cold and lifeless now adorn colorful murals — a reflection of the creativity that now flourishes within. With dance studios, art workshops, and music rooms at their disposal, these once-overlooked, troubled teens discovered their talents and found their voices.

Through art projects, poetry slams, and theater performances, these teens have captivated their community and they're now participants in shaping their own futures. The funding not only repurposed a derelict building, but it lit a brighter future for these inner-city teens, empowering them to strive and thrive.

Example 2: Grant for medical research

Imagine being diagnosed with a life-threatening condition, where every breath feels like a struggle, and every heartbeat is a reminder of your mortality. For these patients, the last round of grant funding paved the way for groundbreaking medical research. It also brought hope and a renewed sense of life to patients suffering from coronary artery disease, heart failure, and arrhythmias.

The grant money has allowed researchers to dive deep into the complexities of these diseases, exploring innovative approaches and pushing the boundaries of medical knowledge. This level of dedication and commitment has not only resulted in improved patient outcomes but has also opened doors to new possibilities in the field of cardiology. Hundreds of patients who were once facing a bleak prognosis now have access to life-prolonging therapies that were once only dreams. These therapies have not only reduced mortality rates but have significantly enhanced the quality of life for these patients.

As we look to the future, let us remember that together we can continue to make a difference and bring hope to those who need it most.

TIP

If your business is just starting out and you haven't experienced success yet, consider crafting personalized stories about your clients, partners, members, donors, and other people involved with your organization. These narratives have the power to make your journey relatable and highlight the potential of your organization.

AI SPOTLIGHT

If you don't have actual stories because your requested funding is for a new endeavor, ask AI for help in creating an "Imagine this . . ." scenario that tugs at heartstrings.

Incorporating stories wisely

Kick off your transmittal letter (more information about that later in this chapter) with an enthralling story instead of the standard opening like most submitters send: *I'm delighted to submit this grant proposal . . .* That's dull and uninspiring. Imagine a first-round reviewer who's sifting through copious proposals searching for those worthy of closer examination. It's effortless for them to set these aside or simply click away from those with mundane openings without giving the proposal a chance. But what if the same reviewer stumbled upon a captivating story — one that would seize their attention? Be the one to seize their attention!

TIP

To make your grant proposal more engaging, include a story both at the beginning and at the end of the proposal. This helps to capture the reader's attention from the start and leaves a lasting impression at the conclusion.

Including dynamic testimonials

Testimonials offer social proof of the credibility and authenticity of the project. They showcase positive experiences and outcomes, building trust and demonstrating the project's potential for success. They validate the initiative and compel decision-makers to invest in a proven venture. When testimonials are scattered throughout the proposal, they reinforce that your organization is trusted, respected, and fully capable of delivering on its promises.

Here's an example of a well-written testimonial:

> *Thanks to [organization], 12 children from our inner-city community had the joy of a two-week adventure in the mountains during the summer. This extraordinary experience provided a break from their everyday concerns and allowed them to immerse themselves in the beauty of nature, resulting in cherished memories that will last a lifetime. With your help, we hope to provide more children with this wonderful opportunity.*
>
> *— James Smith, President of [Organization]*

WARNING

To avoid any potential legal consequences, get written permission before using anyone's testimonial.

Knowing What to Include in the Grant Proposal

The extent of information you include is relative to how large the project is and how much money you request. Following is a detailed list of the parts of a typical grant. Yours may have more or fewer inclusions.

The beginning

Provide the hook. This is the section where you grab the reader's attention or not. Let them know they're about to hear of a very interesting and worthwhile project. Don't promise the moon, but be honest and realistic.

Transmittal Letter

Transmittal letters are either sent as hard copy along with the proposal or via email. If the letter is sent as hard copy, it sits atop the proposal but isn't affixed to it. (Chapter 19 offers lots of information on how to write a business letter.) If it's sent via email, the letter "is" the email and the proposal is attached. In either case, the transmittal letter should convey the following in no more than three paragraphs:

- Open with an engaging story.

- Describe your organization, community, and target population.

- Share the undertaking and two of its major selling points.

- Explain the reasons you're applying for a grant and why you're the best candidate.

- End by thanking them for their consideration.

AI SPOTLIGHT

AI is an exceptional letter-writing tool, capable of producing well-structured, cohesive, and professional writing. It can accommodate specific language, tone, and formatting requests. While the final letter may still require WI, AI can greatly ease the drafting process, saving valuable time and effort.

Title Page

Specific requirements for a grant proposal title page may vary depending on the granting agency. If specifications are given, carefully review them to ensure that the title page is formatted correctly and includes all the required information. If it's left to your discretion, include the following in this order:

- Title of project (in a font larger than he rest)

- Requester's name, address, and telephone number

- Granting agency

- Submission date

Keep this page simple and appealing to the eye. It may even include a photo. Figure 17-2 shows two examples.

AI SPOTLIGHT

Check out Chapter 7 for AI tools that can create a title page appropriate for your grant proposal. You don't need to be an artist; let AI do the work.

Table of Contents

If the proposal is more than 10 pages long, a table of contents (TOC) provides a clear and organized overview of the proposal's structure and allows the reader to easily navigate through the document.

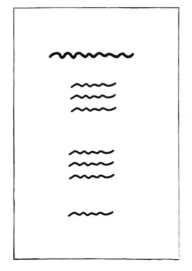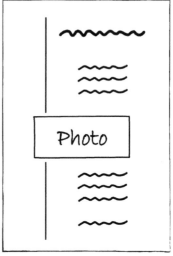

FIGURE 17-2:
Two (of many)
ways to present
a title page.

Executive Summary

REMEMBER

Nearly 90 percent of all funding decisions are made before the potential grantor finishes reading the executive summary. In the first paragraph, set the stage for the story. The *who, where, what, when, why,* and *how* (just like in a news report) that give a hint of direction. During this time the reader is trying get some context, to figure out where you're headed, and how they fit into the journey. Make this section concise, persuasive, engaging, and include charts or tables where appropriate. Limit this to no more than three pages. Here's what to include:

- **Introduction:** Brief overview of your organization and its mission. Explain who you are, what you do, and why your work is important.

- **Project description:** Describe the problem or need that your project aims to address.

- **Methods and approach:** Outline the strategies and methods you will use to achieve your project goals, and the grantor's mission.

- **Expected outcomes and impact:** Highlight the potential benefits and positive changes that will result from your work.

- **Budget:** Include a brief summary of the budget, including the total amount requested and a breakdown of how the funds will be used. Be clear and transparent about how the funds will be allocated.

- **Relevant experience:** Highlight relevant experience, expertise, and partnerships that will contribute to the project's success.

- **Sustainability:** Discuss your organization's long-term plans for funding, partnerships, and community support.

- **Conclusion:** End on a strong note to leave a lasting impression on the reviewers.

To learn more about executive summaries, check out Chapter 16.

The middle

This is the meat and potatoes. It's the section where you educate. It should be informative, persuasive, and assuring. Lavish this section with stories and testimonials to let them know how their much-needed funds will be wisely spent, based on your past (or anticipated) success. These stories may show how your team was so efficient they completed the project ahead of schedule and under budget, or whatever your success story is.

Include what your capabilities are to see the project through, and your organization's enthusiasm for your commitment to the project and the people it's intended to help.

SHERYL SAYS

TAKING IT TO THE NEXT LEVEL

Sometimes the government or a foundation will issue a RFP to publicize the launch of a new initiative or announce deadlines for grants. The RFP may be very robust and require an extensive proposal of perhaps several hundred pages.

I consulted with a company that was responding to an RFP for a $3,000,000 grant. Yes, a large project indeed! They called me in because they'd lost several grants in the past, having been told they'd neglected to address every item in the RFP — which they actually had. To make sure this didn't happen again, I took the TOC to the next level, expanding it to include every item the RFP requested in addition to the page on which it appeared. This would ensure that the reviewers could see that each item was addressed. Here's a brief example of the table:

Entry	Page	Your RFP page and number
Allocated funds	204	Page 30, #30-A

Result: The company received the grant, and I was the hero of their story!

Introduction

In one page or less, introduce the following:

- **Concept:** How this project fits into the philosophy and mission of your organization.
- **Key elements of the program:** This includes the nature of project, timetable, anticipated outcomes, and staffing needs.
- **Overview of the financials:** At this stage you may not be able to pinpoint all expenses, but you can present broad outlines.

Goals and Objectives

Express your goal — the end result — in a powerful sentence. Be sure they're specific, measurable, achievable, relevant, and time-bound (SMART). Support your goal with the long- and short-term objectives, which are the steps along the way. Include the following:

- Measurable milestones you will reach in meeting those goals and objectives.
- How you will know that you're making progress towards your goals and objectives.

Budgetary Needs

You probably won't be able to pin down all the expenses until the details and timing are finalized. For the purpose of writing the grant, sketch out the broad outlines of the budget to be sure the costs are in proportion to the outcomes you anticipate. If it appears that the costs will be prohibitive, scale back your plans or adjust them to remove expenses that aren't cost effective. Also, mention funding from other sources, volunteer services, and the like.

Timeline

State how long this project should take and the steps along the way. If your grant proposal is short and the project is a simple one, you may say: *The project will start within 30 days of receiving the funding and will be completed six months from the start date.*

AI SPOTLIGHT

If the project is intensive, see how AI can assist. Check out Quickbase (https://www.quickbase.com/trial-register), Smartsheet (https://www.smartsheet.com/), Monday.com (https://monday.com/), HoneyBook (https://www.honeybook.com/), Zoho Projects (https://www.zoho.com/projects/login.html), and Hive (https://thehive.ai/).

Sustainability

If the program is proving to be successful and funding runs out, would you seek alternative sources of funding? Detail the following:

- How the program can run on its own.
- Whether you would seek funding from other resources.
- Whether you'd seek additional funding from this grantor.

Promotion

Outline your plans for promoting the program. Through a public relations campaign? Through community affairs organizations? In professional journals? If you have existing marketing literature, send it along.

Target Population

If your target population is a factor, detail who they are (for example, an organization doing research on a specific disease may do a study whose target population is a certain ethnic group of certain ages):

- Gather relevant data and statistics that support the need for the proposed project or program. This will help you demonstrate the significance and impact of your work.
- Make sure your goals are SMART.
- Highlight any existing collaborations or partnerships with organizations or stakeholders that have experience working with the target population and your commitment to working collaboratively and leveraging existing resources and expertise . . . in addition to sharing your findings.

Best Practices

How will you share the success of your project with other organizations or communities? Will you share the "lessons learned" so others can learn from what worked and what didn't work? Also, what lessons learned from others will you apply to this process?

Qualifications

Many groups are vying for the same dollars. Detail why you're more qualified or better able to reach your goal:

- If you've had a breakthrough or success on something similar in the past, be specific about how you met your goals.

- Use percentages and dollar amounts. They can be powerful.

- If you have key people who will lead the charge, include a brief paragraph here, and include their resumes in the appendixes.

The conclusion

Include appendixes, glossary, and other information in the back matter. However, the conclusion is part of the meat and potatoes, offering you one last chance to convince the grantor to fund your initiative. Here are some tips to help you craft a memorable conclusion:

>> Restate the problem

>> Recap the objectives

>> Showcase the feasibility

>> Highlight innovation

>> Express confidence

>> Throw in a testimonial

>> Call to action

Appendixes

This is another opportunity for sharing stories. Consider including a section titled "More About Our Successes." These success stories can be lengthier (a page or more) and can include case studies. Even though this isn't a standard part of a grant proposal, it adds credibility and sets you apart from the competition.

REMEMBER

This section isn't an afterthought or a place to dump random information. It should be a carefully curated selection that adds depth and validation to your proposal. The appendixes may include any of the following:

- Resumes of key people to be involved.

- Stories of past successes that are relevant.

- Testimonials with names (that have been preapproved).

- Validation of claims with research.

- Additional details about the budget.

Glossary

Throughout the grant proposal, keep industry-specific terms, acronyms, or initialisms to a minimum. When you do need to include them, use a glossary for easy reference.

Remembering the do's and don'ts

Do describe your program with facts, statistics, and passion using action-packed words such as: *achieving, cooperative, enhancing, establish, existing, expanding, overall,* and *strategies.* Also, present your goals in visionary terms and your objectives in measurable terms with performance words such as: *decrease, deliver, develop, establish, improve, increase,* and *produce.*

Don't beat around the bush about future funding. Use phrases such as: *creating future fundraising partners, inviting more external funding sources, local fundraising,* and *seeking to identify more stakeholders.* And don't use statements that say the obvious such as *illiteracy is a barrier to employment, clean water is essential, homelessness is a serious issue,* and similar evident statements.

TIP

If submitting a paper copy, use high-quality paper that doesn't appear to be too expensive. You don't want to be viewed as a big spender or you weaken your chances of getting the funding. Consider using recycled paper — even better!

AI SPOTLIGHT

AI can help to write grant proposals by generating ideas, streamlining the writing process, improving clarity and conciseness, using active voice, adding specific examples and evidence, and increasing the chances of securing funding. You can prompt AI to create a tone of empathy and compassion that will resonate with potential funders.

Understanding the Review Process

The review process for large grants can vary depending on the funding organization and the specific grant program. However, there are some common steps and considerations involved in the review process:

» **Eligibility screening:** This step is to ensure that only eligible applications proceed to the next stage of the review process.

» **Peer review:** This step involves the evaluation of the application by a panel of experts in the relevant field.

- **Programmatic review:** This step considers factors such as the relevance of the project to the organization's mission, the potential for impact, and the fit within the overall funding portfolio.

- **Recommendation for funding:** The recommendation may include suggestions for revisions or modifications to the project before funding can be awarded.

- **Final decision:** This review ensures that the recommended projects align with the organization's strategic priorities and available funding. The final decision on whether to award the grant is made at this stage.

- **Award processing:** The grantee and the funding organization work together to establish the necessary administrative and financial arrangements for the project.

Reaching the Finals

Before a decision is reached, several semi-finalists may be called upon to make a presentation. Preparing for the review process of a grant application requires careful attention to detail and effective communication of your organization's qualifications and project's impact.

AI SPOTLIGHT

Here are several ways in which AI can assist you to increase your chances of success:

- **Generating slides and handouts:** AI can assist you in creating professional and visually appealing slides and handouts. Check out Chapter 7 for information on visuals to make sure your slides and handouts are on target.

- **Reiterating your organization's qualifications:** AI can help you articulate your organization's qualifications, experience, and expertise related to the grant's focus area. By leveraging AI, you can highlight your organization's strengths and unique aspects that make it stand out from your competitors. Chapter 8 helps you articulate tone.

- **Aligning your story with the grantor's objectives:** AI can assist you in crafting a compelling narrative that aligns with the grantor's objectives by tailoring your story to resonate with the grantor's mission and goals. Check out Chapter 5 to get you started with materials you can use as prompts.

DARING TO BE DIFFERENT

SHERYL SAYS

Chen attended my presentation workshop. He was to be one of five finalists hoping to win a research grant for his project. He entered the room and walked right up to me and said, "Hi, Sheryl, I'm Chen. The timing for this workshop couldn't be more perfect. I'm one of five finalists seeking a very large grant. We were each asked to prepare a PowerPoint presentation to strengthen our cases. And I present a week from now . . . I printed out the 15 slides I prepared and hope you'll have time to critique them. I really need this grant to continue research I've been doing." After a quick scan, of 15 data-laden slides of charts, tables, and graphs, my response to him was "Yikes!"

Okay, I challenged him: "Imagine this: It's the day of your presentation. You walk into this large conference room with three stern-looking grantors sitting in black leather swivel chairs around a long, black conference table. The room is modern, almost sterile looking. White walls. The only thing hanging is a whiteboard that spans one complete wall. There are no windows, just bright lights. The five finalists are seated facing the projector and large screen in front of the room." (Pause) "Let's assume that you're the fifth and final presenter . . . Do you think the grantors will still be listening attentively by the time you present? Or will they have been so bored by the data-laden presentations of your competitors, they're mentally packing for a trip to Hawaii?" Then I asked him, "Have you ever seen the popular TV show *Shark Tank* where a group of investors hears pitches from people who are seeking funding from them?" He nodded. "Think of your presentation as your shark tank."

He was quite taken aback by my comments because he was planning to blend in with the pack using slides, as he was directed. I encouraged him to see that the villains in this story were his competitors — the sharks swarming around hoping to clutch the pot of gold. I encouraged him to do three heroic things:

- Ditch all his slides.

- Prepare stories and deliver a narrative in conversational format.

- Generate a dynamic handbook for each of the grantors.

At the outset Chen was reluctant. But after going through the workshop, he agreed to deliver a narrative telling stories of the successes of many recipients of his former grants. He left each grantor with a handbook of the stories and other information that made his research worthy of additional funding.

(continued)

(continued)

Here's the outcome: Rather than being the last to present, Chen was the first to present. The grantors were so impressed with the high bar Chen had set, that all the other presenters (who showed data-laden slides) paled in comparison. Chen was memorable. He was awarded the grant! He brought home the gold — Chen was the hero!

Lesson learned: When you use a narrative approach to presenting, your audience pays attention. Don't overburden them with data-laden slides. Tell your story. And if you use slides, let them enhance your story.

Following Up if Your Application is Denied

If your funding application is denied, there are several steps you can take as a follow up:

>> **Request feedback from the grantor asking why your application was denied.** Some grantors will give feedback; others won't. But it doesn't hurt to ask. Feedback can help you understand where your application fell short and what changes you can make to improve future applications.

>> **Review and reflect the feedback.** Pay close attention to areas where you could have provided more detail or made your case more effectively.

>> **Consider reapplying.** If the grantor allows it, reapply. If you do, be sure to incorporate the feedback you received into your new application.

TIP

Look for other funding sources who may be a good fit. Don't give up after one denial or more denials. There are many funding opportunities out there. And consider seeking assistance from the AI sources mentioned in this chapter or engaging a professional grant writer.

5

Producing Personalized and Targeted Writing

Showcase your professional excellence with a bio that serves as your fervent advocate, whether it's a concise single page, a detailed paragraph or two, or an intriguing elevator pitch.

Make a strong impression and forge deeper connections through well-crafted letters that leave a lasting impact.

Develop storyboards to break down ideas into easily digestible chunks of information for your presentations, meetings, or documents.

Craft a comprehensive business plan that outlines your goals, objectives, strategies, organizational structure, and resource requirements, ensuring a well-structured roadmap for achieving success.

Discover the power of writing and publishing a book, enhancing your credibility in ways you never imagined possible.

Chapter **18**

Bios: Being a Shameless Self-Promoter

Your bio is the ultimate cheerleader for your career, pumping up your achievements and skills as if you had a professional ad agency plugging for you. It's not just a list of accomplishments like a dusty resume or a forgotten curriculum vitae (CV). If you're lacking a bio or you have one languishing in your computer's memory, it's high time to give it a makeover. Get ready to unleash your inner rock star and show the world what you're made of. Picture this: You get a last-minute opportunity to be a presenter, and it could be a major game-changer for your career. But uh-oh, you need to send your bio as soon as possible. So you quickly whip one up, but it's not exactly your best work. Avoid such a panic by having a bio ready to go.

Using AI as Your Assistant for Writing Bios

AI SPOTLIGHT

The following tools (among others) use natural language processing (NLP) algorithms to analyze your input and generate well-crafted bios. They consider the context, desired tone, and relevant information provided to create professional and attention-grabbing bios for various platforms. Check them out to learn which will work best for you:

>> Ahrefs Social Media Bio Generator (https://ahrefs.com/writing-tools/bio-generator)

>> Nichesss bio generator (https://nichesss.com/tools/author-bio-generator-zoAkojTt2)

>> Rytr Bio Generator (https://rytr.me/use-cases/social-media-bio)

REMEMBER

When writing a bio it's important to fill out the Kick-Start Brief in Chapter 4 to understand your reader (or audience), purpose, key issue, and the questions your reader will need answered. This Brief provides a foundation for you to customize your content to precisely meet the needs of your reader.

Generating Precise Prompts

AI SPOTLIGHT

Here are some suggestions for creating effective AI prompts, with a particular emphasis on bios:

>> State the purpose of the bio, such as for a professional website, social media profile, networking event, speaking engagement, or whatever.

>> Specify the length, tone, and style.

>> Include your name, profession, education, work experience, skills, and accomplishments.

>> List any notable achievements, awards, certifications, or published books and/or articles.

>> Include information about your hobbies, interests, or personal values, if applicable.

Letting Your Inner Rock Star Shine

Navigating self-promotion can be tricky; it requires a delicate balance between confidently showcasing your achievements and avoiding arrogance. When done thoughtfully and strategically, however, you can highlight your strengths and talents while maintaining a professional image. Perhaps you've hesitated for any of the following reasons:

» You've been taught from a young age to be humble and not boast about yourself.

» You may struggle with imposter syndrome, doubting your own abilities and feeling like you don't deserve recognition for your accomplishments.

» You find it arrogant to incorporate measurable metrics such as *increased sales by 20 percent*, instead of simply stating *improved sales*.

» You fear being judged or rejected, making it difficult to confidently showcase your skills and experiences.

» You can't find the right balance between confidence and authenticity.

Showing You Have a Personality, Not Just a Pulse

If you look at bios of people from certain professional groups, you'll notice they typically sound alike. For example: Certified Financial Planners boast of helping clients to create diversified portfolios, plan for the future, save for children's education, yadda, yadda, yadda. Finding a financial advisor can dictate the path of your financial future for decades. What makes each one different? How do you find one who's right for you?

REMEMBER

Think of your bio as a snapshot of the story behind the person. Your infomercial. Your advertisement. Your personality. Your bio should explain — but not be limited to — your name, current job title, company or personal brand statement, relevant achievements, personal and professional goals, skills, and areas of expertise and interests.

Realizing that one size doesn't fit all

Bios are like fashion statements for your professional persona. Just like outfits, there's no one-size-fits-all solution. Different occasions call for different bios to "suit" the vibe and purpose. From a formal business event to a casual networking meetup or even a creative industry gathering, each setting requires a unique bio that captures the essence of who you are and what you bring to the table. So, embrace the versatility of bios and tailor them to make a lasting impression in any situation. After all, the key to success is being adaptable and showcasing your multifaceted brilliance.

AI SPOTLIGHT

This is where AI comes to the rescue. It can help you draft your bio by analyzing your achievements, personal information, and tone preferences to generate a concise and engaging summary that accurately represents you. Additionally, AI can provide suggestions for improvements based on popular bio formats and language patterns, ensuring your bio stands out and resonates with your target reader.

Showing, not telling

Russian playwright Anton Chekhov said, "Don't tell me the moon is shining; show me the glint of light on broken glass." Showing, not telling is the cornerstone of anything you write or say. This is a technique that lets the reader or listener experience expository details of a story through actions, sensory details, and words that explain (rather than say outright) the person's emotions. A literary example may be:

> **Showing:** *Jimmy froze in place. His heart started ticking like a time bomb as the shadowy figure lurched across the room.*

> **Telling:** *Jimmy was scared as he saw the shadow cross the room.*

UNLEASHING YOUR UNIQUENESS IN A BIOGRAPHY

SHERYL SAYS

When my previous primary care physician (PCP) hung up his stethoscope and retired, I faced the daunting task of finding a new doctor. Unfortunately, many of the doctors recommended by my friends weren't accepting new patients. It became clear that this wouldn't be an easy search, especially since I was looking for a doctor who took a holistic approach to patient care rather than simply prescribing medication. I scoured the Internet and found many healthcare practices willing to set up appointments with doctors of their choosing. That wasn't going to work for me. My body, my choice.

Undeterred, I persisted searching and came across a long list of doctors who were accepting new patients. As I reviewed their credentials, most of them sounded alike. Of course, they graduated from different medical schools, completed internships and residencies at various hospitals, and some even boasted that they came from medical families or had dreamt of becoming doctors for most of their lives. "So what?" I thought. None of their bios gave me any insight into their approach to patient care, and I refused to settle for mediocrity.

I continued my search, knowing that somewhere out there the ideal doctor awaited me. And when our paths would finally cross, I'd have found not just a healer, but a partner in my quest for superb healthcare.

Alas!

Amidst a sea of similarities, one bio shone with distinction. Next to the photo of a young doctor with a warm smile was a quote that caught my attention. "I really value patients who want to collaborate and work together on improving their health." My mindset exactly! I read on.

In addition to having graduated from a prestigious medical school and serving his internship and residency at a leading hospital, this doctor's philosophy is that primary care isn't just a way to keep people healthy, but also to keep them happy and see them through meaningful events in their lives . . . He further states that if patients come in and ask for a prescription, he tries to understand their needs beyond medication. What are their lifestyles? And how do these lifestyle choices impact their health? His hope is to work with patients towards healthier lives, minimizing the need for medications. This is my kind of doctor; I knew it immediately. And at the time, he was accepting new patients. He's been my doctor for several years now, and I'm delighted with his attentiveness and his approach to my healthcare.

The key takeaway is to craft a captivating bio that distinguishes you from your competition, leaving an indelible mark on anyone who reads it. And never overlook the value of a complementary photo with a compelling value proposition to unleash your uniqueness.

Establishing bragging rights

Your bio should sound as though it were written objectively . . . yet it's anything but objective. If you find it difficult to brag about yourself, think of your life as though you were someone else peering in. What would you say about "that" person (you)? Give this serious thought and present the information interestingly:

> **Interesting:** *Six years ago Sam followed his dream, leaving the safety net of his six-figure salary to start his own coaching business.*

> **Lackluster:** *Sam left his job six years ago to pursue his own coaching business.*

Breaking away from the pack

When your bio is longer than an elevator pitch (find out more later in this chapter), convey what makes you different. Interesting. Relatable. It's amazing how many people may connect with you because they share similar interests:

>> What do you enjoying doing when you're not working?

>> Were you raised in another part of the country or world?

>> Do you have a unique pet?

>> Do you have an interesting hobby or unique collection?

>> What projects are you currently doing at work or play?

>> What's your vision for yourself, your company, the world?

>> What volunteer activities are you involved in?

>> What's your passion?

Choosing your voice

When introducing yourself or writing a bio for a social media site, write in the first person. Otherwise, write in the third person, as if someone else wrote (or said) all the wonderful things about you.

First person: *I first entered . . .*

Third person: *Bob first entered . . .*

Third person: *He first entered . . .*

Crafting a One-Page Bio

A one-page bio can be useful on a website, social media page, media and press kit, and more. It allows you to provide a concise and impactful overview of your background, accomplishments, and expertise, helping to create a strong first impression.

SHERYL SAYS

Since my earliest years, I've harbored an insatiable passion for stories. This fervor has shaped much of my professional journey, as storytelling has become the cornerstone of my career and the title of my last book, *Storytelling in Presentations For Dummies* (John Wiley & Sons, Inc., 2023). If you look at the opening paragraph of my bio in Figure 18-1, you'll discover a handful of elements. Notably, it opens with a hook that conveys my identity as a storyteller.

Moreover, I inject a dash of humor by playfully highlighting my idiosyncratic pronunciation of "coffee." This subtle inclusion showcases my lightheartedness and humor, so readers know immediately that I'm not boring. Instead of stating the mundane fact that "I grew up in New York City and relocated to Massachusetts in the early 90s," I opt for a more engaging third-person rendition. I also incorporate my personal motto: "You make more dollars when you make more sense." Many people have commented that my bio has helped them to know me, and several said they sensed my presentations would be anything but dull.

Remembering that there isn't a one-size-fits-all bio, compare the tones of my bio in Figure 18-1 and the one in the "About the Author" section at the back of this book. The bio in Figure 18-1 is the one I include in my workshop materials when I present to academic, biotech, and financial institutions. It emphasizes my expertise and credibility in a more formal way. On the other hand, the "About the Author" bio at the back of this book (which was generated by AI) has a more relaxed, lighthearted tone to create a sense of camaraderie with my readers. Remember, the tone you choose can make a big impact on how others perceive you.

Perhaps you have a personal motto, style, or philosophy that permeates everything you do. Your bio is the place to communicate that. The main thing is that your bio is easy to read and entices people to want to meet you or learn more about you and what you offer. Here are some things to include, as applicable:

>> Name, title, contact information

>> Professional associations and affiliations

>> Published works

>> Notable media appearances or mentions

>> Professional awards

>> Public speaking achievements

>> Community involvement

>> Family (adds a personal touch)

>> Hobbies, passions, and special interests

Sheryl Lindsell-Roberts

You make more dollars when you make more sense.™

Having grown up in New York City, Sheryl still bears traces of her accent, which is very apparent when she says the word "coffee" (or as she pronounces it, *cough-ee*.) Sheryl stayed in New York with her husband and two sons, then moved to the Boston area of Massachusetts.

Communication is key to achievement

Sheryl became an expert communicator because she was raised by a mother who was a stickler for communicating well. That has resulted in Sheryl's stunning 25-year career as a business communications expert and principal of Sheryl Lindsell-Roberts & Associates. She's fiercely committed to helping people engage their readers and audiences in the following ways:

- Cut writing time by 30-50% and get dramatically improved results.
- Make electrifying connections with audiences by using a storyboard approach.
- Create emails with subject lines that shout "read me" and get meaningful responses.
- Communicate crisply with a multi-cultural and multi-generational workforce.
- Deliver key messages at a glance with strong visual impact.

Books and media credits

Television and radio networks throughout the United States have interviewed Sheryl, and she's been featured and quoted in *The New York Times* and in magazines such as *Training Magazine, Profit, Home Business, CIO,* and others. Following are a few of the 25 books Sheryl has written:

Ideal clients — large and small and from a wide variety of industries — are those that believe powerful communication is the key to higher productivity and profitability. Join the thousands who have learned the art of written communication from a professional who has made a lifelong commitment to sharing best practices.

Passions and successes

Writing is one of Sheryl's passions. One day she hopes to write the "great American novel." But in the meantime, she and her team have produced proposals, brochures, websites, video, manuals, technical papers, and more that have helped companies to close multi-million-dollar contracts. The biggest success was writing a proposal that helped an architectural firm close a $70 million school contract.

When Sheryl isn't writing, she enjoys reading, sailing, kayaking, cross-country skiing, snowshoeing, gardening, painting (pictures, not walls), creating pottery, going to the gym, or traveling around the world.

https://www.linkedin.com/in/sherylwrites/

FIGURE 18-1:
My bio with hook, humor, accomplishments, and interests.

Creating a One-or Two-Paragraph Bio

This type of bio is often for an introduction at a workshop, conference, or any event you'll be facilitating. You'll need two versions for this: One version where you'll introduce yourself and another when someone else will introduce you.

The format, style, and content are entirely up to you. Perhaps you have a personal motto, style, or philosophy that permeates everything you do. Your bio is the place to communicate that. The main thing is that your bio is easy to read and entices people to want to meet you or learn more about you and what you offer. The details to include are the same as outlined in the bullet list in the previous section.

GET LINKEDIN

LinkedIn is the largest business-oriented social media site with 500+ million members in more than 200 countries. It provides a platform for professionals to connect with colleagues, industry peers, and potential employers. If you're not on LinkedIn, what are you waiting for? It provides professionals with networking opportunities, access to industry-specific groups, job search and recruitment benefits, research and knowledge-sharing capabilities, and resources for professional development. It's a valuable platform for professionals to connect, learn, and advance in their careers.

If you're already on LinkedIn, does your profile attract other professionals? If not, here are a few tips to jazzing it up:

Photo

Your LinkedIn profile picture is often the first impression you make, so it's important to choose one that's professional looking and makes you appear approachable. Pick a current headshot that reflects your personality and professionalism. It should be clear, sharp, cropped, and taken in a well-lit area.

Headline

Your headline is a public one-liner that gives a quick overview of who you are, what you do, and what you bring to the table. What's your value proposition? What words are relevant? What problems are you trying to solve? What professional attribute makes you stand out? Here are a few thoughts:

Financial Consultant | Fiduciary | Wealth Manager | Retirement Planner | Excellent Listener |

Computer Programming | SQL | Auto Delivery | Communication Skills | Information Technology

(continued)

(continued)

Opening paragraph

A professionally written bio can open doors of opportunities, and it starts with the opening paragraph. Who are you? What makes you tick? What's your current role? What are a few highlights of your success? What's your life like outside of work? What's your story? Here are some ways to get it "write" in the opening paragraph:

- **Lead with your greatest accomplishment:** After leading the company in sales for more than 10 consecutive years, I . . .

- **Open with an anecdote about how your career started:** One of my first memories is . . .

- **Tell how a "theme" has shown up throughout your life:** I've always been the person who . . .

- **Weave a thread of your academic accomplishment:** While studying for my master's degree at [university] I was fortunate to . . .

- **Pitch accomplishments as lessons learned:** I learned early in my career . . .

- **Hook with a short provocative sentence:** I always thought my dream was to be . . . but I later realized . . .

- **Earn credibility by naming specific clients (with their permission, of course):** Over the last several years I've helped companies such as [name several] to . . .

- **Presents your strengths:** My biggest strength is being able to . . .

Avoid clichés such as *passionate, motivated, dynamic, creative, expert, strategic, skilled, focused, guru* — you get the picture.

Preparing a bio for a self-introduction

Think about what your audience expects from your presentation. Why should they want to spend their time listening to you? What will be their valuable takeaways? Why are you the best person to make this presentation? This is a make-it-or-break-it opportunity:

> **Strong start:** *Hello everyone, I'm Jack Miller. I've had more than 20 years' experience in the financial world and help small businesses avoid IRS audits. In fact, throughout my career, I've processed thousands of tax returns without a single audit. This morning you'll learn how you can avoid IRS audits.*

Weak start: *Hi, my name is Jack Miller and I am the VP of ABS Finance Company just outside of Boston. My background includes . . .*

TIP

When introducing yourself, write your bio in the first person and be as succinct as possible. Here's an example of what you may prepare, written in the first person.

Hello, I'm Bruce Adams. I firmly believe that laughter is a bonding force. It has no cultural, social or spiritual exceptions. Laughter is the sweetest human music. The medicine of the soul. The sound of healing. I'm the founder of A Dose of Laughter, and an experienced laughter therapist. I've spent the last 15 years helping people use laughter to relieve stress, reduce pain, improve a sense of well-being, and manage career and personal pressures. This highly interactive two-hour workshop includes laughter exercises, books, games, and puzzles. It's helped hundreds of people cope with the loss of loves ones, serious illnesses, career stresses, and personal setbacks. Okay . . . Let's get started so you can experience all the health benefits of a good belly laugh to last you a lifetime. And this is no joke.

Preparing a bio for someone else to introduce you

When someone else will be introducing you, write your bio in the third person. Here's an example of what you may prepare:

I'm delighted to introduce Bruce Adams. He firmly believes that laughter is a bonding force. It has no cultural, social or spiritual exceptions. Laughter is the sweetest human music. The medicine of the soul. The sound of healing. Bruce is the founder of A Dose of Laughter, and an experienced laughter therapist. He's spent the last 15 years helping people use laughter to relieve stress, reduce pain, improve a sense of well-being, and manage career and personal pressures. His highly interactive two-hour workshop includes laughter exercises, books, games, and puzzles. It's helped hundreds of people cope with the loss of loves ones, serious illnesses, career stresses, and personal setbacks. Experience all the health benefits of a good belly laugh to last you a lifetime. See for yourself. This is no joke. And now . . . here's Bruce.

REMEMBER

When introducing someone else, avoid trite expressions such as:

>> [Name] needs no introduction.

>> You can read [Name's] bio in the program book.

>> Let me read to you what's in [Name's] bio.

>> I've never met [Name], but I hear they're awesome.

Fashioning a Pithy Elevator Pitch

Long before a movie is made, the idea is presented at a pitch meeting. Screenwriters typically have 3 to 5 minutes to propose an idea, but it takes merely 45 seconds for producers to decide whether to invest. Successful screenwriters have a ready pitch that's clear, concise, and engaging. Successful business people must have a similar pitch that's clear, concise, and engaging; it's called an elevator pitch. (The *elevator pitch* got its name because it should take 30 seconds to ride in an elevator from the top to the bottom of a building.) Let's say you're at a networking event. About 30 seconds is about how long you have to introduce yourself and make an impression.

REMEMBER

It's important to remember that while your pitch is about you, people also want to know that you're genuinely interested in them. To ensure this, pay attention to the last bullet when preparing your pitch. Here are some guidelines to follow:

>> Start by stating your name and the name of your company.

>> Highlight the key points of your products or services, emphasizing the benefits.

>> Clearly communicate your value proposition, explaining what sets you apart.

>> Offer your business card as a way of continuing the conversation.

>> Emphasize that you're eager to learn more about the person you're speaking with.

The aim is to create a focused, non-salesy, conversational, and uncomplicated pitch that shows your genuine interest in the other person.

There are many uses for a pitch bio of this length. You can use it for an article you write, a social media profile, a blog you publish, a company directory, or any other place where you need a brief introduction. When using your elevator pitch in this way, change your bio from the first person to the third person and add contact information (phone, email, website, and so on).

> **Example in the first person:** *Hi, I'm Carlo. When I started my journey to fitness, I was anything but the picture of health. I was overweight, had high blood pressure, and wasn't eating well or exercising. I developed a program that has worked for me and hundreds of others — several of whom started running marathons. I'd love to tell you more about my program and learn more about you and what you do. Perhaps we could set a time to meet for coffee?* [Hand your business card and get one in exchange.]

Example in the third person: *When Carlo started his journey to fitness, he was anything but the picture of health. He was overweight, had high blood pressure, and wasn't eating well or exercising. Carlo developed a program that has worked for him and hundreds of others — several of whom started running marathons. Carlo would love to tell you more about his program and learn more about you and what you do. You can contact Carlo at [contact information].*

AI SPOTLIGHT

Composing an elevator pitch can be daunting because there's so much you want to share but so much you must leave out. So how do you stand out? This is where AI comes to the rescue. Check out the following tools for further help:

>> Logic Balls (https://logicballs.com/tools/elevator-pitch-generator)

>> Topai (https://topai.tools/s/elevator-pitch-generator)

>> Writer Buddy (https://writerbuddy.ai/free-tools/elevator-pitch-generator)

IN THIS CHAPTER

» **Using AI as your letter-writing assistant**

» **Generating precise prompts**

» **Discovering the true value of a letter**

» **Opening and closing a letter**

» **Writing fundraising and collection letters**

» **Writing letters of complaint**

Chapter **19**

Letters: Forging a Personal Connection

I n this whirlwind of a digital era, where information zips around at lightning speed, the humble letter shines brighter than ever. It's like a charming time traveler, bringing with it a touch of nostalgia and a personal touch that no email or text message can replicate. With every stroke of the pen or click of the key, letters weave emotions, sentiments, and crucial details into a tapestry of thoughtfulness and intention. And let's not forget the magic they hold as physical keepsakes, serving as cherished mementos that outshine any fleeting digital exchange. In this fast-paced electronic world, letters truly reign supreme, reminding us of the power of genuine, heartfelt connection.

The Direct Marketing Association has come up with astonishing numbers as to why letters haven't lost their importance. Did you know that the average response rate from direct mail is 4.4 percent? Compare that to the 0.12 percent average response rate of e-marketing. That's a staggering 37 times higher! So, don't dismiss the power of a well-crafted letter — embrace it.

I've written several books on all aspects of business writing. Among them, my bestsellers have been focused on letter writing. These books have been so popular they've been translated into multiple languages, which demonstrates the high demand to learn more about this valuable mode of communication. This chapter offers highlights of some of the most challenging aspects of letter writing: fundraising, collecting outstanding funds, and letters of complaint.

Using AI as Your Assistant for Letter Writing

Put your best foot forward and write letters that engage — in multiple languages if necessary. Many of the tools that help with a variety of writing tasks will compose masterful letter content. Here are a few of the popular AI tools:

>> Anyword (https://anyword.com/)

>> ChatGPT (https://chat.openai.com/auth/login)

>> Copy.ai (https://www.copy.ai/)

>> Grammarly (https://www.grammarly.com/)

>> HyperWrite (https://www.hyperwriteai.com/)

>> Jasper (https://www.jasper.ai/)

>> Rytr (https://rytr.me/)

>> You.com (https://you.com/)

When writing letters, it's important to fill out the Kick-Start Brief in Chapter 4 to understand your reader, purpose, key issue, and the questions your reader will need answered. This Brief provides a foundation for you to customize your content to precisely meet the needs of your reader.

Generating Precise Prompts

Here are some suggestions for creating effective AI prompts, with a particular emphasis on letters:

>> State the purpose of the letter (sales, complaint, request for information, thank you, or other).

>> Include the recipient's information and your relationship (client, a business partner, colleague, for example) as this will influence the tone and formality.

>> Outline of the main points or information you want to include.

>> State a call to action (CTA), if there is one.

Why Write a Letter?

Have you ever gone through an old box of cards and letters? They're treasures that can't be deleted. Countless possessions throughout history have been destroyed, but fragile letters have been protected — powerful handwritten words that are worth reclaiming again and again. They're personal acts of authorship. Letters exchanged between Napoleon and Josephine, John and Abigail Adams, Henry VIII and Anne Boleyn, George (Sr.) and Barbara Bush, Oscar Wilde and Lord Alfred Douglas, and hosts of others through the centuries survive to this day.

While phone calls and emails have their merits and their place, people are leery of telemarketers and email scams. Therefore, letters offer a unique opportunity to connect with people on a deeper level and leave a lasting impact. There are several reasons why:

>> **Tangible presence:** A physical letter has a lasting presence that can be held, revisited, and shared with others.

>> **Less intrusive:** Unlike phone calls, which can interrupt busy schedules, letters can be read at the recipient's convenience. They allow recipients to engage with your message on their own time without feeling pressured or overwhelmed.

>> **Attention to detail:** Crafting a well-written letter demonstrates attention to detail, professionalism, and effort. It shows that you've taken the time to personalize the message and tailor it specifically to the recipient, making them feel valued and appreciated.

TIP

Type your business letters on letterhead in a 12-point font in Times New Roman or Arial, using a block format (everything justified to the left). The key parts are the date, recipient's address, salutation, message, complimentary closing, and signature. Note that the subject line is placed below the salutation.

HANDWRITTEN NOTES: THE SECRET SAUCE OF PERSONAL GRATITUDE

Maya Angelou said, "I've learned that people will forget what you said, people will forget what you did, but people will never forget how you made them feel." That's the essence of a handwritten note — letting someone know you're grateful for something they said or did. It makes them feel good. It's a genuine expression that can't be replaced by an email, text, or social media thank you. And the thoughtfulness won't be lost on the recipient. Whether you find yourself expressing gratitude for a thoughtful gift, conveying appreciation after a job interview, commending an employee, or simply wanting to show someone how much you value them, taking the time to write a heartfelt note can forge a deep and meaningful connection. The power of a few timeless words such as, "I'm very grateful for. . ." has the remarkable ability to evoke genuine emotions and make recipients truly feel valued.

Writing Salutations and Closings

Your salutations and closing should align with the purpose and tone of your letter, your relationship and familiarity with the recipient, the culture and expectations of the recipient, and the consistency and clarity of your message. By providing the correct tone, you're setting a formal or informal tone that will carry through your letter.

Saying hello

Salutations are important because they set the mood and determine the attitude your reader should adopt when responding. It's somewhat like body language in writing.

Always start with *Dear Someone* (even though the person probably isn't dear to you). If you're writing to someone you don't know well, use *Dear Mr., Mrs., Ms.,* or *Dr.* and the last name, followed by a colon. If you call the person by their first name, end with a comma. If you're unsure of the person's gender, use the first and last name followed by a colon:

Formal: *Dear Mr. Gentry:*

Informal: *Dear Leslie,*

Unsure of gender: *Dear Pat Smith:*

Never use generic salutations such as *To Whom it May Concern* or *Dear Sir or Madam*. They're cold and impersonal. When you personalize your letter by addressing it to a specific person, you increase the chances of your letter being read and taken seriously.

For mass mailings, tools such as Mailchimp (`https://mailchimp.com/`), Constant Contact (`https://www.constantcontact.com`), and others can merge addresses with letter salutations, so each recipient feels you're writing directly to them. You can also use Microsoft Mail Merger; check it out at `http://tinyurl.com/3zz9bktt`.

Bidding adieu

A complimentary closing ends the letter with a professional touch. It demonstrates that the writer is adhering to standard communication etiquette.

Formal: *Respectfully, Sincerely, Sincerely yours.*

Semi-formal: *Best regards, Cordially, With appreciation.*

Informal: *Cheers, Best wishes, Take care.*

The closing doesn't end there. It's the beginning of a block of information that has the name of the sender and the person's title that can be expressed in either of the following ways, leaving enough room for your signature:

Sincerely yours,   *Sincerely yours,*

James Botticelli   *James Botticelli, Manager*
Manager

Fundraising: Capturing Hearts and Opening Wallets

Fundraising letters play a pivotal role in giving you a chance to showcase your financial needs, involve donors (or potential donors), share your emotional story, demonstrate the significance of their contributions, and foster long-term relationships. While phone calls and emails are often used for this purpose, it's crucial to approach phone calls with caution. People have grown wary of telemarketers and email scams, so they're less effective for connecting with potential donors. When you send a letter, you cultivate a personal and authentic experience that captures the attention and support of those you aim to engage.

Go online and search "fundraising letter examples." You'll find more than you can ever use.

TIP

Getting them to open the envelope

The best written letter won't get results until the recipient opens it. Here are some tips for piquing interest on the envelope:

>> **Paper stock:** Try heavier paper stocks, vellum, glassine, or polybag-type envelopes.

>> **Size matters:** Instead of a standard-size #10 envelope, try a 4"x6", 6"x9" or 9"x12".

>> **Use an off-white color:** An ivory, beige, or light grey envelope will stand out from the standard whites.

>> **Include a teaser:** Place a dynamic message on the envelope's front or back. It should provoke curiosity but not give everything away. *Your Gift Inside, Urgent Reminder, Limited time only, Gift Card Enclosed,* or *Last Chance.*

>> **Personalize the address:** Make the recipient feel special by using a legible script font or actual handwriting. This gives the mailing a personal touch.

>> **Use a stamp:** Affix a stamp with a customized design that aligns with your message, as opposed to an *indicia* (imprinted postal marking) that shouts mass mailing.

Including a SASE

The jury is out on whether to include a self-addressed, stamped envelope (SASE). Some experts feel that a SASE makes it easier to reply, so you'll get a larger number of responses. Others feel that volume isn't the key — serious donors are. Therefore, if the donor uses their own stamp, they're more serious about supporting the organization or cause and may donate more generously. So much for the experts.

Try sample mailings with and without a SASE to see which yields better results. Collect what you perceive as junk mail for a week or two. Look at the envelopes, study them, or be whimsical and turn them into paper airplanes. But try to incorporate into your mailing envelopes what appealed to you and drew your attention. Let these envelopes become a canvas for your imagination, drawing people in and sparking their curiosity.

Grabbing attention with a captivating opening paragraph

TIP

Start your letter with something that will captivate attention: A bold question, statement or story of a specific person or situation that your charity has helped. This gives the reader a glimpse into your world and reminds them why your mission is important. Appeal to their hearts by giving specific details that are short and pithy. Here's an example:

> *Every day, countless children in our own community go to bed hungry. With your help, we can continue to provide nutritious meals to these vulnerable children and give them a chance for a brighter future.*

AI
SPOTLIGHT

AI can create enticing openings for fundraising letters by leveraging data insights, emotional appeal, and persuasive language to captivate the reader's attention to "donate."

Presenting the "ask"

There's an old expression: "Ask and you will receive." This ask or CTA is a clear directive that guides the reader's focus towards the desired action thereby eliminating any confusion or ambiguity:

> *Join the fight*

> *Send a check*

> *Call us*

> *Stop by*

> *Your compassion and support will help us transform lives and create a better future for all these children. With your generosity, together we can make a real difference. Please send a check or pay by credit card, PayPal (Venmo, or Zelle).*

Ending with a postscript

Did you know that a postscript may be the most read part of your letter? It stands apart from the body of the letter and grabs the recipient's eye. Don't miss out on this opportunity to grab their attention by adding this section to your fundraising letter:

> *Don't forget, your donation is tax-deductible!*

> *Can't donate at the moment? Consider volunteering your time and skills.*

> *Jim, did you know that your donation will be doubled?*

TIP

Consider sending a letter on behalf of a previous recipient to tug at the recipient's heartstrings. Here's an example:

> *I'm lucky. Thanks to the generosity of people such as you, I've lived with [xxx] for the past 10 years. I've gotten married and my son was just born. With continued generosity, I hope to see him grow into adulthood.*
>
> *Won't you please [call to action]. Thank you so much.*
>
> *Most sincerely,*

AI SPOTLIGHT

Here are some of the top-rated AI generators for fundraising: Donor Perfect (`https://www.donorperfect.com`), CharityTracker (`https://www.charity tracker.com/`), GiveButter (`https://givebutter.com/`).

SHERYL SAYS

FUNDRAISING LETTER THAT CREATED A LASTING BOND

Louise and I formed a unique bond that began with a heartfelt fundraising letter. While working on a book about letter writing, I stumbled upon a letter written by Jay, Louise's beloved son. Jay, a courageous and compassionate gay man, had penned a letter to raise funds for the AIDS foundation. I asked for permission to print it in my book.

Little did I know that Jay had tragically lost his battle with AIDS just weeks before my book was published. Filled with an overwhelming desire to honor Jay's memory, I reached out to Louise to express my deepest condolences and offer her a copy of the book. In response to my gesture, Louise sent me a letter that touched my heart in ways I could never have anticipated. Her words, filled with gratitude and warmth, opened the door to a profound and meaningful friendship I shared with her and Jay's siblings. Here's an excerpt from that letter:

> *Dearest Sheryl, Your memorial to Jay is more than a small comfort. I read your letter and Jay's over and over. Tears flowed, but they were tears of pride and comfort that through your book Jay will never be forgotten. I wish you could have known him . . . I close, hoping that someday we may meet as you hold a special place in my heart.*

My tears flowed as well . . . I called Louise, and we met for lunch the following week. She and I became fast friends. It was a friendship that lasted until she died a few years later at the age of 92. I framed her cherished letter and it sits on a shelf in my office in a very prominent place.

Collection Letters: Payback Time

There are people who go to extremes to avoid honoring their debts. I've heard all kinds of excuses from, "I had the paperwork in my hand and a gust of wind blew it into the river. I nearly drowned trying to go after it" . . . to "I was on the way to the post office to mail your check when I slipped on the ice. The envelope got lost in a snow bank and I'll have to wait until the snow melts to find it."

Buying is the heart of business, and collection is its lifeblood. Settling an account quickly is to everyone's benefit. The longer an account remains unpaid, the less likely is it to be paid. There are generally several stages of collecting funds, each getting progressively firmer. Some companies send a reminder followed by an ultimatum. Others send a series. Following is a series of four collection letters, typically sent 2–3 weeks apart.

First: Gentle reminder

The first letter should be a gentle reminder because a missed bill is often an oversight. Here's what to include in the first reminder:

Have you sent payment for your [date] invoice? If it's on its way, thanks. If not, please send it out today.

Second: Inquiry

This takes a different approach, asking why the account hasn't been settled. If the customer responds with a valid reason, payment assistance may be offered. If there's no response, consider the following:

>> **Reaffirm the good relationship.** *We look forward to continuing the wonderful relationship we've enjoyed over the last several years.*

>> **Stress the customer's financial obligation.** *This is the second reminder. If your check is on its way, thanks. If not, please put it in the mail today.*

>> **Employ sales tactics.** *When you send us your payment in full by [date] why not include your summer order?*

Third: Appeal

This letter must be persuasive and appeal to a sense of self-respect, duty, justice, fairness, cooperation, and self-interest. Ask for an explanation or hint that there may have been an error. You may say the following:

We're puzzled that you haven't answered our first two letters. Please call us immediately so we can discuss what prevents you from paying this invoice. Is there a problem with the invoice? Were you dissatisfied with the merchandize? We look forward to hearing from you immediately to settle this account.

Fourth: Final warning or ultimatum

After the customer has ignored your first three letters, your final attempt takes on a different tone. Even at this point you want to salvage the relationship, so you're giving them one last chance:

>> **Give a firm deadline.** *We must have your check no later than [date] or you'll force us to place this in the hands of a collection agency.*

>> **Stress the danger of a bad credit rating.** *You've been an upstanding member of the business community, so this puzzles us. Your credit reputation is of great value, and you'd be doing yourself a great disservice by blemishing it.*

>> **Offer one last chance before turning over to a collection agency.** *This is the last time you'll be hearing from us. Remit payment by [date] or the next communication will be from the collection agency.*

Making Complaints: Grin, Don't Grunt

When you're dissatisfied with a product or service, first discuss your concerns with a manager or other representative of the company and try to get satisfaction. If you don't, then it's time to put your complaint in writing. A letter is important because it:

>> Documents your complaint so there's a permanent record.

>> Helps preserve any legal rights you may have.

>> Puts the company on notice that you're serious about getting satisfaction.

Don't write an angry, sarcastic, or threatening letter. Remember that the person receiving the letter is probably not the one responsible for the problem. They're the one you're hoping resolve the problem. Also, never use *To whom this may concern*; that's a non-person. Get a name.

Find the proper recipient

The higher up you go on the company ladder, the better your chances are of getting satisfaction. Go on the company's website to find key company officers listed. (I go right to the CEO and have had lots of success. It's not necessarily the CEO I hear from, but from some high-ranking person within the company.)

Copy other relevant individuals so everyone involved is aware of the complaint you're registering. And that may include the manager you spoke with who gave you no satisfaction.

Stay focused on your complaint

In the first paragraph, include all the basics (who, what, when, where, and why). Be honest and straightforward, resisting the temptation to include unimportant details. Explain the negative experience without veering off with tangential comments about the company's employees or products:

> On May 5 I purchased at your Boston store a leather sofa and matching love seat. Enclosed is a copy of the receipt so you can see the details of the purchase. The sofa was delivered on June 15, and we've had it in our home for four months. Already the webbing underneath has given way and some of the springs are starting to drop down, as you can see from the attached photo. On October 20, I went back to the store and spoke with [name], the store manager. They told me there's nothing they can do.

Photos are excellent supplemental information to include, such as in the example just mentioned.

Include clear details and documentation

Include information about the product or service such as the date of the event, location of the store, product or serial number, person or people you spoke with, and so forth. Attach any paperwork such as receipts and previous correspondence.

Make a specific request

State exactly what you expect and how long you're willing to wait for a response. Be reasonable. Don't rely on the company to propose a solution. Instead, be clear as to what you expect. An apology. A refund. A replacement. And a timeframe:

I checked the warranty which guarantees the material and workmanship for one year. Therefore, please have someone call me within the next two weeks so we can arrange to have new pieces of furniture delivered to my home. Thank you.

Provide contact information

State how you expect the recipient to follow up, whether it's through a phone call, letter, email, or any other preferred method of communication.

REMEMBER

In addition to voicing your complaints when things go wrong, it's equally important to praise and commend when they go right. Whether it's someone going the extra mile or a product that exceeds your expectations, acknowledging these positive experiences is crucial for companies to not only address their shortcomings but also celebrate their successes. You can reach out to the CEO or the company's higher-ups through a heartfelt letter or post a glowing review on the company's website or on popular online review platforms.

TRANSMITTAL LETTERS: THE SUPERHEROES OF COMMUNICATION

A well-written transmittal letter (also known as a cover letter) and dressing for a job interview are like the dynamic duo representing the need to make a lasting first impression! Just as you dress to impress at a job interview, a well-crafted transmittal letter showcases your professionalism and communication skills. So, whether you're donning your best garb or penning a killer transmittal letter, remember the critical value of first impressions.

People often spend copious amounts of time writing and polishing their reports, resumes, business plans, grant proposals, and so forth, then throw together an on-the-fly transmittal letter without paying special attention to the high value of this communication. This is similar to showing up to a job interview in sloppy clothes but answering all the questions correctly. While you may have the right qualifications and knowledge to ace the interview, the initial impression left a lasting impact — and not the one intended.

Here are some things to consider:

- Offer key information at a glance.
- Limit the letter to one page.
- Focus on the main points.
- Display your professionalism.

And don't forget to let AI help you draft these all-important letters, applying your own finishing touches.

Chapter **20**

Storyboarding: Bringing Your Presentations to Life

A *storyboard* is like a map that takes your creative ideas on an adventure — breaking down your genius into little bite-sized frames, detailing what you'll tell and what you'll show. It's like crafting a visual masterpiece, one frame at a time. So, whether you're standing in front of a crowd or working behind the scenes on a video, get ready to dive into the world of storyboarding and watch your ideas burst into epic life.

REMEMBER

Storyboarding isn't just for presentations. This amazing tool is like a trusty compass, leading you through a world of endless creative possibilities. It's the secret ingredient that adds an extra zing to business meetings, grant proposals, training sessions, commercials, ad campaigns, marketing and advertising, product and design development, e-marketing, and so much more.

The versatility of storyboarding knows no bounds. It seamlessly weaves its way into many corners of business writing. So, get ready to unleash your creativity and let storyboarding take your business writing to new heights!

Using AI as Your Assistant for Creating Storyboards

AI SPOTLIGHT

By leveraging AI technology, storyboarding can be made more efficient and more accessible. Here are some ways AI is used in storyboarding:

>> Analyzing scripts and narratives and generating a sequence of storyboard frames.

>> Producing images, objects, scenes, and characters.

>> Providing suggestions for the layout and composition of storyboard frames.

>> Enabling multiple team members to work on the same storyboard simultaneously.

>> Learning from previous work and suggesting elements and styles that align with the creative vision.

>> Saving you time for more pressing matters such as ideation and perfecting your final product.

And you don't need to be a graphic artist . . . you just need the right tools, some of which are:

>> Boords (https://boords.com/)

>> FrameForge (https://www.frameforge.com/)

- >> Lumen5 (for videos) (`https://storyboarder.ai/`)
- >> MakeStoryboard (`https://makestoryboard.com/`)
- >> PanelForge (for animation) (`https://www.panel-forge.com/`)
- >> Storyboarder (`https://storyboarder.ai/`)

REMEMBER

When generating a storyboard, it's important to fill out the Kick-Start Brief in Chapter 4 to understand your reader (in this case, your audience), purpose, key issue, and the questions your audience will need answered. This Brief provides a foundation for you to customize your content to precisely meet the needs of your audience.

Generating Precise Prompts

AI SPOTLIGHT

Here are some suggestions for creating effective AI prompts, with a particular emphasis on storyboarding:

- >> Include what the finished product is to be: face-to-face presentation, business meeting, proposal, film, video, animation, and so forth.
- >> If you're producing a film, video, or animation, include details about the composition, camera angles, lighting, colors, and any specific visual effects or transitions.
- >> State the genre or style.
- >> Describe the key topics, subtopics, scenes, or events.
- >> Pinpoint any visuals that accompany the narrative.
- >> Specify the tone, emotions, and any important details related to the narrative.
- >> Mention timeline or sequence, time constraints, or pacing requirements.
- >> Incorporate images, videos, or existing storyboards.

STORYBOARDING HAS A HISTORY THAT GOES WAY BACK

In 1898, a Russian theatre practitioner, Konstantin Stanislavski, developed storyboards for his production plans for the performance of Chekhov's *The Seagull* at the Moscow Art Theatre. Yes, storyboarding dates back that far!

Better known, however, is Disney's Webb Smith who's considered the father of modern-day storyboards. In 1933, he started to draw rough sketches to animate *Three Little Pigs*. He pasted the sketches up on a wall to show how a storyline comes together.

In 1939, *Gone with the Wind* became the first movie to be completely drawn with a storyboard.

Storyboarding has evolved through the centuries and is now widely embraced by business communities.

Getting to Know Your Audience

Before you prepare to storyboard, there are four key words to remember: *It's not about me!* When your audience walks into a room or picks up what they'll read, they're thinking, "What's in it for me?" Perhaps you already think you know your audience, but do you actually understand their (hidden) agendas? What keeps them up at night? Ask yourself the right questions. Take a look at Figure 20-1. It has two "audience" columns.

>> In the first audience column there are questions about your audience that you should ponder, such as: "What are their major concerns?" and "What tough questions should I expect?"

>> In the second audience column there are questions you anticipate the audience will need answered during the presentation, such as "What are the alternatives?" and "When does this take effect?"

TIP

In addition to filling out the Kick-Start Brief in Chapter 4, use this example as a guide as you prepare the storyboard. Delete the questions that don't pertain to your audience and add in those that do.

	Your (About Audience)	Audience's Questions
Who...	• Will be supportive and make supportive comments? • Will be adversarial and make combative comments? • May feel threatened by my recommendations? • Is my contact person for logistical and other issues? • Should I bring in as a subject matter expert?	• Is responsible? • Will be impacted by the change?
What...	• Are the major concerns of my audience? • Can I tell or show to help them address those concerns? • Stories can help them remember key points? • Do they know about the topic? • Is my relationship with them? • Obstacles may I encounter? • Discussion points should I encourage? • Tough questions should I expect?	• Are the alternatives? • Are the advantages and/or disadvantages? • Are the next steps? • If we do nothing?
When...	• Is the best time to deliver this presentation? • Should I distribute the handouts?	• Does this take effect? • Do you need a decision?
Where...	• Can the audience get more information? • Can I get more information?	• Will the funding come from? • Can I get more information?
Why...	• Is the audience attending? • Was I chosen to make this presentation?	• Are you recommending this?
How...	• Much time should I spend on providing background? (Do they need any background?) • Will I open/close the presentation? • Does this relate to the strategic impact on the organization?	• Will we measure success?

FIGURE 20-1:
Questions you need to address before storyboarding.

Getting Ready to Storyboard

TIP

Before you begin storyboarding, capture what you've documented in the Kick-Start Brief (see Chapter 4) to ensure that your audience will remember your essential message amidst the supportive points:

I am presenting _____ (key point — narrow subject)

to _____ (specific reader/audience)

in order to _____ (call to action — what I want my reader/audience to think, do feel, or consider)

Types of Storyboard

The type of storyboard you use depends on factors such as the complexity of your project, your needs, or your preferences. Storyboards aren't mutually exclusive. You may use thumbnail sketches to start your project, then progress to a written or digital storyboard. The goal is to create a visual representation that helps you plan and communicate the intended presentation skillfully and professionally — whether you're working alone as a solo presenter or on a more complex project with a collaborating team. There are several different types of storyboarding, each with its own purpose and format.

Traditional storyboard

The traditional storyboard used in business is a series of hand-drawn or digitally created frames, arranged in chronological order in two columns. In the first column (which you fill in first) document your narrative, your *Tell*. In the second column (which you'll fill in afterwards) include anything you plan to *Show*. Take a peek at the following figures:

>> Figure 20-2 is the first page of a simple presentation on how to make a PB&J sandwich, depicting scenes or actions along with notes and descriptions.

>> Figure 20-3 is the first page of a storyboard outlining a business presentation. The Show column includes actions to be taken in addition to what's to be shown.

Filling in the Tell column

At this early stage, you're using the storyboard to create a preliminary draft of what you want to tell your reader/audience — your initial thoughts. This is your chance to express yourself without being critical of anything you write. You can censor yourself later. Your task right now is to document all the thoughts swirling around in your head. Avoid going back over what you wrote; save that for later. The most important thing is to keep moving forward. Depending on your level of comfort, you can use cryptic notes, bullets, or verbatim text.

Filling in the Show column

When preparing for a business presentation, it's important to consider what to show that will best support the narrative. The following are examples of what you can show for face-to-face and/or virtual presentations: slides, audio, video, demo, handouts, polls, chats, Q&A, whiteboard, brainstorming, interactive games, and individual/group activities.

Additional types of storyboard

Other types of storyboard include the following:

>> **Written:** This is descriptive text with scenes, actions, and dialog. It can be useful for planning a meeting, as you see in Figure 20-3 (as the first page of the meeting's plan).

>> **Thumbnail:** As shown in Figure 20-4, this is similar to traditional storyboards, only it's quick sketches for arranging the flow.

>> **Digital:** These are created using software or specialized apps that allow for easy manipulation of images, adding annotations, and even creating simple animations, as you see in Figure 20-5.

>> **User eXperience (UX):** This type of storyboarding as you see in Figure 20-6 focuses on depicting actions, emotions, and the context of use. It helps designers understand and communicate how a product or service fits into a user's life and can solve their problems.

How to Make a PB&J Sandwich
30-minute Presentation for Martians

<table>
<tr><th>Tell</th><th>Show</th></tr>
<tr><td></td><td>1-1/2 minute Video on YouTube
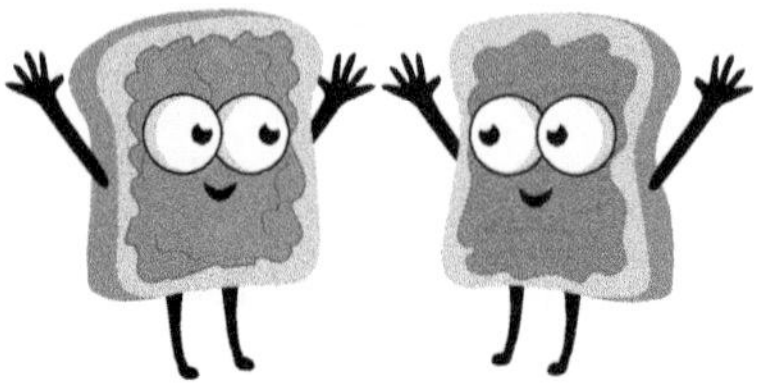</td></tr>
<tr><td>• Welcome and brief intro.
• Please feel free to jump in with any questions as we go along.</td><td></td></tr>
<tr><td>Tell story of how PBJ& started.

Boast of National PBJ& Day on April 2 for this all-American sandwich.</td><td>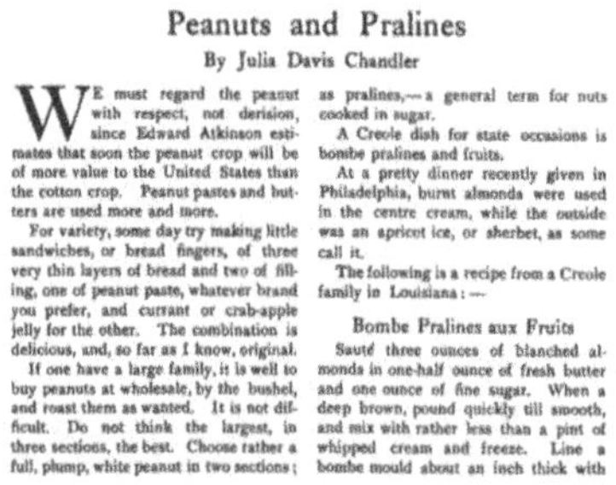
Peanuts and Pralines
By Julia Davis Chandler
WE must regard the peanut with respect, not derision, since Edward Atkinson estimates that soon the peanut crop will be of more value to the United States than the cotton crop. Peanut pastes and butters are used more and more.
For variety, some day try making little sandwiches, or bread fingers, of three very thin layers of bread and two of filling, one of peanut paste, whatever brand you prefer, and currant or crab-apple jelly for the other. The combination is delicious, and, so far as I know, original.
If one have a large family, it is well to buy peanuts at wholesale, by the bushel, and roast them as wanted. It is not difficult. Do not think the largest, in three sections, the best. Choose rather a full, plump, white peanut in two sections; as pralines,—a general term for nuts cooked in sugar.
A Creole dish for state occasions is bombe pralines and fruits.
At a pretty dinner recently given in Philadelphia, burnt almonds were used in the centre cream, while the outside was an apricot ice, or sherbet, as some call it.
The following is a recipe from a Creole family in Louisiana: —
Bombe Pralines aux Fruits
Sauté three ounces of blanched almonds in one-half ounce of fresh butter and one ounce of fine sugar. When a deep brown, pound quickly till smooth, and mix with rather less than a pint of whipped cream and freeze. Line a bombe mould about an inch thick with
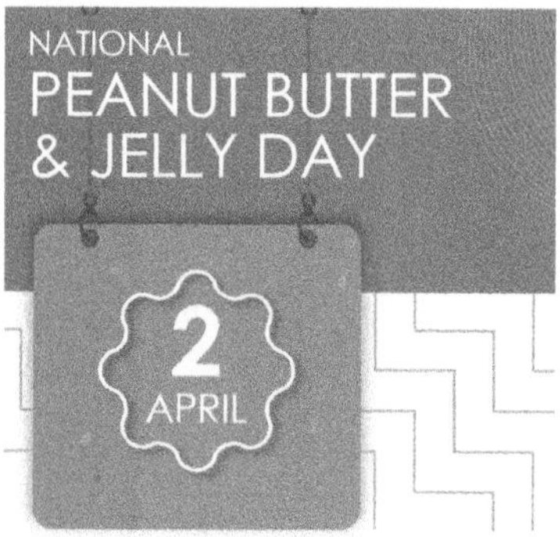
</td></tr>
</table>

FIGURE 20-2: Traditional storyboard for a presentation.

© LIGHTFIELD STUDIOS/Adobe Stock

Tell	Show
9:00 Informally welcoming our guests and chatting while enjoying coffee and pastries	• Coffee and pastries on table in back of room • Posters positioned strategically around the room, highlighting testimonials from delighted customers … with key emphasis on the outstanding support we provide during installation and thereafter • Handouts on the conference table for Brooke to distribute before lunch
9:20 (Sit at conference table) **Brooke** (who set up the meeting) will formally introduce our team. **Jon** will say a few welcoming words and invite the visitors to share their concerns and needs. ** A key issue they've had in the past (as we learned at the trade show) is they haven't gotten proper support from previous vendors for this very expensive, complex equipment. <u>We must focus on our outstanding customer support.</u>	<u>Rectangular table arrangement</u> Rosa will sit at the head of the table; Ramesh at the opposite end, facing her. Jon and Brooke will sit on one side in the middle; Jesse will sit on the opposite side, facing them.
10:00 Q&A: Open discussion of how we can help them to solve their problems. **Jon, Brooke, and Jesse** will share stories of how we've helped customers solve these same issues, such as having a senior member of our technical team at their facility during installation in addition to the high levels of ongoing support throughout the period of ownership.	Pointing discreetly to posters highlighting our superior customer support
10:45 **Jesse** takes visitors on tour of application labs to showcase the equipment, the processes, the staff, and answer questions.	Lab tour

FIGURE 20-3: Traditional storyboard for a business meeting.

FIGURE 20-4:
Thumbnail
storyboard for
arranging flow.

© GroupO FRL/Adobe Stock Photos.

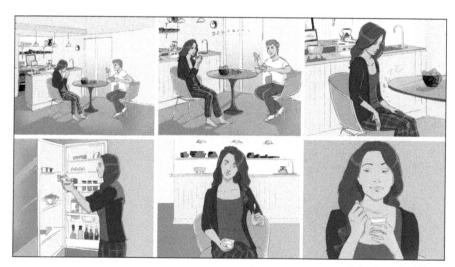

FIGURE 20-5:
Digital storyboard
using an AI
generator.

© skmp/Adobe Stock Photos.

© skmp/Adobe Stock Photos.

FIGURE 20-6:
UX storyboard
showing
emotions.

Storyboarding in Other Business Contexts

Although the original concept of storyboarding came from the film industry, businesses often find scenarios that aren't too dissimilar. They might juggle resources, plan a marketing campaign, or design a new product. But all of these situations involve collaborating with a team to map all the different parts of the plan on paper (or the computer) from start to finish. That's why companies have adopted storyboarding for business — helping them to write down their ideas and plans in a logical order.

Storyboarding is used in various business contexts to enhance communication, planning, and visualization of ideas. It allows businesses to tell their stories, align teams, and improve the overall effectiveness of their projects and processes. Here are just a few specific uses for storyboarding:

>> **Marketing and advertising:** Storyboards are commonly used in advertising and marketing campaigns to create compelling narratives, conceptualize and present ideas, and visualize how their products or services will be presented to their target audience . . . so they heed the call to action.

>> **Savvy presenters:** Presenters use storyboards to detail the flow of the narrative and visuals instead of torturing audiences with "Death by PowerPoint."

>> **Business process improvement:** Storyboards can help identify bottlenecks, visualize workflows, and communicate proposed changes to stakeholders. This can be particularly useful in lean and agile methodologies.

>> **Product design and development:** Businesses involved in product design and development create storyboards to visualize the user experience and iterate on design concepts. Storyboarding can help teams identify potential issues, make improvements, and create user-centered products.

>> **UX design:** UX designers use storyboarding as a way to map out user journeys and interactions with digital products. Storyboards help designers empathize with users, identify pain points, and design intuitive and engaging experiences.

>> **Training and education:** Storyboarding is used to create interactive and engaging learning materials, such as e-learning modules and instructional videos. They help instructional designers to structure content and ensure effective communication of information.

>> **Videos:** Videos often accompany sales and marketing campaigns. Videographers use storyboards to play and visualize their scenes, shots, and sequences before production. They help the production teams communicate their vision and ensure everyone involved is in alignment.

Working Step by Step, Frame by Frame

The storyboard is a visual blueprint for your story. It allows you to plan and communicate your vision clearly and effectively. It serves as a guide for the production team and helps ensure that everyone involved is on the same page. So, embrace your creativity, experiment with different ideas, and let your storyboard bring your story to life!

TIP

Here's a step-by-step process to help you create an effective storyboard:

1. **Get to know your audience.** Fill out the Kick-Start Brief in Chapter 4 and the questions in Figure 20-1. They'll will help you identify your audience, purpose, key issue, and questions you need to answer.

2. **Understand the sequence.** Be sure to have a clear understanding of the sequence and key moments. Think first of what you need to tell, then how and where visuals may enhance the narrative.

3. **Create a template.** This can be a series of rectangular boxes arranged vertically or horizontally on a piece of paper or using digital tools.

4. **Divide your storyboard into segments.** Each scene should represent a specific event or action that moves the story forward.

5. **Bring in the key elements.** You can use stick figures, cartoon-like characters, or whatever you can create that captures the essential details and actions that convey the story visually.

6. **Add dialogue and captions.** This helps to clarify the story and guide the audience or viewer.

7. **Arrange and rearrange the frames.** This ensures the flow is logical and coherent. Consider the pacing, transitions, and overall visual composition of the frames.

8. **Consider camera angles and shots.** If this will be a video, experiment with different camera angles and shots to add visual interest and enhance the storytelling. Use close-ups, wide shots, and other techniques to create a dynamic and engaging storyboard.

9. **Review and revise.** It may take many interactions to ensure the story flows smoothly, the visuals are clear, and the key moments are effectively conveyed.

Naming Your Presentation

REMEMBER

Names matter! If the title of your presentation is boring, your intended audience will think your presentation will be boring as well. There are a number of tried-and-tested tips professional writers and journalists use to fashion headlines. Some of them go to a *swipefile* (a collection of creative pieces, such as blog posts, emails, landing pages, and social media posts that are gathered to serve as inspiration and reference). They can pull out which headline works best for the current topic, and create slight variations. Others rely on AI for selecting names. The next time you pick up a magazine, notice how many alluring headlines (titles) seem to appear again and again.

Here are a few tips:

» Include a tempting benefit: *How to [do] . . .*

» Tell a story: *Go From . . . To . . .*

» Use the number three or any odd number: *Three Tried-and-Tested Ways to . . .*

» Inject curiosity: *New Research Reveals . . .*

» Start with an -ing verb: *Propelling Your . . .*

» Use alliterations: *Seven Simple Steps . . .*

>> Rhymes: *Meet and Repeat*

>> Pose a question: *Why do . . .*

AI SPOTLIGHT

The allure of an interesting or intriguing title often becomes the deciding factor for many people when choosing to attend workshops, underscoring the impact a powerful title can have in attracting an audience. Let AI help you create a title that resonates with and captivates your anticipated audience, whether it needs to be professional, lighthearted, intriguing, or whatever. You can gear your prompt in the right direction by asking to create a title in the form of a question (for example). Learn more about prompt writing in Chapter 23.

The name of your presentation may determine if you talk to a smattering of people or to a standing room only (SRO) crowd. Think of the last time you attended a presentation or workshop. You looked at the title and name of the presenter, formed an impression, and opted to sign up or not. Here are some weak and strong titles. Which would appeal to you?

Titles	Reactions
Weak: *Plan for Your Retirement NOW!*	Oh no. Not another one. (Zzzzzzzz — snoozer!)
Strong: *Three Ways to Ensure Financial Independence in Retirement*	Hmm! Ensure? Just three ways . . . May be worth checking out.
Weak: *Fourth Quarter Update*	Vague. Couldn't they just send the report?
Strong: *Fourth Quarter Exceeds Expectations*	Great news. Waiting to hear if we get end-year bonuses.
Weak: *Latest Software Update*	What's it this time?
Strong: *Long-Awaited Software Update to Close Security Risks*	Finally! Let's find out how to make this happen.
Weak: *Maric Building Status, Parcel II*	Too busy to attend.
Strong: *Maric Building Project Parcel II — Behind Schedule*	We need to brainstorm on how to make up the time.
Weak: *Shed Pounds During Lunchtime*	Oh sure!
Strong: *Lunch crunch*	Interesting name? I can spare an hour.
Weak: *Networking 101*	What's this? High School?
Strong: *Mingle Makers*	Catchy! I'll give it a try.

» Generating precise prompts

» Capturing your ideas and planning your content

» Creating a simple business plan

» Adding clarity and direction

» Avoiding common pitfalls

Chapter **21**

Business Plans: Preparing Blueprints for a Thriving Business

n 1994 Jeff Bezos — and we all know who he is — left his job in finance and founded Amazon, operating it exclusively as an online book retailer. He formulated his business plan on a cross-country drive from New York City to Seattle. Today Amazon is a multi-trillion-dollar company. So, whether you're a mom startup, you're opening a factory, you're operating online, or any combination, heed the words of Benjamin Franklin: "If you fail to plan, you are planning to fail."

Think of it in this way: Embarking on a long-distance trip without a GPS is like navigating the treacherous waters of entrepreneurship without a well-crafted business plan. Just as a GPS provides direction and prevents you from getting lost on unfamiliar roads, a business plan serves as your navigation aid, ensuring that no detours or wrong turns lead you astray.

Therefore, a business plan is essentially the road map to running your business. It helps to define your goals, objectives and strategies, and incorporates what you hope to accomplish, how you intend to organize the business, and the resources you need to meet your goals. This chapter helps you to efficiently plan your route.

Using AI as Your Assistant for Writing Business Plans

AI SPOTLIGHT

An AI business plan generator is a good starting point. It can simplify the process, save time and money, and provide valuable guidance and structure. Here are three of the popular generators:

>> 15minuteplan.ai (https://www.15minuteplan.ai)

>> Bizplan (https://www.bizplan.com/)

>> Upmetrics (https://upmetrics.co/)

WARNING

Although AI business plan generators are a good place to start, writer intelligence (WI) is critical. AI models rely on large datasets to learn patterns and make predictions. If the AI data is incomplete, biased, or lacks diversity, the AI model might not have a comprehensive understanding of your company's goals, leading to incorrect or flawed plans. AI lacks nuances, and relies on statistical patterns without fully understanding underlying concepts. Although the plan may be technically correct, it takes WI to fully consider the broader implications and consequences. As you'll see throughout this chapter, creating a business plan requires WI. While AI can automate certain tasks and provide recommendations, it lacks the ability to fully understand complex business dynamics, make subjective judgments, and ensure ethical decision making.

REMEMBER

When writing a business plan, it's important to fill out the Kick-Start Brief in Chapter 4 to understand your reader, purpose, key issue, and the questions your reader will need answered. This Brief provides a foundation for you to customize your content to precisely meet the needs of your reader.

Generating Precise Prompts

AI SPOTLIGHT

Here are some suggestions for creating effective AI prompts, with a particular emphasis on business plans:

>> State whether this is for a startup, an existing business, or a specific project.

>> Specify the industry or sector.

>> Identify the target audience (potential investors, lender, partner, or internal use).

>> Outline the key sections such as an executive summary, company description, market analysis, product or service description, marketing and sales strategy, organizational structure, financial projections, and funding requirements . . . or any additional sections relevant to your specific business or industry.

>> Add details about your business, such as the unique value proposition, target market, competitive advantage, pricing strategy, distribution channels, and growth potential.

>> Include financial projections and provide relevant financial data such as revenue projections, cost estimates, profit margins, and funding requirements.

>> Specify the time period and any assumptions to be considered.

>> Discuss succession planning (also known as exit strategies).

>> Indicate formatting or style requirements, if any.

Brainstorming the Plan and Determining Content

Whether you're doing this by yourself as a solo practitioner or with a team, it's essential to brainstorm the business plan before you start writing it. Here are some ideas to help you get started:

>> **Define your vision:** Start by clarifying your long-term goals and vision for your business. Consider where you want your business to go, what it will look like in three, five, ten, or however many years, and how it will grow and evolve.

>> **Identify your target market:** Understand your target audience and their needs. Determine who your ideal customers are, their demographics, and what problems your business can solve for them. This will help you tailor your products or services to meet their specific needs.

>> **Focus on business ideas:** Encourage creativity and open-mindedness. Consider different industries, trends, and emerging markets. You can also explore your own passions, skills, and expertise to find a unique business idea.

- **» Evaluate the feasibility:** Consider factors such as market demand, competition, scalability, and financial viability. This evaluation will help you narrow down your options and select the most promising idea for your business plan.

- **» Create a business model canvas:** Identify key elements such as customer segments, value propositions, revenue streams, and cost structure. It encourages creativity and innovation while providing a structured approach to developing your business plan.

- **» Design a marketing and sales strategy:** Conduct market research, define your target buyer personas, and determine the most effective marketing channels to reach your audience. Consider your pricing strategy, distribution channels, and promotional activities.

- **» Include financial projections:** Outline your expected revenue, expenses, and profitability. Consider factors such as start-up costs, operating expenses, sales forecasts, and cash flow projections. This information is crucial for attracting investors and securing funding.

The key to successful brainstorming is to encourage free thinking and capture as many ideas and opinions as possible. One way is to conduct a SWOT analysis (Strengths, Weaknesses, Opportunities, and Threats — outlined later in this chapter) to assess the internal and external factors that may impact your business. This analysis will help you understand your competitive advantage and potential challenges. Another type of brainstorming is using sticky notes as you see in Figure 21-1. They provide a flexible and interactive way to organize thoughts effectively.

TIP

Once you've brainstormed, it's time to develop the content. Determining the length can vary depending on factors such as the purpose of the plan, the complexity of the business, and the intended audience. While there's no fixed rule for the exact length of a business plan, here are some considerations:

- **» Purpose:** If the plan is intended for internal use within your business (such as The Crunchy Crust business plan shown in Figure 21-2), a shorter plan may be sufficient. On the other hand, if you're seeking external funding or presenting the plan to potential investors, a more comprehensive and detailed plan is needed.

- **» Complexity:** A simple business with straightforward operations may only need a short plan, while a more complex business with multiple products or services, market segments, and operational considerations may require a more extensive plan.

- **» Intended audience:** If you are presenting the plan to investors or lenders who are familiar with your industry, you may be able to provide a more concise plan. However, if your audience is less familiar with your industry or business model, a more detailed plan may be necessary to provide a comprehensive understanding. Be sure to define any terms they may not understand.

FIGURE 21-1:
Using Post-it
notes to
brainstorm
the plan.

>> **Quality over quantity:** Focus on providing relevant and concise information that effectively communicates your business concept, strategies, and financial projections. Avoid unnecessary repetition or excessive details that may detract from the main points of the plan.

Writing a Simple Business Plan

A simple business plan is a concise overview, typically one or two pages long, that covers key elements such as the company's vision or mission, product or service offering, target audience, revenue streams and sales channels, structure and operations, and financial forecasts. It provides a clear and focused outline of the business's goals and how it plans to achieve them.

**AI
SPOTLIGHT**

I used You.com to generate the simple two-page business plan you see in Figure 21-2. The plan is for a sandwich shop for a sole proprietor who plans to open two more locations in the future. This chatbot even generated the name of the shop. (Quite catchy, huh!)

The Crunchy Crust Sandwich Shop Business Plan

Executive Summary

The Crunchy Crust aims to provide high-quality, delicious sandwiches to customers in a convenient and friendly environment. With a focus on fresh ingredients, unique flavor combinations, and excellent customer service, we believe our sandwich shop will quickly become a favorite among locals. This business plan outlines our vision, goals, and strategies for success, including the expansion of our brand with two additional shops in the future.

Mission Statement

Our mission is to provide our community with high-quality, sandwiches and sundries in a warm and welcoming dine-in environment with take-outs as an option. We are committed to supporting local farmers, using non-GMO products, promoting sustainability, and creating a space where people can connect and enjoy exceptional repasts.

Business Description

The Crunchy Crust will be located in a bustling commercial area with high foot traffic. We will offer a diverse menu of sandwiches, including vegetarian and vegan options, as well as sides, beverages, and desserts. The shop will have a modern and inviting atmosphere, with comfortable seating for dine-in customers and a quick-service counter for takeout orders.

Market Analysis

There is a growing demand for quick, healthy, and affordable dining options, making the sandwich industry an attractive market to enter. We have conducted thorough market research and identified our target audience as professionals, students, and families who prioritize convenience and quality. By offering a wide range of sandwiches to cater to different dietary preferences, we aim to capture a significant market share.

Competitive Analysis

While there are several sandwich shops in the area, we believe our unique menu, emphasis on freshness, and exceptional customer service will set us apart from the competition. We will also differentiate ourselves by offering seasonal specials and introducing new, innovative sandwiches regularly. Additionally, we will leverage digital marketing platforms and social media to boost our online presence and attract a larger customer base.

Operations Plan

Our sandwich shop will operate six days a week, from early morning to late evening, to accommodate breakfast, lunch, and dinner customers. We will focus on efficient inventory management, ensuring that we always have fresh ingredients on hand. Staff will be trained to provide friendly and prompt service, and we will implement technology solutions to streamline order processing and payment systems.

FIGURE 21-2:
Simple two-page business plan.

Marketing and Sales Strategy

To attract customers, we will implement a multi-channel marketing strategy. This will include online advertising, social media engagement, local partnerships, and targeted promotions. We will also offer loyalty programs and discounts to encourage repeat business. Additionally, we will actively seek feedback from customers to continuously improve our offerings and service.

Financial Projections

Our financial projections indicate steady growth and profitability. We anticipate an initial investment of ($) from personal savings to cover the start-up costs, including equipment, inventory, and marketing expenses. With increasing revenue and careful cost management, we expect to achieve positive cash flow within the first year. The profits generated will be reinvested into the business, enabling us to open two additional sandwich shops within the next three years.

Management

Marc Erics, the sole proprietor, has had 10 years' experience in the restaurant industry and holds an MBA from Northeastern University. He is a former partner at Sammy's Sandwich Shop that was forced to close due to the pandemic. He is now ready to incorporate all his experience into this new business venture.

In conclusion… The Crunchy Crust is poised for success in the competitive market, thanks to our unique menu, excellent customer service, and strategic marketing efforts. By focusing on quality, convenience, and customer satisfaction, we are confident that our brand will thrive in this commercial, high foot-traffic area. With a strong foundation and a clear vision for expansion, we believe our sandwich shop will become a go-to destination for sandwich lovers in the area.

FIGURE 21-2:
(continued)

Creating a Robust Business Plan

A robust business plan is the cornerstone that provides a clear pathway for your business, guiding you through each stage of starting, managing, and growing. It provides clarity and direction, can attract investors and partners, proactively mitigate problems before they start, and aid in strategic decision making. This section looks at some of the topics you may need to include.

REMEMBER

Pay attention to the presentation and formatting. Poorly formatted documents with inconsistent fonts, headings, or layout can create a negative impression and make it difficult for readers to navigate through the plan. Take the time to ensure that your plan is visually appealing, well organized, and easy to read. Place your business plan in a three-ring binder — don't get too fancy because you want to show that you're financially responsible, especially if you're trying to attract funders.

Review your business plan as needed. If your plan isn't working, review each section and make revisions. If economic conditions or your business model change, update the plan. And have your lawyer, accountant, and trusted advisors review your business plan — they may find something you overlooked or underemphasized.

Executive Summary

Use the executive summary to capture the highlights of your business — it's the gateway to your entire plan. (Learn more in Chapter 16.) The executive summary must stand on its own and show passion. Include charts, tables, and graphs, when appropriate. Here's what to include:

- **The hook:** Share something creative about your company, an interesting fact, or just a very well-crafted description of your business. Give potential investors or partners something that makes your company stand out and be memorable among a sea of other business plans vying for the same dollars.

- **Company description summary:** Now that you've hooked the reader, they need to understand what your company does, what products or services you offer, and who's managing the company.

- **Market analysis:** What's the demand for your products or services? Who are your competitors? What advantages do you have that make your business unique in comparison to others?

- **Business model:** The revenue stream, cost structure, and key partnerships that drive the business's financial success.

- **Financial information and projections:** Provide an overview of your current business financials. Include highlights of your current sales and profits (if you have any), as well as what funding you're hoping to acquire and how this will affect your financials in the next few years.

- **Future plans:** Are you hoping to open another location? Expand your product line? Be financially independent in two years, five years, or whenever?

Mission Statement

This is a one-paragraph description of why your company exists. It explains what the company does, who it serves, and what differentiates it from competitors. If it's applicable to your business, include a social and environmental impact statement that's in line with current expectations of corporate responsibility. While keeping this section brief, include the following:

- What your company does.

- What sets you apart from your competition.

- What needs and benefits you provide.

- What excites you about the company's future.

For example:

At [Company Name], our mission is to [specific purpose]. We are dedicated to [core values that guide the business]. Through our [products/services], we offer [unique value proposition]. We are committed to delivering [quality, innovation, or excellence]. Our goal is to [long-term vision and aspirations]. By consistently upholding our mission, we aim to [desired outcome or result such as growth, profitability, or exceeding customer satisfaction].

Business Description and Concepts

This is where you may want to be boastful. Show your passion for your business. Passion is *the* thing that can turn a so-so business into a great one. Explain why you care. Highlight your vision and include personal anecdotes and brief stories. This is the time to boast about how you started your business in your garage, how you grew your business, and where you plan to take the business. Include charts, graphs, or tables as necessary. But there's more . . .

Business Description

- Provide a concise summary of your company's concept and offerings.

- Explain the benefits your business provides to customers.

- Highlight what sets your brand apart from competitors.

- Describe the industry your business operates in and how it distinguishes itself within that industry.

Target Market

- Identify your target market and describe the specific customer segments you aim to serve.

- Provide insights into the needs, preferences, and behaviors of your target audience.

- Explain how your business meets the demands of your target market and solves their problems.

Unique Selling Proposition (USP)

- Clearly define your unique selling proposition, which is the factor that differentiates your business from competitors.

- Highlight the specific features, benefits, or qualities that make your product or service stand out.

- Emphasize how your USP addresses the needs and desires of your target market.

Business Model

- Explain your business model, which outlines how your company generates (or will generate) revenue and sustains profitability.

- Describe the key components of your business model, such as pricing strategy, distribution channels, and customer acquisition methods.

Products and Services

In jargon-free terms, help the reader to see, taste, smell, and feel your product or service. Explain the concept for your business, along with all aspects of purchasing, manufacturing, packaging, and distribution. You'll go over suppliers, costs, and how what you're offering fits into the current market and stacks up against your competitors:

- How will it improve lives?

- How can you do it better or more cost effectively than others?

- Do you have a patent or is one pending?

- What makes this product or service unique or better than what's already available in the market?

- Have you had the product tested or certified, or gotten approvals from industry experts?

- Where are you currently with this product or service?

- How will you sell it? Online or in retail stores? Have you lined up any vendors?

- How will you fulfil orders or deliver the service?

- Do you envision future products or services to extend the business once it's successfully launched?

Market Analysis and Strategy

Show that you have a solid understanding of the marketplace, including industry characteristics and trends, anticipated growth, complementary products or services, barriers of entry, and so on. You must absolutely understand where your business sits in the marketplace now and in the future before you start to write the business plan. Address this from two sides:

- **Industry analysis:** Assess the general industry environment in which you compete.

- **Target market analysis:** Identify and quantify the customers that you'll be targeting.

AI SPOTLIGHT

Check out `https://www.capterra.com/sem-compare/marketing-analytics-software` to discover AI tools for detailed market analysis, including customer behavior and competitive landscape.

Sales Forecast

This section helps to project future revenue and provides insights for managing the business effectively. Here are some key elements to include in:

- **Product or service list:** List all the goods and services your business offers.

- **Sales volume:** Estimate the number of units or quantities of each product or service that you expect to sell over a specific period of time.

- **Pricing:** Determine the price point for each product or service. Consider market demand, competition, and your business's pricing strategy. Multiply the sales volume by the price to calculate the total revenue for each product or service.

- **Sales growth:** Consider anticipated growth (or decline) in sales over time. This could be based on market trends, industry performance, or regulation changes.

- **Market analysis:** Conduct a thorough analysis of your target market, including customer demographics, preferences, and buying behavior.

- **Seasonality and trends:** If your business is seasonal, take into account any fluctuations or trends that may impact your sales.

- **Competitor analysis:** Assess the competitive landscape and consider how your competitors' actions may affect your sales.

- **Sales channels:** Explain the various channels through which you'll sell your products or services, such as online platforms, retail stores, or direct sales. Consider the potential sales volume and revenue from each channel.

AI tools such as Zoho (`https://www.zoho.com/crm/enterprise/solutions/artificial-intelligence.html`), Varicent (`https://www.varicent.com`), and Aviso (`https://www.aviso.com/`) can help with forecasting sales.

Marketing Plan

Provide a marketing, advertising, and/or public relations plan. Indicate specific actions you plan to take, distribution channels, product and service warranties, tracking methods, and pricing. Start with the least expensive marketing tactics and proceed to the most expensive. Include the sales literature you plan to use. Detail your marketing materials, and clarify the role your website will play in your sales efforts:

- Who are your customers? What are your products? Who is your competition (direct and indirect)?

- What pricing, packaging, and distribution strategies have you determined?

- Will your advertising include public relations? Web presence? Social media? Focus groups? Face-to-face interaction? Telephone campaigns? Trade shows? Distribution channels?

If you're an existing company preparing for expansion, use customer complaints to your advantage. This will help you understand the specific needs and preferences of your target audience. Tailor your marketing messages to address these concerns and highlight how your product or service can solve their problems or meet (exceed) their expectations. Personalized marketing resonates better with customers and can lead to increased engagement and conversions.

Tools such as Branding 5 (`https://www.branding5.com`), Single Grain (`https://www.singlegrain.com/blog/ai-marketing-strategy/`), and others can help you formulate a robust marketing strategy.

Operations Plan

You need an operations plan to help others understand how you'll deliver on your promise to turn a profit. This is where you outline that you understand what's involved in operating this type of business. Include buildings, equipment, labor requirements, and all the "bricks and mortar." And depending on the nature of your business, you may integrate sustainable practices to appeal to eco-conscious investors and customers.

Here are things to include:

- General operational details that help investors understand the physical details of your vision.

- Information about any physical plants, equipment, assets, and so on.
- A list of all levels of the operation that must be done to start turning a profit.

Financial Plan

Your financial projections will help you see if your business plans are realistic, whether you'll have any shortfalls, and what financing you may need. If you're a start-up company, remember that you'll have to pay your suppliers before your customers pay you. You may also have to rent a facility, purchase equipment, and so on. These are key expenditures for which you'll need up-front money.

You must understand how to project, forecast, estimate, and calculate all aspects of your finances:

- Break financial projections into annual projections, three-year projections, and five-year projections.
- Calculate your costs of goods and services as well as your anticipated fixed overhead costs.
- Develop a balance sheet which will give you a handle on cash, accounts receivable, inventory, machinery and equipment, land, and so forth.
- Plot expected revenues, expenses, assets, liabilities, and equity.

AI SPOTLIGHT

Here are some AI tools to help with financial calculations:

- Cube Software (https://www.cubesoftware.com)
- Domo (https://www.domo.com/)
- Kepion (https://www.kepion.com)
- PlanBuildr (https://planbuildr.com)
- LivePlan (https://www.liveplan.com)
- Microsoft (https://www.microsoft.com/en-us/power-platform/products/power-bi)

Management Team and Key Members

Don't underestimate the importance of collective genius. Describe your team's abilities, experiences, special skills, publications, patents, books published, and anything else that shows strength. If someone on your team has had serious entrepreneurial success, you earn double points.

Risk Assessment

Starting a new business is always risky. Managing an existing business also has its share of risks. Remember, though, if you're not taking risks, you're not growing your business. There's an old expression: Lead, follow, or get out of the way. Some business people are willing to take big risks; others, not so much. To help determine risk, consider doing a SWOT analysis, which stands for strengths, weaknesses, opportunities, and threats:

- **Strengths:** Identify the internal factors that give you an advantage over your competition. This can include unique specialty or resources, expertise, competitive advantages, geographic location, and potential for franchising or expansion.

- **Weaknesses:** Identify the internal factors that give you a disadvantage compared to your competition. This can include any limitations such as less-than-stellar brand recognition, lack of resources, limited geographic reach, or areas that need improvement.

- **Opportunities:** This takes into account external factors that can be leveraged to benefit your company. They can include market trends, emerging technologies, or new customer segments.

- **Threats:** These can potentially harm an organization and may include new competition, economic downturns, and regulatory changes.

Exit Strategies

Consider and plan for an exit strategy from the early stages of your business. This allows you to make informed decisions and take actions that align with your long-term goals. Options may include the following:

- **Sell to investors or another company:** This can provide a substantial profit if the business is successful.

- **Initial public offering (IPO):** This takes the company public by offering shares to the general public through a stock exchange. It allows the business owner to sell shares and potentially generate significant capital.

- **Management buyout:** This gives the existing management team the ability to purchase the business and provides smooth transition of ownership and continuity of operations.

- **Liquidation:** This is where business is closed down, and its assets are sold to pay off obligations. This is typically used when the business is not performing well or when the owner wants to close the business entirely.

- **Merger or acquisition:** Merging or selling to another company can provide opportunities for growth and expansion while allowing the business owner to exit the company.

Appendixes

Include resumes, promotional material, testimonials, product photos or sketches, list of inventory and fixed assets, price lists, copies of legal agreements, articles about your product or service, and any other documents that add strength to your business plan.

Knowing What to Avoid

WARNING

Knowing what to avoid is as critical as knowing what to include. Avoid the following in your business plan:

>> **Unrealistic financial projections:** Your financial forecasts should take into account market conditions, competition, and other relevant factors. Overly optimistic projections can undermine the credibility of your plan and make it less likely to attract investors or lenders.

>> **Lack of market research:** Without this information, your business plan may lack a solid foundation and fail to address key market opportunities or challenges.

>> **Ignoring potential risks:** Your business plan should include a thorough analysis of potential risks, such as competition, regulatory changes, economic downturns, and technological advancements.

>> **Waiting until the last minute:** This isn't like college where you can drink lots of coffee and cram all night. Your business plan must be well thought out. Take the time to do it right, and involve as many people as you need to make that happen.

>> **Worrying about being original:** Even an unoriginal idea can be propelled by a superior management team. So, focus on finding highly capable people — people who may be able to attract investors and partners.

>> **Being a windbag:** Try to keep your business plan to no more than 50 pages. Stick to the essential facts and stay focused.

Chapter **22**

Nonfiction Books: Establishing Bragging "Writes"

t doesn't matter if you're a rocket scientist or a professional pancake flipper, write a book! Publishing a book is like sprinkling magic on your name. Suddenly, you become the guru, the master, the go-to person in your field. It's like getting a shiny badge of credibility that opens doors for you. You'll land speaking gigs left and right because everyone wants to hear from the author-extraordinaire. You can make sweet passive income from those book sales. (Who doesn't love to make money while sleeping?) You expand your kingdom by reaching more people than ever before.

So grab that pen or laptop, fire up your creative juices, and get ready to conquer the world with your amazing book!

Use AI as Your Assistant to Writing a Nonfiction Book

AI SPOTLIGHT

AI tools can help to generate ideas and provide research assistance, create outlines, edit and proofread, provide feedback and suggestions, publish, design a cover, and assist with book promotions. They include but aren't limited to the following:

>> Cloud Ghostwriting (`https://www.cloudghostwriting.com/`)

>> Jasper (`https://www.jasper.ai/`)

>> Sudowrite (`https://www.sudowrite.com/`)

>> Writer (`https://writer.com/`)

While AI can be a valuable tool to assist in the writing process, it can't replace *you* to reflect your own voice and perspective. AI lacks creativity, emotional understanding, and storytelling capabilities, which are vital aspects of compelling writing.

REMEMBER

When writing a nonfiction book, it's important to fill out the Kick-Start Brief in Chapter 4 to understand your reader, purpose, key issue, and the questions your reader will need answered. This Brief provides a foundation for you to customize your content to precisely meet the needs of your reader.

Generating Precise Prompts

AI SPOTLIGHT

Here are some suggestions for creating effective AI prompts, with a particular emphasis on nonfiction books:

>> Define the topic, subject, or scope.

>> Identify the target audience such as beginners, experts, or a specific demographic.

>> Specify the main chapters, sections, or topics.

>> List key points, subtopics, or specific information in each chapter or section.

>> Provide reference materials, research papers, or sources.

>> Indicate the desired tone and style such as formal, conversational, academic, or journalistic.

>> Provide examples and illustrations.

DON'T PUT IT OFF ANY LONGER

Commitment is the cornerstone of any successful endeavor, and writing a book is no exception. It requires dedicating time and energy to the process, even when the initial excitement fades and the challenges arise. Without a steadfast commitment, the idea of writing a book remains nothing more than a fleeting thought, easily forgotten amidst the chaos of everyday life.

Having a plan is essential to navigate the complex world of book writing and publishing. A well-thought-out plan provides structure, guidance, and direction. It outlines the necessary steps, from research and outlining to drafting and editing, ensuring that the journey to publication remains focused and purposeful. A plan also helps to stay organized and motivated, preventing you from getting lost in the overwhelming sea of possibilities.

In the end, it's those who have commitment, passion, and a solid plan who will turn their aspirations into tangible achievements. Writing a book is a monumental task, one that requires dedication and perseverance. So, if you are one of those people who constantly utter the words, "I'm planning to write a book," take a moment to reflect on your commitment, passion, and plan. You don't want to look back many years from now and say, *I woulda, coulda, shoulda.*

Knowing Who Your Readers Will Be

If you already have a blog, podcast, or other online presence, then you'll already know who your readers are. If not, you need to learn about them. Here are some strategies to help you determine who your readers may be and what they want:

>> **Research your target audience.** Understand who your target audience is and what their interests, needs, and preferences are. This will help you tailor your book to their specific desires and expectations. Conduct surveys, interviews, or focus groups to gather insights directly from your potential readers. Ask them about their interests, challenges, and what they would like to learn or gain from a nonfiction book on your topic.

>> **Study market trends and reader preferences.** Stay up to date with current market trends and popular topics in your genre. This will give you an idea of what readers are currently interested in and what topics are in demand. Read books in your genre and analyze their reviews and ratings. This can provide valuable insights into what readers liked or disliked about similar books and what they are looking for in a nonfiction book.

>> **Analyze reader feedback and reviews.** Look for reviews and feedback on similar books in your genre. Pay attention to common themes or recurring comments from readers. This can give you an understanding of what readers appreciate or expect from a nonfiction book. Engage with your potential readers through social media, forums, or online communities. Ask for their opinions, suggestions, and feedback on your book topic or ideas. This direct interaction can provide valuable insights into their preferences and expectations.

Getting to Know the Marketplace

Before you begin to write your book, you must explore the market, the competition, and how your book will be better or present more or extensive information than what's already published.

AI SPOTLIGHT

AI can help with competitive analysis by identifying competing books, analyzing book summaries and descriptions, evaluating book reviews and ratings, assessing market demand, and identifying other titles' strengths and weaknesses. A good place to start is at `https://booxai.com/ai-tools-for-book-sales-optimization/`.

Also, check out online booksellers, go to libraries, and to local bookstores (the few that are left.) Learn to use Amazon's "Also bought" results to show books that are potentially similar to yours. And check out Goodreads (`www.goodreads.com`). Learn everything you can about books that compete with yours:

>> What are their strengths and weaknesses?

>> Are they self-published or traditionally published?

>> Does the author have local or national prominence?

>> Why is the author believable?

>> How does the information in these books differ from the information that will appear in yours?

Look at ten books you consider to be direct competition to yours — books that cover the same type of information or that tell the same type of story, then narrow the competition down to five you feel are closest in subject matter. These should be the most direct competition. List by title, subtitle, author, publisher, copyright year, number of pages, paperback/hardcover, and online price.

ESTABLISH YOUR CREDIBILITY

SHERYL SAYS

I met an engineer at a conference. When he heard I'm an author, he jumped in to tell me he was writing a book on travel. "Why a book on travel, when you're an engineer?" I asked. He responded, "Because I travel a lot." Now . . . if the contributing editor of the travel section of a newspaper or magazine were writing a book on travel, that would be a credible person. But an engineer who travels, not so much. Know what makes you credible:

- Are you well known in your field?

- Are you considered a thought leader?

- Have you had a success that's widely known?

- Have you invented something?

- Have you developed a tried-and-tested process?

- Have you received an award or citation for your talents in the genre your book fits in?

You must have credibility in order to be credible. (Redundancy deliberately included.)

TIP

A broad readership will increase your chances of appealing to a publisher:

>> Does your topic appeal to a broad-based audience?

>> Does it present useful and timely information?

>> Does it answer questions or solve problems that are meaningful and significant to your readers?

Remember, there are very few topics that haven't been written about. So know how your book will be different, better, or fill a need.

Selecting a Title

The title of a book is significant for several reasons. The title is the first thing people see. It can grab attention or not. A well-crafted title can give readers a sense of what to expect from the book, hinting at its genre, style, or subject matter. It sets the tone and creates anticipation, influencing whether a reader decides to pick up the book or not. A title can create a lasting impression by conveying the author's voice, style, and perspective. A well-written title can increase the book's visibility in a crowded marketplace.

TIP

Establish a working title early on because it can serve as a guidepost to help you focus. This isn't necessarily the title you'll end with; it's a place to start. A working title provides a sense of direction. It can spark creativity allowing you to explore different angles and perspectives. And it can help you organize your thoughts and structures.

The title of a book can play a significant role in its success. A well-chosen title can attract readers, create intrigue, and convey the essence of the book's content. On the other hand, a poorly chosen title may fail to capture readers' attention and hinder the book's success. Although there's no guarantee, here are some tips for creating book titles that sell:

>> **Add an intrigue factor:** Titles that capture the audience's attention and leave them intrigued are more likely to sell. Consider using titles that evoke curiosity or mystery. (Example: *Cloud Cuckoo Land* by Anthony Doerr.)

>> **Be clear and clever:** A clever title is great if it's clear, but a clear title is always preferable. The best approach is to have a title that is both clear and clever. This gives readers an understanding of what the book is about while also piquing their interest. (Example: *Visual Intelligence* by Amy E. Herman.)

>> **Enhance discoverability:** This means choosing a title that's easily searchable and stands out among other books in its genre. (Example: *Storytelling for Presentations For Dummies* by Sheryl Lindsell-Roberts . . . A little shameless self-promotion!)

AI SPOTLIGHT

This is where AI can be invaluable. Sites such as BookRaid (`https://bookraid.com/ai/book-title-generator`) and others found online can help you generate interesting titles. You can use them as-is, or tweak them to make them your own. Figure 22-1 is an example from You.com.

A title consists of the most important words you may ever write. Think of John Gray's original book title *What Your Mother Couldn't Tell You and What Your Father Didn't Know*. When that book didn't sell, Gray changed the title to *Men are From Mars, Women are From Venus*. That book became an overnight success. Another title that struck gold was Seth Godin's book *Purple Cow*. The subtitle is "Transform Your Business by Being Remarkable." The book teaches how to stand out from the herd. A clever title can make your book stand out from the herd.

1. "From Dream to Reality: A Guide to Starting Your Own Day Care Center"
2. "Little Hearts, Big Dreams: The Ultimate Handbook for Opening a Day Care"
3. "Creating a Safe Haven: A Step-by-Step Guide to Launching Your Day Care Center"
4. "The Day Care Entrepreneur: Unlocking Success in the Childcare Industry"
5. "Nurturing the Future: The Essential Guide to Building a Thriving Day Care Business"
6. "From Diapers to Diplomas: A Journey into Launching Your Own Day Care Center"
7. "Caring for Our Community: A Comprehensive Manual for Starting a Day Care"
8. "The Day Care Playbook: Strategies and Secrets for Opening a Successful Center"
9. "Growing Together: A Roadmap for Starting and Running a Day Care Center"
10. "Little Steps, Big Impact: The Definitive Guide to Starting a Day Care Center"

FIGURE 22-1:
AI-generated titles.

Unless you're a known author and your name alone sells your books, you'll need a well-thought-out title and subtitle. The title should open the door and the subtitle should stimulate curiosity or interest.

REMEMBER

Sometimes the title you thought was perfect when you started to write the book doesn't work as well by the time you finish. The title isn't carved in granite until the book goes to press.

Creating a Roadmap

If you were planning to drive from New York to California, you would undoubtedly start with a roadmap. Even though you were planning to use your GPS, it would be helpful to envision your route. You also need to create a roadmap to write your manuscript. It keeps you focused and on track. Your roadmap can be in the form of a table of contents or outline. It's where you transform your ideas into a structured format a reader can understand at a glance. As you go through the writing process, you'll add, delete, and change many things . . . but this is a starting point.

AI SPOTLIGHT

AI can come to your rescue. Figure 22-2 shows how You.com prepared an extensive outline. The figure shows just the first page.

Title: "Building Blocks: A Guide to Starting and Running a Successful Daycare Center"

Chapter 1: The Foundation of Your Daycare Center

- Why start a daycare center?
- Defining your mission and vision
- Understanding the legal requirements and regulations
- Choosing the right location and facility

Chapter 2: Planning for Success

- Conducting market research and identifying your target audience
- Developing a comprehensive business plan
- Creating a budget and securing funding
- Building a team: Hiring qualified staff and educators

Chapter 3: Designing an Engaging Curriculum

- Developing age-appropriate educational programs
- Fostering child development through play and structured activities
- Incorporating STEAM (Science, Technology, Engineering, Arts, and Math) subjects
- Promoting inclusivity and diversity in your curriculum

FIGURE 22-2:
AI-generated
chapter outline.

Writing Copy for the Back Cover

REMEMBER

If your book will be sold as a printed product, the back cover copy is one of the most important selling points for your book. It's like a billboard — million-dollar real estate. However, books that are exclusively available as e- books don't have back covers.

The decision of when in the process to write the back cover copy differs from author to author:

>> Writing the back cover copy before writing the book

- Serves as a roadmap or guide helping to focus on the key themes, main points, and overall message of the book.

- Helps to refine and clarify ideas by distilling the essence of the book into a concise and compelling description.

- Provides motivation and inspiration throughout the writing process.

>> Writing the back cover copy after writing the book

- Gives a clearer understanding of the content, structure, and tone of the book.

- Highlights specific aspects of the book that are most important or compelling.
- Ensures that the description accurately reflects the content of the book.

AI SPOTLIGHT

If you want to condense your key points in the back cover, turn to any of your favorite chatbots. You can prompt for the length, tone, and salient points.

Here are some ideas to include on the back cover:

>> **Description:** The average number of words can vary depending on the genre, book size, and font size. While there's no specific industry standard, it's generally recommended to keep the wording to no more than 150–200 words.

>> **Bio:** Write a brief bio that highlights your credentials, expertise, or any relevant accomplishments in no more than 100 words. This helps establish your credibility and gives readers a sense of who you are as a writer. And don't hesitate to include a headshot. It gives potential readers the feeling that they know you. Check out Chapter 18 in this book for writing your bio.

AI SPOTLIGHT

AI can be of great value in helping you write a stellar bio. You can prompt for a serious bio, a conversational one, a humorous one, or whatever fits the genre of your book. Chapter 23 offers lots of good advice about writing prompts.

>> **Testimonials:** If you have received positive reviews or endorsements, consider including a few testimonials on the back cover. These can help build trust and credibility. Choose testimonials that highlight the strengths and unique aspects of your book.

>> **Awards and other books:** If your book or other books you've written have received any awards or recognition, mention them. This can help create a positive impression and generate interest.

>> **Eye-catching design:** Use visually appealing graphics, fonts, and colors that align with the overall theme and tone of your book. A well-designed back cover can attract attention and make a positive impression on potential readers. (Find out more about visuals in Chapter 7.)

TIP

Look at what appears on the back cover of your favorite books. Notice the key points and what enticed you to buy (or pick up) the book.

Writing the Draft

Don't be concerned about where to start. You don't have to start with the introduction or opening chapter. Start with the section or chapter that's easiest for you to write. Then go to the second easiest, and so forth. Before you know it, you'll have major chunks completed. Your reader will never know whether you started at the beginning, middle, or end.

AI SPOTLIGHT

Check out Part 2 of this book that includes many references on how AI can be valuable throughout the entire writing process — from title to draft to completion.

MY BUMPY ROAD TO SUCCESS

Here's something I penned for a writers' group I lead. It amusingly tells of my frustrating journey to finding my first publisher. Perhaps you'll relate to it.

What do I have in common with Dan Brown, Beatrix Potter, Martha Mitchell, Stephen King, J.K. Rowling, George Orwell, and a host of others? Cascading waterfalls of rejections. Rejections are a collective familiarity in the world of traditional publishing.

Nearly every best-selling author has travelled the bumpy road paved with rebuffs — from contests to agents to editors at publishing houses. Rejections suck! There's the feeling of being gutted like a filleted fish, underscoring an author's worst qualms: *Who do I think I am? A writer?*

During attempts to publish my first book, some rejections appeared in the form of black holes. Nothing. Nada. Zippo. Others were handwritten notes, form letters, or emails I printed out. I pounded a nail into the wall and posted them all. It gave me something in common with my favorite writers . . .

When a publisher said *No,* I said *Next.*

Over a period of two years, when the nail could no longer support the weight impaled upon it, I replaced it with a spike. When the spike got too heavy and some of the not-so-subtle rejections pummeled me on the head, I reminded myself of those notables who left their footprints along this bumpy road to success.

I learned patience and perseverance. But, most importantly, I learned that, as writers, we're more than rejections. And we're much *more* than acceptances. If we wait for others to define us, we'll be saddled with their expectations. Our work ethic, values, imagination, voice, and narratives are valid with or without getting published. *We write for ourselves. We write to embrace memories. We write for those who listen.* If we get published in the traditional sense, it's a bonus!

So, the next time you send writing into the vast, bleak abyss or you get a response that reads "Thanks, but no thanks," remember: Rejections are signs that you may be on your way to getting traditionally published. If you haven't received legions of them, perhaps you haven't submitted your writing often enough. And if you don't get traditionally published but choose to self-publish, you still are a valid writer. Relish the joy of your glorious self-expression any way you can.

By the way, the same holds true for submitting articles. Believe in yourself! Don't give up!

6

The Part of Tens

IN THIS PART . . .

Learn to craft powerful prompts to enhance
the quality and relevance of AI's responses.

Gain insights into the common pitfalls that cause
business documents to fall short, and discover
strategies to elevate them to superstar status.

Chapter **23**

Ten Tips for Writing Powerful Prompts

Writing effective AI prompts is akin to driving a masterful golf ball for a hole in one. Just as golf demands preparation, aim, technique, focus, and keeping an eye on the end result, crafting AI prompts that get the desired results requires similar skills and attention to detail. And you can finally put aside the good manners that were drummed into your head when you were a kid. AI tools don't care about polite words such as "please" and "thank you;" they don't have feelings or emotions. You can get straight to the point and trust AI's wizardry to work its wonders.

TIP

Chapter 7 delves into the world of crafting prompts for artwork. So whether or not you're an artist, you can unleash your artistic potential. In Parts 3, 4, and 5 you discover chapter-specific prompt recommendations for each topic. This chapter offers some general pointers to get you started.

Appreciating the Importance of Prompts

Garbage in, garbage out (GIGO) was coined by George Fuechsel, an IBM computer programmer and instructor, in the 1960s. The phrase quickly gained popularity in the early days of computing, and remains relevant today. It underscores the importance of high-quality prompts. If the input prompts are vague, incomplete, or misleading, AI's output may be irrelevant or of poor quality. Well-structured prompts will

>> minimize ambiguity

>> reduce the need for follow-up clarifications

>> enhance the overall user experience

>> encourage creativity

>> enable AI to generate more insightful and contextually appropriate content

Understanding the Capabilities of Chatbots

AI chatbots have varying capabilities, so it's important to understand the strengths and limitations of the AI tool you're working with. For example, if the tool shines in generating creative narratives, you can design prompts that encourage story-telling to enhance documents such as grant proposals and bios. On the other hand, if the AI tool is more adept at providing factual information, you can craft prompts that require the AI to research and present accurate data on a given topic.

AI SPOTLIGHT

Try out some of the popular chatbots such as ChatGPT (`https://chat.openai.com/auth/login`), Microsoft's Copilot (`https://copilot.microsoft.com/`), and Google's Gemini (`https://gemini.google.com/app`), as well as others to learn of their diverse strengths, weaknesses, and capabilities. This will expand your understanding of the evolving AI landscape.

SHERYL SAYS

Oh, how the landscape keeps evolving! When I started writing this book, Microsoft's AI product was like a sprightly Copilot (formerly Bing), while Google's AI product pranced around like a merry Bard. There were other situations along the way where I had to shout "Hold the presses," such as the announcement that

ChatGPT had gone haywire. So hold onto your hats, for the world of AI keeps spinning and evolving. Who knows what other surprises await, even after this book has been printed? It's a whirlwind of excitement and change!

Communicating with AI as You Would a Person

AI can seamlessly accept both voice and written prompts, catering to different preferences and needs. When communicating with AI, you can engage in a dialogue just as you would with a human assistant. Perhaps they need more information or clarification. Perhaps they missed the point or veered off topic. It's the same with AI. When you need to continue the thread of a conversation, you can re-prompt with something like the following:

» shorten into two paragraphs

» be more specific

» make the tone more conversational

Asking for One Single Task at a Time

It's best to ask for one thing at a time; AI can't multitask. So focusing on a single request helps the chatbot to understand and respond accurately. Otherwise your prompt can lack clarity, making it difficult for AI to generate a meaningful response:

Lacking clarity: *I need information on the benefits of exercise, different types of exercises, how to create a workout routine, and the best diet plan to follow.*

Simplified single task: *What are the benefits of exercise for overall health and well-being?*

Providing Specific Guidelines and Instructions

This can relate to word or page count, number of bullet points, formatting requirements, tone, or any specific elements or themes. Here are some examples of well-written prompts:

>> *Write a persuasive 2-paragraph email to [name of client] who has shown an interest in purchasing [product] but can't commit because of budget constraints. List three purchase options.*

>> *Write a series of 3 emails to follow up on a post-purchase to make customers know they're valued.*

>> *Create an engaging two-paragraph introduction for an article on the pros and cons of [topic] starting with a pertinent analogy.*

>> *Compose a 500-word blog on [topic].*

>> *In two pages use an academic tone to summarize [topic].*

Asking Open-Ended Questions

When you ask AI for open-ended questions, you open the floodgates of creativity and imagination. It's like giving wings to a bird, allowing it to soar freely across the vast expanse of its potential. With open-ended questions, AI can delve into uncharted territories, exploring ideas and concepts that you may have never considered before. This can spark a chain reaction of thoughts, leading to unexpected and fascinating outcomes. It's in these uncharted territories that AI truly shines, pushing the boundaries of what is known and venturing into the realm of what could be:

Open-ended prompt: *How do you envision the role of AI in shaping the future of healthcare?*

Closed-ended prompt: *Do you envision that AI will re-shape the future of healthcare?*

TIP

Close-ended queries, such as those requiring "yes" or "no" answers, are effective when you need specific answers, concise responses, or feedback that can be easily analyzed. They provide a focused approach to communication and can help you get the information you need efficiently.

Using Specific Keywords or Phrases

You can enhance AI's ability to generate more relevant ideas by incorporating specific keywords related to your industry, niche, or topic. As an example, if you're asking about dog breeds, include terms such as breed, size, training, and temperament. If you're talking about gardening, include keywords such as organic, plants, soil, or fertilizer. Here are a couple of examples of prompts using some of these keywords:

» *Share tips on how to create a thriving organic garden.*

» *Write an informative 500-word article about the best plants for beginners to grow in their garden along with essential care instructions.*

» *Tell me about small dogs with good temperaments.*

» *Which large dogs are obedient and easy to train?*

Encouraging Research

When writing AI prompts that encourage research, give clear and specific instructions while leaving room for the AI to explore and generate its own ideas. For example, you can ask AI to *Explore the impact of climate change on marine ecosystems, considering both short-term and long-term effects.* This prompt prompts the AI to research and provide a comprehensive analysis. Next, continue the conversation by asking AI to support its responses with evidence or examples. You can write, *Provide three examples of scientific studies or research papers that support your analysis.* Other examples may include the following:

» *Create an agenda for a meeting with my team. The meeting is about [insert meeting info]. Provide examples of what should be included in the agenda.*

» *Conduct market research on consumer preferences for eco-friendly products. Provide insights on current trends. You can then re-prompt for information on consumer buying behavior.*

» *Investigate sustainable energy solutions for reducing carbon emissions in urban areas.*

Using a Checklist

Using a checklist to prepare AI prompts helps to organize and structure the prompts and ensures that you've included all key components. This improves the accuracy of your prompts and gets you the results you want. Ask yourself the following questions:

>> Are your instructions clear, leaving no room for ambiguity?

>> Have you included precise, detailed information such as length and tone?

>> Have you provided the necessary context with ample detail?

>> Is the prompt well organized and clearly structured?

>> Have you used straightforward, succinct language?

>> Have you included helpful examples and ideas, if relevant?

>> Did you proofread?

Making the Document Your Own

REMEMBER

Beyond the pointers, remember that while AI has made remarkable strides in generating coherent and contextually relevant text, it needs writer intelligence (WI) — the essence of individuality, creativity, and personal experience that gives your writing its soul. Infuse your own unique voice, perspectives, and emotions into the content generated by AI to ensure that your writing remains genuine, engaging, and distinctly yours. By way of example, if AI's response includes a phrase such as "Utilize this only when . . ." and you would typically say "Use this only when . . ." make the change to ensure the text aligns with your style.

Chapter **24**

Ten Reasons Why Business Writing Fails

The art of writing is a skill we've all fancied ourselves masters of since our humble days of scribbling with crayons and forming our first ABCs. Yet many among us remain blissfully unaware of our weaknesses. Some factors are poor grammar, bloated sentences and paragraphs, burying the key message, rambling, failing to understand the target audience, lacking clear objectives, and more.

REMEMBER

Research by Grammarly and The Harris Poll in 2022 estimates an annual loss of $1.2 trillion (yes, trillion!) among U.S. businesses due to poor communication. That's approximately $12,506 per employee each year. Different reports show different numbers, but they're all staggering. This often leads to missed deadlines and meetings, conflicts within a team or other employees, confusion and misinterpretations, inefficiencies, omission of key steps in a process, poor morale, high employee turnover, loss of grant money, and perhaps legal issues.

So, approach the craft of writing with humility and a willingness to improve. After all, recognizing your weaknesses is the first step towards honing your skills and becoming a better writer. And who knows, with a little practice and a touch of self-awareness, you might just surprise yourself with the wonders you can create through the written word.

Not Using AI as Your Writing Assistant

AI SPOTLIGHT

Lots of AI tools have been discussed in this book — from chatbots to comprehensive high-end tools — that can help you to write successful documents. They can assist with everything from generating ideas and creating valuable headlines, to proofreading and editing, and a whole lot more. A few popular general-purpose tools are ChatGPT (https://chat.openai.com), Grammarly (https://app.grammarly.com/), Jasper. Ai (https://www.jasper.ai/), and You.com (https://you.com/).

Be sure to give Chapter 23 a read to find helpful tips on general prompt writing. Additionally, explore the individual chapters in Parts 3, 4, and 5, where you'll find a variety of AI tools and suggested prompts that are specifically tailored to the topic at hand.

Failing to Address the Target Reader

Failing to understand your target reader can have significant repercussions. Imagine a ship setting sail without a compass: it drifts aimlessly, missing its intended destination. Similarly, without a clear understanding of who your reader is, your communication efforts may fall flat. Here are some critical consequences of not knowing your target reader:

>> Misaligned messaging

>> Wasted resources

>> Ineffective calls to action

>> Lost sales opportunities resulting in lost revenue

>> Brand misperception

TIP

You must see your target so you know where to aim. Check out Chapter 4 for more on getting to know your reader.

Poor Planning

"Give me six hours to chop down a tree and I will spend the first four sharpening the axe." Those were the words of President Abraham Lincoln during a time the United States was in great crisis. If Lincoln didn't spend time planning, perhaps we'd be living in a very different country today.

Yes, you may be working against a tight deadline and feel you don't have time to plan. The bottom line is . . . no matter how tight the deadlines are, time spent planning is never wasted. The temptation to start writing immediately may be strong, but the result is often lengthy and muddled content. Decide what information is essential, what information is desirable, and what information is not necessary.

AI tools can help you plan your entire document from titles, headlines, and bullets, to research and so much more.

Lacking Clear Objectives

Documents without clear objectives will lack focus and fail to achieve their intended purpose. Here's what may happen:

>> Tasks become disjointed, leading to inefficiency.

>> The project balloons beyond its intended boundaries.

>> Resources are squandered on irrelevant stuff.

>> Stakeholders interpret things differently.

>> Deadlines are missed.

>> Quality suffers.

You're the one who must determine the objective of your document. AI can support your objective but can't create it for you.

Where's the Beef?

The iconic phrase "Where's the beef?" originated in a 1984 television commercial for the fast-food chain Wendy's. In the ad, actress Clara Peller was frustrated by a tiny hamburger patty in a competitor's oversized bun. Famously she said, "Where's the beef?" Since then, that's become an all-purpose phrase when questioning the substance of an idea, event, or product. Readers won't wonder "Where's the beef?" when your document has the following:

>> An introduction that grabs their attention.

>> Headlines that tell the story at a glance.

>> A conclusion that leaves a lasting impact and drives the call to action.

Through data analysis, pattern recognition, predictive modeling, decision support, and automated reasoning, AI can help get to the core of an issue and generate "the beef."

Lacking Visual Interest

When people think of visual aids, they think of charts, graphs, and tables. These can enhance understanding and make complex information more accessible. While they're important and often necessary, remember that visual aids also mean the following:

>> Ample white space.

>> Strong headlines that tell the story.

>> Paragraphs limited to about eight lines of text.

>> Sentences limited to about 20 words.

Check out Chapter 7 to learn more about the wide range of visual aids that make documents strong and understandable, and how AI can be of assistance.

Inconsistent Tone

Inconsistency in tone and style can lead to disjointed and unprofessional documents. To ensure coherence and clarity, it's crucial to maintain a consistent tone and style throughout each document — even if different sections were written by various contributors. Whether you're crafting emails, reports, or marketing materials, adhering to consistent punctuation, numerals, and hyphenation enhances professionalism. (Check out Chapter 8 to learn more about tone.)

Being consistent is a two-part journey. Use AI to follow conventions and rules while making sure you do a final check. Here are some highlights:

>> Use clear, understandable wording.

>> Use positive words and phrases unless there's a reason to emphasize the negative.

>> Use the active voice unless you want to focus on the action and not on the person performing the action.

>> Use *you* and *your* more than you use *me* and *my*.

>> Use inclusive language.

>> Be sensitive to cultural and regional differences.

>> Be judicious about using humor.

AI SPOTLIGHT

AI tools can analyze text and provide insights into the overall tone of a document as well as the tone of each sentence within a message. However, never overlook the value of writer intelligence (WI).

Spelling and Grammatical Errors

With so many AI tools available, there's no need for a document to have any spelling or grammatical errors. AI can be a wonderful resource, but you still need humans to do a final check. AI won't pick up misspellings of names, transposition of numbers, or anything that's been omitted.

AI SPOTLIGHT

Check out Chapter 9 to learn how to polish your text. Many of the tools listed earlier in this chapter will be of great value.

Insufficient Supporting Evidence

Documents that lack supporting evidence or references may fail to convince readers of their validity. By harnessing the capabilities of AI, you can ensure that your documents are backed by solid evidence and references that make them more persuasive and compelling to readers. With AI's assistance in gathering, analyzing, and summarizing evidence, you can make well-informed decisions and drive progress across various fields with greater efficiency and accuracy.

REMEMBER

Be sure to support all your evidence by conducting thorough research, gathering reliable sources, and double-checking the sources as well as the information.

Management-speak, Buzz Words, and Jargon

Are you tired of hearing trite expressions such as *24/7, synergy, cutting edge, at the end of the day*, and the like? I know I am. Creating trite-free and jargon-free documents makes them understandable and accessible to a wider range of readers. Jargon-free documents promote inclusivity, facilitate comprehension, and enhance the overall readability and usability of the information.

REMEMBER

If there are many terms you need to explain, consider including an index or list of terms. If there are only a few, here's how to handle acronyms and initialisms within the document:

The Coalition Forces Land Component Command (CFLCC) will be meeting on [date].

When you mention them afterwards, you can simply refer to the abbreviated term.

Index

A

A/B testing, 153, 159
abandoned cart emails, 157
abstracts and executive summaries
 about, 239
 active voice in, 250
 components of, 244, 248–249
 creating, 29
 creating prompts, 240
 influence of abstracts, 241–244
 necessities of executive
  summaries, 247–248
 positive attitude in, 249–250
 purpose of, 241, 247
 sequencing in, 250–252
 technical terms in, 249
 types of abstracts, 244–247
 using AI for writing, 240
academic articles, writing, 213–214
academic conferences, 217
academic writers, 18
accessibility, 158
accuracy, proofreading for,
  122–123
active voice, 109, 250
Adobe Creative Cloud Express, 88
Adobe Photoshop, 86, 146
Adobe Sensei, 86
advertising, storyboards for, 313
advertising writers, 12–13
Adzooma, 169
Agent GPT, 16
Ahrefs Content Idea Generator, 223
Ahrefs Social Media Bio
  Generator, 276
AI Blog Idea Generator, 223
AI ethics, 22
AI patterns, 33
AI Revolution, 48
AI Spotlight icon, 3

AI Technical Writing Certification
  Course, 17
AI tools
 chatbots compared with, 44
 choosing, 46
 for readability, 127
 for social media marketing, 171
 for text marketing, 166, 168
 for web marketing, 169–170
 for writing drafts, 78
AI Writing Courses for Bloggers and
  Digital Marketers, 17
AISEO, 127
algorithm, 22
Alpaca, 86
alternative (alt) tags, for SEO, 181
Altman, Sam (OpenAI founder), 18
AmpliFund, 254
Amplitude, 161
Anyword, 45, 104, 290
appendices
 in business plan, 331
 in grant proposals, 268
 in reports, 235, 236
approach, in abstracts and executiv
  summaries, 244, 264
appropriateness, of emails, 135–136
Art Effects, 86
ArtDraw, 86
articles
 about, 211
 academic, 213–214
 benefits of writing, 215–217
 blogosphere, 222–223
 creating
  prompts, 212–213
  query letters, 220–222
  titles, 219
 following publisher's
  guidelines, 218
 hypothetical threads, 214–215

 non-academic, 213–214
 reading masthead, 217–218
 using AI for writing, 212
Articoolo, 13
artificial intelligence (AI)
 about, 8, 21–22
 communicating with, 349
 relationship with writer intelligence
  (WI), 46–47
 terminology for, 22
 using
  to assist writer intelligence
   (WI), 9–10
  for creating storyboards,
   304–305
  for email campaigns, 152–153
  for emails, 132–134
  for first drafts, 76–77
  for proofreading and editing,
   118–119
  for tone, 104–105
  for visuals, 86
  for writer's block, 76–77
  for writing abstracts and
   executive summaries, 240
  for writing articles, 212
  for writing bios, 276
  for writing business plans, 318
  for writing grant proposals,
   254–255
  for writing instructions
   procedures, 192
  for writing letters, 290
  for writing nonfiction
   books, 334
  for writing reports, 226–227
  for writing web content, 175
 The Art of Possibility (Zander and
  Zander), 249–250
 "ask," presenting the, 295
 audience analysis, 52
 audience segmentation, 23, 162

expected outcomes/impact, in executive summaries, 264

experience, in executive summaries, 264

expressions, tone and, 108

EZTesting, 168

F

fact-checking, 26

failure, reasons for, 353–358

FAQs, in instructions and procedures, 208–209

feasibility, evaluating, 320

Federal Communications Commission (FCC), 166

feedback, 32, 336

FeedHive, 171

15minuteplan.ai, 318

final decision, 270

financial information/projections, in executive summaries, 324

financial projections, 320, 329

financial scams, 148

findings, in abstracts, 244

finesse, in emails, 149–150

first drafts
  about, 75
  polishing, 84
  sequencing, 83–84
  using AI for, 76–77
  writing, 24, 81–83
  writing for nonfiction books, 342–343

first person, sharing stories in, 71

Flesh-Kincaid, 127

flowchart, 93, 95

focused message, 179

follow ups, for email campaigns, 153

formal reports, sequencing, 232–236

formal tone, 105

formatting, 32, 201–203

forums, 217

four pillars of storytelling, 68–70

FrameForge, 304

Frase AI, 15

freelance writers, 14

freewriting, 78–79

front matter, of reports, 233–234

Fronty, 86

Fueschel, George (computer programmer), 348

fundraising, 293–296

future plans, in executive summaries, 324

G

Gap Scout, 52

garbage in, garbage out (GIGO), 348

Gemini, 43, 348

Gen X, 59

gender-neutral pronouns, 112–113

General Data Protection Regulation (GDPR), 187

General Motors, 28

general-use comprehensive AI tools, 45

generational differences, bridging, 58–60

generative AI, 22

GetAccept, 15

Getresponse, 152

Ginger Software, 119

GiveButter, 296

glossary
  extracting, 30
  in grant proposals, 269
  in reports, 235, 236

goals and objectives, in grant proposals, 266

Godin, Seth (author), 338

Google Translate, 119

Google Workspace, 134, 194

grammar, 25, 28, 31

Grammarly, 12, 14, 15, 18, 31, 45, 104, 118, 134, 175, 212, 222, 240, 290, 354

grammatical errors, 357

grant proposals
  about, 253–254
  components of, 262–269
  creating prompts, 255
  denied applications, 272
  dynamic testimonials, 262

emotional appeals, 260–261

finals for, 270–272

human touch in, 255–257

incorporating stories, 261

preliminaries for, 257–259

review process, 269–270

using AI for writing, 254–255

Grantboost, 254

grantors, finding, 258

graphics, 145–147, 183

Graphmaker.ai, 93

Gray, John (author), 338

green, 96

GrowthBar, 14, 223

H

HAL, 8

hallucinations, 20, 22

handwritten letters, 292

header rows, in tables, 91

headlines, 24, 97, 143–145, 183

Hemingway App, 169

Hemingway Editor, 119

Herman, Amy E. (author), 114

HeyGPT, 16

highlight abstracts, 246–247

HighQ, 16

Hive, 266

Hix.ai, 78

homepages, 174, 176–179

HoneyBook, 266

hook, in executive summaries, 324

Hootsuite Insights, 171

Hostinger AI Website Builder, 175

HourOne, 210

house list, 159

HubSpot, 134, 152, 164

HubSpot AI Writer, 18

HuggingChat, 43

human emotion, 19

humor, tone and, 114–115

hyper-personalization, 161

HyperWrite AI, 15, 78, 290

Hypotenuse AI, 14

hypothetical threads, 214–215

using
    AI for, 104–105
    gender-neutral pronouns,
        112–113
    industry-related jargon, 113–114
Topai, 287
tracking changes, 32
trade shows, abstracts for, 241
traditional storyboard, 308–311
Traditionalists, 59
traffic analysis, 52
training, 17, 314
translators, 15–16, 83, 119–121
transmittal letters, 232–233,
    262–263, 300–301
Trello, 194
trends, in sales forecast, 327
Turing, Alan, 8
Twilio, 168
2001: A Space Odyssey (film), 8
two-paragraph bios, 282–285

U

Udemy, 17
Uizard, 86
Unbounce, 175
Unique Selling Proposition (USP),
    175, 326
unsubscribe, 159
Upmetrics, 318
U.S. Copyright Office, 47, 90
user experience (UX), 15, 27, 309,
    313, 314
UserGuiding, 196
Userpersona, 52
utilitarian, 12

V

Varicent, 328
Venngage, 88
version control, 32
videos, 26, 209–210, 314
Vimeo, 209

vision, defining your, 319
Visla, 210
Visme, 88
visual appeal, creating for emails,
    143–146
visual cues, in emails, 146
visual formatting, 32
Visual Intelligence (Herman), 114
visual interest, importance of, 356
visual search optimization, 27
visuals
    about, 85
    adding tables/charts, 90–95
    color, 95–96
    copyright, 90
    creating
        about, 24–25
        prompts, 87–88
    data, 25
    headlines, 97
    for homepages, 177–178
    infographics, 88–90
    lists, 98–101
    paragraph length, 96–97
    sentence length, 96–97
    using AI for, 86
    white space, 96
vocabulary, 28, 31
voice, for bios, 280
voice search optimization, 27
VWO, 165

W

Warning icon, 4
Wave, 210
web content
    about, 173–174
    anatomy of landing pages,
        179–180
    competition and, 182–184
    conversion tracking, 186–187
    creating homepages, 176–179
    creating prompts, 175–176

mission statement, 179
    optimizing for SEO, 180–182
    sensitivity to international visitors,
        184–185
    terminology for, 174–175
    using AI for writing, 175
    writing for comprehension,
        185–186
web content writers, 18
web marketing, 168–170
websites, 17, 217
welcome emails, 158
white space, 96
whitelist, 159
WhiteSmoke, 119
wisdom, absorbing, 37–38
Wistia, 209
Wix, 175
Wizehive, 255
Wordsmith, 13
Wordtune, 45, 127
Writer, 104, 334
Writer Buddy, 287
writer intelligence (WI)
    about, 7
    power of, 80–81
    relationship with artificial
        intelligence (AI), 46–47
    using artificial intelligence (AI)
        to assist, 9–10
Writer.com, 170
writer's block
    about, 23–24, 75
    brainstorming, 79
    freewriting, 78–79
    mind mapping, 79, 80
    outlining, 79–80
    using AI for, 76–77
Writesonic, 14, 45, 64, 104
writing
    abstracts, 241–247
    academic articles, 213–214
    closings, 293
    for comprehension, 185–186

About the Author

Sheryl Lindsell-Roberts is a proud New Yorker with an unmistakable accent that lingers even after many years of living near Boston. Her pronunciation of the word "coffee" (or as she charmingly says, "cough-ee") is a giveaway as to where she's from. Sheryl was raised by a mother who had an unwavering obsession with perfect grammar and impeccable speech. At the tender age of five, her mother taught her to spell complex words like "schizophrenia" and "antidisestablishmentarian" and proudly showcased Sheryl's linguistic prowess to anyone who'd listen.

Little did Sheryl know that this early exposure to the power of words would ignite a lifelong passion. Armed with a Master's Degree in Business and English, she embarked on a journey to establish her own communications company, aptly named Sheryl Lindsell-Roberts & Associates. Her career has been a tapestry of diverse roles, ranging from technical writing and training facilitation to directing marketing campaigns and crafting compelling narratives for video productions. Sheryl's innate ability to deliver key information with visual impact and engage readers has made her a sought-after training facilitator, coach, and business communications aficionado.

Throughout her career, Sheryl has authored an impressive repertoire of 25+ books, spanning the business and humor markets. While she dreams of one day penning the great American novel, her current creative outlets include interior decorating, writing poetry, and indulging in outdoor adventures such as kayaking, hiking, cross-country skiing, and snowshoeing. A true renaissance woman, Sheryl also finds solace in gardening, painting (canvas, not walls), practicing yoga, power-walking, playing the violin, and exploring the wonders of the world through her globetrotting escapades.

Sheryl's expertise hasn't gone unnoticed, as she's graced the airwaves of radio and television across the United States. Her insights and wisdom have been featured in prestigious publications such as *The New York Times*, solidifying her reputation as a respected voice in the industry. As an ongoing contributor to *Training* magazine, Sheryl continues to share her knowledge and inspire others on their own communications journeys.

To learn more, visit Sheryl on LinkedIn at `https://www.linkedin.com/in/sherylwrites/`.

By the way, this spirited bio was crafted by Sheryl's favorite chatbot with the help of prompts she provided. `You.com` *worked its magic to bring this bio to life!*

Dedication

To my mother, my guiding light and master of words. I can never thank her enough for the priceless lessons she instilled me. From the time I could talk she made sure I spoke clearly and articulately, even if it meant endless hours of pronunciation practice. Her unwavering faith in the transformative power of language has molded me into the person I am today and guided me towards varied professions where communication reigns supreme. Whether I'm leading workshops, captivating audiences with my public speaking skills, tackling writing projects, or simply engaging in everyday conversations, I carry her cherished teachings with me.

Author's Acknowledgments

Guess who I've had the pleasure of teaming up with for the third time? That's right, Tracy Boggier, the Acquisitions Editor extraordinaire! Tracy's confidence in me is like a warm hug on a cold winter's day. I hope we'll continue our bookmaking adventures together. Also Meir Zimmerman, my trusty Technical Editor. I'm forever grateful for the valuable insights he's brought to each of my books.

But hold on to your hats, because we've got a new addition to the A-team! Introducing Dan Mersey, the Development Editor from jolly old England. Collaborating with an editor from across the pond was a new experience for me, but it turned out to be a seamless partnership. Despite some slight differences (with me using "zee" and Dan using "zed" to end the alphabet) we remained perfectly in sync from "A to Y" throughout the entire project. It was even more impressive that Dan committed to not spell "color" as "colour." That level of dedication truly exemplified our shared commitment to the cause!

Publisher's Acknowledgments

Acquisitions Editor: Tracy Boggier
Development Editor: Dan Mersey
Technical Editor: Meir Zimmerman
Managing Editor: Murari Mukundan

Production Editor: Tamilmani Varadharaj
Cover Images: © Zorica Nastasic/Getty Images, © ismagilov/Getty Images, © imaginima/ Getty Images